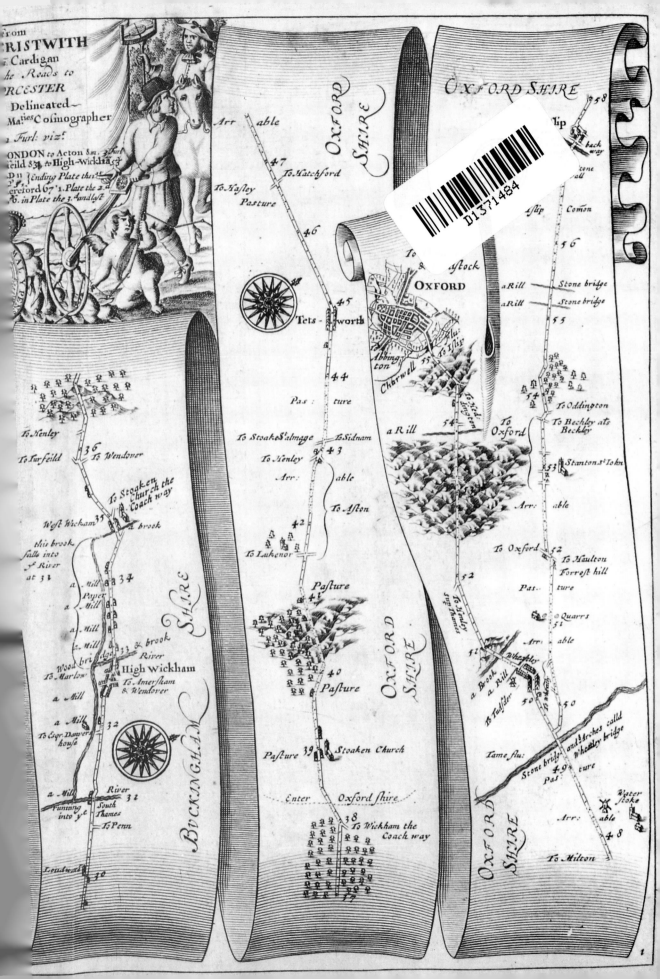

From
[A]RISTWITH
[&] Cardigan
[the] Roads to
[WO]RCESTER
Delineated —
[by his] Maties Cosmographer

[in] Furl: viz!
[L]ONDON to Acton 8m. 3 furl
[Acton]feild 83½. to High-wickt14 c ?
[Ending] Plate ther st
[H]ereford 67 ½. Plate the 2.d
[&c] in Plate the 3. and last

OXFORD SHIRE

OXFORD SHIRE

Arr   able
47 To Hatchford
To Hasley Pasture
46
45
Tets - worth
44
Pas :   ture
To Stoake S'almage   To Sidnam
To Henley
Arr :   able   43
To Aston
42
To Lakenor
Pasture
41
40
Pasture
Pasture 39 Stoaken Church
Enter Oxford shire
38 To Wickham the Coach way
37

58
[I]slip back way
[St]one [w]all
[I]slip   Comon
56
a Rill   Stone bridge
a Rill   Stone bridge
55
To [Wo]stock
OXFORD
Abbing ton   To Islip
Chirwell 55
a Rill   54
To Oxford
54   To Oddington
To Bechley ats Beckley
53   Stanton s.t Iohn
Arr :   able
To Oxford   52   To Haulton
Forrest hill
52   Pas   ture
Quarrs   51
Arr : able
51   Wheatley
a Brook   50
a Rill
To Tusfeld   50   50
Tame flu: Stone bridge and Arches calld
49 Wheatley bridge
Pas 49 ture
Arr :   able   48
Water Stoke
To Milton

OXFORD SHIRE

BUCKINGHAM SHIRE

To Henley
To Iurfeild 36 To Wendover
To Stoaken Church the Coach way
West Wickam 35 a brook
this brook falls into y.e River at 31
a. Mill 34
Paper Mill
a. Mill
a. Mill 33 & brook
Wood bridge   River
To Marlow High Wickham
To Amersham & Wendover
a Mill
a Mill 32
To Esqr. Dowers house
a Mill   River 31
Running   South
into y.e   Thames
To Penn
Loudwat 30

TRAVELLERS
IN BRITAIN

Other books by Richard Trench

FORBIDDEN SANDS
LONDON UNDER LONDON
ARABIAN TRAVELLERS
LONDON BEFORE THE BLITZ

RICHARD TRENCH

TRAVELLERS
IN BRITAIN
Three Centuries of Discovery

AURUM PRESS

For Barbara Davis

AUTHOR'S NOTE

Wherever possible I have tried to retain the original language for the direct quotations from contemporary accounts. This explains eccentricities of spelling and grammar. However, where the usage proved too arcane, or the spelling too difficult to be easily understood, I have modernized the language, without, I hope, losing too much of its original sense. In other cases, earlier editors had already brought the language into more modern usage. Some of the extracts have also been abridged.

ACKNOWLEDGEMENTS

The author and publishers are grateful to the following for permission to reproduce illustrations: Bodleian Library, pp. 12 (ms Bodley 264 f81), 58 (Poole 117, Box 762), 63 (210 b252), 181 (G A Gen Top b33, vol. iv); Bridgeman Art Library, pp. 41, 120, 121, 123, 125, 148, 150, 151, 156, 161, 163, 164, 166, 168, 171, 193, 194, 197, 198, 200, 202, 205, 206, 209, 211; Bristol Art Gallery, p. 120; British Library, pp. 11, 14, 16, 18, 20, 22, 24, 28, 32, 34–5, 46, 49, endpapers; British Museum, pp. 76–7, 80, 85, 88, 96–7, 102, 111, 114, 117, 124, 131, 142, 145, 182, 184, 186; Mary Evans Picture Library, pp. 53, 72, 79, 92, 110, 113, 135, 141, 154, 174, 189; National Portrait Gallery, pp. 104, 210; Soane Museum, p. 108; York City Art Gallery, p. 148.

First published 1990 by Aurum Press Limited, 33 Museum Street,
London WC1A 1LD
Copyright © 1990 by Richard Trench

Maps by Chartwell appear on pp. 6, 10, 78, 167 and 192

British Library Cataloguing in Publication Data

Trench, Richard
Travellers in Britain
1. Great Britain. Social life, history
I. Title
941

ISBN 1 85410 102 1

Typeset by Wyvern Typesetting Ltd, Bristol
Printed by Butler & Tanner Ltd, Frome

CONTENTS

GENERAL MAP OF ENGLAND

—PROLOGUE—

SPECULUM BRITANNIAE

'And this also,' said Marlow suddenly, 'has been one of the dark places of the earth.'

Joseph Conrad, 'Heart of Darkness'

FOR A THOUSAND years, from the Roman withdrawal to the beginning of the Renaissance, Britain possessed no identity. People travelled, on the pilgrim route to Canterbury, Walsingham and St Michael's Mount, and on the trade routes to London, Bristol, Norwich and York; but they rarely recorded what they saw. Dragons, saints, earthquakes and invoices the medievalists did record. Commonplace topography was hardly mentioned. Search all *The Canterbury Tales* and you will find not one description of Canterbury.

From the twelfth-century chronicles of the Benedictine monk, William of Malmesbury, come occasional chinks of light, but they are few and far between. 'Contemplate yourself as in a glass,' he wrote; but the glass is never wide enough to illuminate the whole island. Like his fellow-chroniclers he was a historian, not a geographer, and any topographical knowledge that emerges comes by accident. The world was flat and made by God, and everything that needed to be known was known already.

By the early fifteenth century manuscripts were giving routes and distances to the Holy Land, together with useful advice for pilgrims. Maps, some of them of England, were being copied.

Maps had existed since the thirteenth century when Mathew Paris, a Benedictine monk at St Albans, drew four maps of England, a map of Italy, a route map to the Holy Land and a map of the world. England is hardly recognizable. East Anglia and Kent have sunk into the North Sea, the Thames has been diverted into Southampton Water and Yorkshire is squeezed into the space for Rutland. It was more accurate, however, than the map of the world in Hereford Cathedral painted by Richard of Haldingham fifty years later, the *Mappa Mundi*. Centred on Jerusalem, it showed Britain on the edge of the world, and shaped like a banana.

By 1335 England and Wales were clearly recognizable on the maps of the time. Painted on two skins of vellum, the Gough map (named after its discoverer) showed a reasonably accurate coastline, the major towns, cities, roads and rivers. Only at Scotland did it lose its accuracy, giving the country an unfortunate resemblance to a condom.

England – and Scotland, too, for different reasons – was slowly becoming conscious of itself. Not only did it have its first maps, it had its own language. But this new consciousness was only beginning. Local dialects made the language incomprehensible from one county to another. A 50-mile journey was a major undertaking. The roads were appalling and in constant need of repair. The bridges were neglected by the monasteries that were supposed to maintain them. Wayfarers were in constant danger from landless outlaws, at one end of the social scale, and 'over great subjects', at the other. Still, a consciousness was there, even if it seemed no more than a rumour.

1
A RUMOUR OF BRITAIN

THE FIRST TRULY topographical record produced in England came at the very close of the Middle Ages. Its author was a retired confidential secretary in his mid-sixties. His name was William Worcestre. He had been born in Bristol in 1415 and went up to Oxford at the age of seventeen, lodging at Great Hart Hall (later part of Balliol) for six years. An Oxford education in the 1430s meant studying Latin, grammar, logic and mathematics. Unlike the infidel universities, such as Fez and Cairo, where geography was regarded as a primary subject, geography as a science was unknown at Oxford.

With his studies completed, Worcestre gained a post as secretary to Sir Thomas Falstolf, serving him, from 1459 until Falstolf's death, in London, in Castle Combe (where Falstolf was on the bench) and at Caistor Castle in Norfolk (where he was the castle governor for a time). Falstolf left Worcestre nothing when he died in 1477, so the confidential secretary moved first to Cambridge, where the cost of living was lower than in London, and then to Norwich, where he took up freelance clerical work and lived a life of genteel poverty.

Yet he was never quite the retired confidential secretary he seemed, ready simply to advise on a lawsuit or write a letter for a friend. Every so often, about once a year, he went wild, drunk up his money for days on end and woke with a hangover and an empty purse. People thought it was out of character, but to William Worcestre that must just have shown how mistaken people were about character. Sir John Falstolf had been a mean and malicious man. Worcestre felt he had been treated unjustly; and there was a bitter streak in him. In the two years of lawsuits that followed, the lawyers were the only winners. Worcestre still had a patch of land in Bristol, and another in London. It was enough to keep him out of God's Hospital, the vast almshouse for the old and destitute in the cathedral precincts of Norwich, but hardly enough to enjoy retirement. You could see the bitterness on his swarthy face, its deep lines caging the violence within.

Norwich was the third largest city in England after London and Bristol. Within its walls were 10,000 souls and a maze of topsy-turvy corkscrew streets enclosed by overhangs and unexpected gables. Its alleyways were packed with flint cobbles encased in mud, though sometimes there were no cobbles at all. The drains, where they existed, ran down the middle of the streets. The whole place stank. Rising above the rooftops

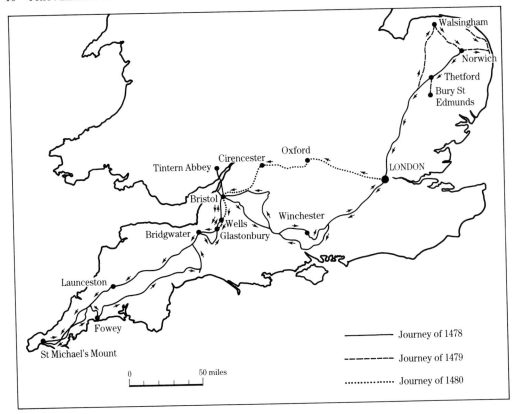

Walsingham

Norwich

Thetford

Bury St
Edmunds

Oxford

Cirencester

Tintern Abbey

LONDON

Bristol

Winchester

Wells

Bridgwater

Glastonbury

Launceston

Fowey

St Michael's Mount

0   50 miles

——————— Journey of 1478

- - - - - - - - Journey of 1479

.... Journey of 1480

were the spires and towers of fifty-three churches. A fifty-fourth was built while William Worcestre lived there. It was attached to the Great Hospital, and was called St Helens. Worcestre watched it going up, as he had watched King's College Chapel in Cambridge going up. It was an era of new building.

Overawing the city, and representing an older style in architecture, was the castle. There were stories of it being founded by Julius Caesar, but William Worcestre was an educated man, and such stories held no weight with him. Beneath the castle sprawled the cathedral and its precincts. In spite of the predominance of the castle it was to the cathedral, set in its close on a loop of the River Wensun, that the eye turned. It was low-lying, reflecting the contours of the land around, and its spire, 315 feet high – the second highest in England – seemed to emphasize that lowness. Nave, transepts and tower were Norman, an immovable expression of twelfth-century muscular Christianity. The east end was enclosed by a chorus line of flying buttresses. Inside, the entire nave was a forest of scaffolding. There had been a fire in 1463 and much of the Caen stone rising up from the aisles, through the triforium to the clerestory, had been blackened. Other parts had turned pink in the heat, but there were vast stretches untouched by the fire, where wall paintings hundreds of years old of crucifixions and resurrections, saints and sinners glowed in the shadows of the grey arches. The fire had completely destroyed the roof and ceiling, and now the ceiling was being vaulted. The vaults were being kept in place with painted bosses that told the story of the Bible in simple pictures: a religious comic strip for people who could not read or write.

Worcestre looked up at the bosses, but they were only blurs, and he had no idea how far away those blurs were. He was no longer able to judge distances. Perhaps it had something to do with the accident he had had years earlier when he lost an eye. Maybe that was why he was so obsessed with taking measurements, like a deaf man reading a music score.

From Norwich, in his mid-sixties, he made three pilgrimages: the first, in 1478, to St Michael's Mount in Cornwall, where an apparition of St Michael had appeared in 495; the second, in 1479, to Walsingham, where an apparition of the Virgin Mary had appeared in 1061; and the third, in 1480, to Glastonbury, where King Arthur and Joseph of Arimathea, and maybe even Christ, had come, and where the Holy Grail had been buried.

His hobby was topography. William Worcestre wanted to know his own world, so he wrote down what he knew. He did not write any great tome, but wrote down his itineraries, his notes on his itineraries and – ever the reliable secretary – a careful account of the cost of his itineraries. But he was an educated man, and his one eye saw a lot; and he must have known the story of one-eyed Cyclops, king in the land of the blind.

*   *   *

'On Monday, 17 August I began my journey from Norwich to St Michael's Mount in Cornwall,' he blandly notes. The first stage to London took three days. He spent his first night at Thetford, a sizeable town with five monastic houses and a grammar school founded for choirboys. Monasteries were good to travellers in the fifteenth century, and gave them rooms for the night, especially if they were pilgrims. The alternative was a tavern, not the most salubrious of places. The clientele at the inn Piers Plowman passed through included a porter, a tinker, a rabbit-catcher, a family of tinkers, a rat-catcher, a fiddler, a priest and his mistress, a ropemaker, a seamstress, a butcher's girl and a whore. Sleeping arrangements were sorted out amid puddles of vomit and cheap wine.

Bed-making in a medieval inn, beating the fleas out of the mattress the morning after.

His second day took him through Suffolk into Cambridgeshire. The landscape was typically East Anglian, not entirely flat, but low-lying and broken by streams and rivers. It was good farming country, and since the Black Death had cut the population by one-third, the old medieval strips had been annexed by the plague's survivors. Small farms were growing up cultivated by yeomen, and large landowners preferred hiring labourers to demanding days of work from resentful small farmers. Feudalism was dying. But the forests and open spaces were disappearing almost as fast as the old feudal strips, and the more wealth there was to be made from the wool trade, the faster the forests disappeared. Everyone needed wood. Most countryfolk's houses were made of wood, effectively log cabins; and rich and poor needed wood as winter fuel. Soon there would be none left.

William Worcestre would not have needed William of Malmesbury's description of East Anglia, for he was familiar enough with the area, but he was bound to have known of it. Topography and old manuscripts were his pastime.

> This province on the south and east is surrounded by the ocean; on the north by deep lakes and stagnant pools, which, stretching out a vast distance in length, with a breadth of two or three miles, afford abundance of fish for the use of the inhabitants; the soil is admirable for pasture and for hunting; it is full of monasteries, and large bodies of monks are settled on the islands of these stagnant waters; the people are a merry, pleasant, jovial race, though apt to carry their jokes to excess.

The day's journey ended at Walden Abbey in Essex. The abbey was Benedictine and stood on the River Cam about a mile and a half west of Saffron Walden. William Worcestre passed through the village on his way to the abbey. It was all timbered or half-timbered, and in the background were the ruins of a Norman castle. Next morning, with the sound of the monks chanting matins still lingering, he set off south.

The landscape was getting hillier. The flatlands of East Anglia were behind him. Everywhere there were rabbits – to be crossbowed, trapped, smoked, dug out, hunted. There was a plague of rabbits. He spent that night on the road, at an inn at Harlow. Rising early next morning he rode through Epping Forest and, passing over Bow Bridge, he already knew that he was approaching London. As he came up to

The rabbits' revenge: rabbits were one of the cheapest meats in medieval England.

Whitechapel the road was lined with houses. Beyond Whitechapel the street was packed with iron foundries. The continual banging, knocking, filing and denting from the workshops was so noisy that you could hear yourself go mad. The whole place stank, stank of humanity, sewerage, charcoal, but most of all it stank of the new-fangled 'seacoal' coming to London in ships from Newcastle. Behind the foundries on the south side of Whitechapel Road the land was still rural, and the milk the London milkmaids collected from the farms was still warm from the cows' teats. Further on towards the City were the walls of the Order of St Claire Nunnery. The nuns were named Minoresses and the quarter was named the Minories.

He passed under the Aldgate into the City of London about midday. Fenchurch Street lay straight ahead. It was cut by Gracechurch Street, which went on past a building with a lead roof owned by the Corporation, called Leaden Hall. It was one of the City's biggest markets, selling poultry, cheese and butter. There were sacks of grain, and stalls selling wool and leather. Crossing over Gracechurch Street, from Fenchurch Street, Worcestre came into Lombard Street, where the Italian bankers were. Lombard Street led to the Stocks Market, the fish and flesh market where the pillory stood, which marked the beginning of Westcheap, or Cheapside, as it was sometimes called. This was the biggest market in London. Each trade had its own quarter: the fishmongers in Friday Street, the bakers in Bread Street, the shoemakers in Cordwainer Street, the dairymaids in Milk Street and the chicken-sellers in Poultry.

This was the very heart of the City. Its markets fed 40,000 people, making London one of the biggest cities in the world. Shanty-town suburbs spilled out over the walls into the Liberties, forming little villages separated from each other by the lands of the monasteries and religious houses that surrounded the walls: Smithfield, Holborn, Whitechapel, Southwark. Within the walls, and outside in the Liberties, there were over 100 churches. Above them rose the cathedral, St Paul's, 'worthy of being numbered among the most famous of buildings', according to William of Malmesbury. Its nave was Norman, twelve bays long, its choir was Early English and took up another twelve bays. It was so long that people used the transepts as a short-cut from Queenhythe to Newgate Street.

The overwhelming impression was of London's density. Thirty thousand people – three-quarters of the total – were packed into a square mile, and not one domestic building was over three storeys high. Only a few rich people, and the livery companies, had houses built of stone. The rest lived in overcrowded and overhanging timber and wattle buildings, the top floors used as bedrooms, the ground floors as workshops.

William Worcestre stayed six days in London. Fortunately for him, inns were not a problem, as they were in the country. In London the inns were famous, and you knew exactly what you were getting. If you wanted to get laid you went to the taverns around Cock Lane, such as the Saracen's Head, the Boar's Head or the Cross Keys. If you wanted to get drunk you went to the Star or the Lion-at-the-Door. If you wanted a good night's sleep you went to the Goat, or the Bell. The newest inn was the George and the Hoop by Salter's Hall. It had thirty-three beds and as many stables, and it had only been open for a year. Even across the bridge in Southwark, owned by the Bishop of Winchester and with so many whores they were called 'Winchester Geese', everybody knew exactly what inn they were going to. The best that could be said for the majority of them was that they were a good place to swap syphilis stories; but the Walnut Tree had an impeccable reputation, and so had the Tabard: they needed it, for they catered for the pilgrim trade.

London Bridge and its arches, which 'wise men went over and fools shot under'.

At the end of six days, six days in which he meticulously wrote down everything he spent, Worcestre crossed London Bridge into Southwark and rode on along the south bank of the river and across open marshy country to Wandsworth. The bridge, packed with shops, houses, guard towers, drawbridge and even a chapel, was one of the wonders of the world. Spanning 900 feet, its eighteen pillars were thicker than its nineteen arches, so that it acted like a dam, and in a lowering tide the water was higher upstream than down and shot under the arches with irresistible force; which explained the saying about wise men going over the bridge and fools going under. Wandsworth was an industrial area where the hurrers, who made hats, and the fullers, who bleached cloth, argued incessantly about water rights on the River Wandle. In Worcestre's time the fullers were winning. Wandsworth had no religious house, so Worcestre made do with an inn.

Next morning he rode off, south-west through Kingston, Guildford and Farnham to Alton, where he spent the night at yet another inn. The following morning saw him in the ever-diminishing forest land, riding past strip farms cut out of forests, to the Bishop of Winchester's house at Bishop's Waltham, where he arrived in time for dinner. He continued after dinner to Southampton, which he reached late in the evening.

Southampton had one of the best natural harbours in the country. Here King Canute's courtiers watched their king wet his feet; and here the army of Richard Coeur de Lion embarked for the Holy Land, and the army of Henry V for France; here too – in Worcestre's own lifetime – the defeated English army, driven out of France by the French, returned to England. William Worcestre came in from the north, over two moats and through the Bargate, which held the Guildhall above its arch. He came down the High Street. Southampton Keep rose up on his right and the Star and the Dolphin, sailors' inns for a sailors' town, marked by the half-timbered street front, on his left. Further on the left was the Holy Rood Church, its spire seeming to reach the clouds, its walls gracefully buttressed and decorated with all twists and turns in the Decorated manner. Beyond that was the Red Lion. The street ended at the quayside, which was lined with French, Portuguese, Venetian, Genoan, Maltese and even Turkish ships, exchanging wool for the riches of the Orient. The line of masts curved round to the north-west with the arcaded city walls. On top of the battlements in the French *quartier*, where the 300-year-old merchant's house supported the city wall, emplacements for 'gonnes' looked out over the sea. In the middle of the quayside, a little to the east of where the High Street met it, was God's House, the Hostel of St Julian, which provided beds for travellers.

Worcestre stayed in the port all next morning and rode out in the afternoon through the Blue Anchor Postern in the French *quartier*, and continued north-west for the seven or eight miles along the banks of the Test to Romsey Abbey. The abbey's church was Norman, its west end very early Early English, though it still had a stretch of tenth-century wall from an earlier Saxon nunnery in the nave. The two great east windows had been punched through a century earlier and filled with coloured glass. The Norman mouldings in the choir's triforium were exquisite. South of the nave the cloisters squared off, and beyond them were the abbey's buildings, the library, kitchens, dining room, dormitory and guest house. There William Worcestre spent Saturday night, leaving early next morning after Mass and riding the seventeen miles to Salisbury before noon.

He approached the city over low meadows. High in the sky rose the cathedral spire, the tallest in England. The cathedral beneath it looked beautiful in late August: perfectly proportioned, in the Early English style, the only cathedral in the country built to a uniform design. He came in from the south-east, which gave a splendid view of the cathedral's east end and south transept. Inside was all lancets, clustered marbled columns and pointed arches. South of the nave the stonework in the cloisters looked as though petals had been cut out of it.

The town came with the cathedral from Old Sarum, a couple of miles to the north, 250 years earlier. This made it that rare thing, a planned medieval city. Its streets formed an irregular grid and they were fed by narrow, shallow canals. The High Street, running north, took Worcestre from the cathedral to Bridge Street, where he crossed the bridge over the Avon and continued for four miles to Wilton, a half-empty and inhospitable village, one time the capital of Wessex, its population decimated by the Black Death and not yet recovered. From here in the early afternoon he set off north across Salisbury Plain, riding within a couple of miles of Stonehenge, across the bleak and undulating clay and chalk plain to a village called Cheverell, about five miles to the south of Devizes, where he spent the night.

Monday, 31 August took him through Devizes – which was a keep, two churches and a market place with an infill of houses between them. There he veered north over the Marlborough Downs to Clyffe Pypard, huddled around a church at the bottom of a wooded cliff, then turned sharp west to Chippenham. By the time he arrived there it was the afternoon, but he was in no hurry, and continued leisurely for another four miles to Castle Combe. He came in along a wooded valley on a road that cut straight through the town. It was a rich town, rich from the wool trade, its high Perpendicular church, St Andrew's, brazenly displaying its wealth. He must have had mixed feelings in Castle Combe, for Falstolf had been on the bench there and Worcestre had spent a lot of his early adulthood in Castle Combe in Falstolf's service.

Dawn came up and he set off over the rolling landscape for Bristol, arriving in the city where he had grown up at 6 p.m. It was the second largest in England, with a population of some 12,000. It had grown rich in Saxon times from the Irish slave trade,

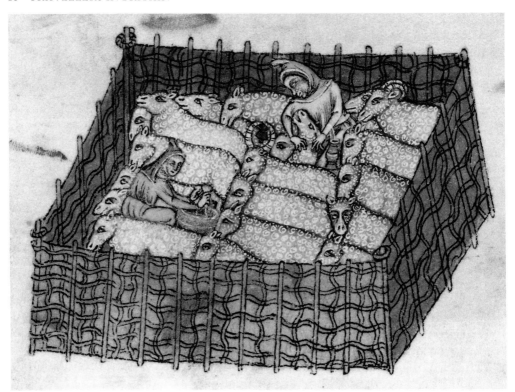

Milking sheep, whose wool provided England with her 'golden fleece'.

but by Worcestre's time was richer still from the wool trade. All but the very poor had courtyards and orchards surrounding their houses, and all year round the quays were crowded with ships trading Bordeaux and Spanish wine for wool and finished cloth. Within Bristol's walls were seventeen parish churches. Outside, as with London, the city was girdled with religious houses: the Hospital of St Mark, the Hospital of St John, the Augustinians (Austin friars), Carmelites (Whitefriars), Franciscans (Greyfriars) and Dominicans (Blackfriars). The abbey was Augustinian. Most of the abbey church was Norman, but the chancel was Decorated. It was broad, light, airy, used flying buttresses in unconventional ways, and was lit by huge windows in the nave. On the other side of the city was St Mary Radcliffe, large enough to be a cathedral. Its edifice had passed through every stage in the Gothic era, and it was the most beautiful church in Bristol. Already people were saying it was the most beautiful church in the country. Worcestre, unable to see the perspectives and proportions with his one eye, carefully measured it: sixty-three yards long without the Lady Chapel, seventy-seven with, and thirty-eight across the transepts.

William Worcestre stayed in Bristol for two days. He had family there. Meticulous with his accounts, he estimated that his stay in the city cost him five shillings and a penny halfpence, including a penny for horse-shoeing and tuppence for horse medicine. On the third day he rode out through the gates, down by the River Avon, and took a ferry across the Bristol Channel to Chepstow, then he pushed on up the Wye Valley to Tintern Abbey. The setting in the valley amid clusters of trees was beautiful, but Tintern was a very unexceptional Cistercian abbey except for the west front. The monastic buildings – library, cloister, kitchen, infirmary, dormitory, abbot's house, chapter house and guest house – lay between the Early English Gothic church and the river. He paced everything, as usual. 'The cloisters are thirty-seven yards long, the whole church has fourteen arches on each side' (in fact there are eleven). Then he paced the infirmary and the infirmary chapel, each sixty steps, and measured the chapel house, eighteen yards by five. He enjoyed visiting the library, getting information from old manuscripts about Wales, and ended up staying for the weekend, hearing Mass in the abbey church on the Sunday.

The following Tuesday he was back in Bristol for the Feast of the Nativity. He stayed only one night, and left at noon the next day, passing over the Mendips. It was all stone: stone houses, stone walls, stone farmhouses and stone paths.

He arrived at Wells that evening. Inevitably he crossed the market place, lined on the north side with modern buildings built by Bishop Bekynton and with a stone water conduit in the middle, and passed through the Penniless Porch into the cathedral precincts. The west front was a colourful mass of 300 saints with Christ and the Apostles in the centre, as bright as an illuminated manuscript. In the Early English nave his eyes went straight to the scissor-arches at the crossing, built 150 years earlier to prevent the tower from sinking. 'The length of the cathedral church of Wells is two hundred of my steps,' he wrote unemotionally. He returned across the market place to his lodgings. Wells was an expensive place, Worcestre discovered next morning. He was charged eight shillings and a halfpenny for bed, board and food for the horse. He was not a rich man, and paying must have hurt.

He left Wells, descended into the Somerset Levels and rode on to Glastonbury, aiming for the lone tower of St Michael's on top of the tor, a landmark for travellers from one end of the flatlands to the other.

The Benedictine abbey of Glastonbury was the oldest religious house in England. Its buildings reflected its age. The abbey, cloisters and living quarters were Norman and looked very ancient, which only increased the abbey's grandeur. According to William of Malmesbury, with whose history of the abbey William Worcestre would have been familiar, it had been founded on the island of Avalon (Glastonbury Tor) by Joseph of Arimathea and a dozen followers.

> They, quick to obey the Divine precepts, completed a chapel according to what had been shown them, fashioning its circular walls with twisted twigs; a chapel, it is true, of uncouth form, but to God adorned richly with virtue.

Whether the young Christ had been there, whether Saints Patrick, Columba and Dunstan had worshipped there, or whether King Arthur found spiritual refuge there – 'disputable matters,' hedged William of Malmesbury – Glastonbury remained one of the richest religious houses in Christendom.

Financially Glastonbury proved nearly as painful as Wells. Worcestre lost two shillings and tuppence, and try as he could to account for it, his mind was a blank. He stayed for two days, before riding on to the Polden Hills, which had once been islands rising up from the marshes. That evening he arrived at a tiny hamlet just before Bridgwater, where he dismounted and found a room for the night.

Next morning he rode through Bridgwater, crossed the River Parrett and continued on, alternating riding and walking beside his horse, across rolling moorland. He breakfasted in Taunton, a prosperous market and weaving town with a population of 1,000, overlooked by a simple Norman castle. He remounted, and after riding hard through the western reaches of Somerset and the eastern marches of Devon, spent the night in the village of Halberton about three miles east of Tiverton, another prosperous wool town where the two rivers, the Exe and the Lowman, join.

He rode over the high ground past Tiverton towards Okehampton. He was now between two moors, Exmoor to the north and Dartmoor to the south. It was bleak and windswept, the landscape broken and rocky. To a man from Norwich it must have appeared almost mountainous. It took the whole day, and he did not arrive at Okehampton until early evening.

The following morning's ride took him to Launceston, high in the rocks above the Tamar Valley, just inside Cornwall. Its anarchic streets seemed to get narrower the closer you got to the centre, a claustrophobic contrast with the open moorland. Everything except castle, churches and a few public and guild buildings was built of timber or half-timber. He had time to get lost in the town, which he did. Being tired after his ride across the moors, he spent the rest of the day and the night there, staying at the local Augustinian priory, where he heard Sunday Mass the following morning.

That day took Worcestre twenty miles, skirting to the north of Kilmar Tor and Dozmary Pool, where Excalibur was supposed to have been thrown, and across the gaunt and craggy Bodmin Moor, its water-soaked earth clothed in heather, to Bodmin, the largest town in Cornwall, famous in the recent civil wars for its support of the Yorkist cause. There he visited St Petroc's, one of the most modern churches in the land, completed only six years earlier. The saint himself, Worcestre wrote, not quite accurately, 'lies in a beautiful shrine in Bodmin Church facing St Mary's Chapel'. The canons of St Petroc's showed him their new library, which specialized in scientific books, and he had a long conversation with Dom William, the librarian 'who has knowledge and pleasure in physics, and I – through his kindness – saw several ancient books of physics with him'. He did not stay there though, for the cannons did not have the facilities, but instead spent the night at the Franciscan friary, where travellers traditionally found a bed.

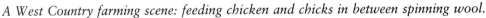

A West Country farming scene: feeding chicken and chicks in between spinning wool.

He was in the saddle all that Tuesday, from Bodmin to Truro, mostly walking his horse through high and inhospitable land, broken by tumbling woody valleys, where tiny villages sheltered under spires. The Cornish people were prosperous people, prosperous from wool and tin-mining, but they were not English, and had their own customs and their own language. William Worcestre must have found it very lonely: at times the only people he could communicate with were village priests, speaking with them in pidgin Latin.

He travelled the twenty-five miles to St Michael's Mount via Penryn the next day. He looked out from the shore towards the mount, and the western ledge of the granite rock where St Michael had appeared to Cornish fishermen in 495, then rode across the sand, uncovered at low tide, to the mount itself. He walked round it, and noted that it was about a mile in circumference, then visited the church. It had been built in the thirteenth century after the Norman church had crumbled in an 'earthquake' (probably a landslide). Of the earlier Saxon church, which had occupied the site from the eighth century to the Norman Conquest when the Benedictines took over, there was no sign. The Benedictines had now gone. Bridgetine nuns were the only occupants, apart from the convent's priest, the only male on the island.

William Worcestre had completed his pilgrimage. Oddly enough, for a man so fascinated by places, Land's End only twelve miles away did not interest him. He lived on the verge of a new era. Beyond Land's End was a New World. But he was still a medieval man, and the New World was not yet known. Land's End meant an abyss, so he gave it a miss. 'The same afternoon I rode back to the town of Penryn.'

He was in Bodmin again the following night, Saturday, 19 September, and the next day made a short excursion south down the Fowey Valley to Fowey, a centre for piracy, protected by high cliffs. There he took the ferry over the Fowey estuary and continued inland to Liskeard twelve miles away. He reached it in the middle of the afternoon and, hardly stopping, went on to the Benedictine abbey at Tavistock on the River Tavy. The town, like the enormous abbey which owned it, was built entirely of volcanic green-grey stones. It was the centre of the tin-mining industry, one of the 'stannary' towns. Here mine courts were held, and guildsmen have been responsible for the weighing and stamping of the tin since the reign of Edward I.

Next morning he set off across Dartmoor, passing close by Rough Tor, at the very centre of the moor, where craggy outcrops contrasted with oceans of blue and purple heather. He would not have crossed it alone. Too poor to hire his own guide, he would have ridden with a company of travellers, who either knew the route or clubbed together to pay for a single guide. By the time they had crossed it, and William Worcestre had gone on through Moretonhampstead and Dunsford, and down the River Teign to Exeter, it was late afternoon. You did not need a guide to get to Exeter – it was a big place, and its cathedral's twin towers rose high above the houses and city wall, as much a landmark as Glastonbury Tor. It was a rich town and had been so for a long time, and William Worcestre would have been familiar with William of Malmesbury's description of its riches.

Though the barren and unfruitful soil can scarcely produce indifferent oats, and frequently only the empty husk without the grain, yet owing to the magnificence of the city, the opulence of its inhabitants, and the constant resort of strangers, every kind of merchandise is there so abundant that nothing is wanting which can conduce to human comfort.

Good husbandry before the Enclosures; from the fourteenth-century Luttrell Psalter.

He awoke next morning and visited the cathedral. It was comparatively small, he discovered by measuring it. His eye would have told him nothing. The west front was crowded with layers of saints, and both the inside of the cathedral and the cloisters that squared off to the south of the nave were in a Decorated Gothic style.

He came out into the daylight, untethered his horse, mounted it and set off through the streets, passing the Hospital of St John of Jerusalem at the East Gate, and on into open country, reaching Ottery St Mary about mid-morning. The towers on the church there were like the towers on Exeter Cathedral, only smaller. He rode only a short distance that day, as he wanted to give his horse and himself time to recover from the day's ride over Dartmoor, and when he reached Newenham Abbey, just outside Axminster, in the early afternoon he took advantage of the monks' hospitality to stable his horse and himself. The memory of the moors and its fauna still haunted him. 'Sage and bindweed have flowers like bells,' he wrote that night.

From Newenham he rode north through Chard and Taunton to Bridgwater, where he spent the night, and swung south-east next day, travelling the ten miles to Muchelney Abbey, which had once been an island amid marshes and now stood like Glastonbury Tor on a hill in the Somerset Levels. It had been a Benedictine monastery since 693. The abbey and the abbey buildings were Norman. They looked very old. It was a rich monastery, very rich, which made its tiny community of a dozen monks very wealthy men, but they were not entirely corrupt, and did not begrudge good food and comfortable shelter to travellers like William Worcestre, respectable folk returning from a pilgrimage.

On his way to Muchelney he had met John Selwood, Abbot of Glastonbury, who invited him to return to the monastery. He was there the next night, and stayed all Sunday morning and most of the afternoon, before going to Wells in the early evening. From Wells it was a day's ride north over the Mendips to Bristol, where he stayed for two days.

He left on Friday, 3 October, passing through Keynsham and Bath, where he measured the length of the principal bath (the King's Bath) as forty steps long and thirty across, before spending the night in an inn. He came out of Bath on the Saturday morning by the south, rode the nineteen miles south-east to Warminster, and continued on through the afternoon to Stockton, 'where I was arrested'. The information comes as a jolt, and William Worcestre tells us no more about it. Something must have happened, perhaps some serious drinking, or maybe his swarthy face and one eye just frightened children. He was released within hours, so it could not have been that bad. Whatever it was, it brought an end to his day's travelling, so though a free man he was obliged to stay in the village for the night. When he left Stockton next morning he rode hard, along the Wylye Valley which marked the south-west border of Salisbury Plain, and continued first to Salisbury and then to Stockbridge on the Test. Next day, while the sun was still low, he rode into Winchester.

In its youth Winchester had been the capital of England, but by the time William Worcestre came in through the West Gate and rode down the High Street, the town had grown middle-aged. It stood on the west bank of the River Itchen, in a depression at the bottom of the valley slope, so the cathedral abbey hardly rose above the skyline. You came across it unexpectedly and it was not until you were close that you became aware of the cathedral's immensity. Most of it was Norman, though there were parts east of the crossing that were Early English. The west end was Perpendicular, and the work on it was still going on when William Worcestre saw it. The interior was spectacular, spanned by rich fourteenth-century vaulting. Beneath the vaulting gangs of craftsmen were transforming the nave from Norman to Perpendicular. The size was unforgettable. It was one of the longest churches in Christendom, and the side chapels blazed with wall paintings. The abbey buildings lay to the south of the cathedral, the library over the passageway between the south transept and the chapter house, and overlooking the cloisters. It was one of the most comprehensive libraries in England and contained an illuminated Vulgate 300 years old. The Bishop's Palace and castle stood by the city walls a little to the east of the abbey buildings overlooking the river. The abbey's decline reflected the city's decline, for though the monastery was built for seventy Benedictine monks, there were only twenty-nine left.

It was not the only religious house in decline. To the north of the city in the suburbs was Hyde Abbey – where the bones of King Alfred had been laid – a shadow of its former self; while south of the city was the Hospital of St Cross. It was 300 years old and its buildings had been rebuilt thirty years earlier by Cardinal Beaufort, but it too was short of numbers and there were insufficient religious to look after the sick. Worcestre left the cathedral and rode past the Hospital of St John of Jerusalem, crossed Soke Bridge and continued north and east between Magdalen Hill and St Giles's Hill towards Alton.

He spent the night at Alton, from where he followed his earlier route through Farnham and Guildford to London. After a short time in London he made the three-day ride back to Norfolk. It had been a long journey for an old man.

*   *   *

The next year, 1479, William Worcestre set out on a journey through East Anglia. In May he was visiting the great Benedictine abbey of Bury St Edmunds, one of the six richest in the country, so rich that in 1381, the year the peasants revolted and chopped the head off the abbot, the monks had one-and-a-half servants each. The whole town was owned by the abbot, which possibly accounted for its rare street plan, a rigorously imposed grid which had been designed by an abbot after the Conquest. Here Sigebert, first Christian king of the Angles, founded a monastery, and here the barons and Archbishop Langton met in 1214 and swore before the high altar to impose on King John the Magna Carta. The abbey itself was being rebuilt after a fire. It was still a

The lame, the sick and the halt, on their way to the Virgin Mary's shrine at Walsingham.

magnificent sight, over 500 feet long, with the proportions of a cathedral, and part-hidden behind wooden scaffolding. Inside, some of the most splendid stone vaulting of the late Perpendicular period was being set in the ceiling.

In early July he was in Walsingham, passing through Swaffham, Castle Acre (where there was a Cluniac priory) and Fakenham on the way. An Augustinian priory, built of Norfolk flint, guarded the Walsingham shrine and was so rich from pilgrims that it was even wealthier than Bury St Edmunds. The shrine where the Virgin Mary had appeared in 1061 was marked by a little chapel to the north of the priory church; and to the east of the church were two wells where the diseased, lame, handicapped, mad and desperate sunk and swam in the water amid the prayers and ribaldry of the pious and profane.

*   *   *

A year later, in 1480, William Worcestre made his third pilgrimage, a journey back to his own youth, to Oxford, where he had been a student, through the Cotswolds to Bristol, where he had been born, and on to Glastonbury again.

The first part of the journey, to London, was through familiar territory, leaving Norwich on 30 July, spending one night at Thetford, where he paid fourpence for food for himself and his horse, and a second night at Walden Abbey. He stayed in London for a week and from there rode west to Oxford, where he stayed a second week.

Oxford had been important long before it became a university centre. It stood on the border of Wessex and Mercia, protected on three sides by the Thames and the Cherwell. Already at the time of Domesday it had over 1,000 houses. It was England's first university, founded by students from the University of Paris in 1167, who chose the town for its reputation for learning, a reputation built up by the hundreds of monks and friars in the religious houses that surrounded the town. Benedictines, Franciscans, Carmelites, Dominicans and Augustinians enriched the university, giving it some of the greatest scholars of the Middle Ages: Duns Scotus, Robert Grosseteste, Bradwardine, Fitzralph and Roger Bacon.

The centre of the town was Carfax or *Quatrevois*, by the pre-Conquest Church of St Martin. West from Carfax stood the castle (built by Henry I, and where his daughter Matilda took refuge from her cousin King Stephen), the remains of Beaumont Palace (where Richard Coeur de Lion had been born), and the vast abbey of Osney. East was St

Michael's Church, standing on Cornmarket by the Bocardo Gate. Beyond the gate were the Church of St Mary Magdalen, the Blackfriars, and the road to Woodstock. South from Carfax was St Aldgate, running in a straight line past the Austin cannons' building and St Frideswide's Augustinian priory, with its Norman church and Perpendicular cloisters, to Folly Bridge. There the great Roger Bacon had studied the stars from the roof of the bridge gatehouse, and had sought order in the darkness of the universe. East was The High, gently curving as it went out of the city to the bridge over the River Cherwell by Magdalen Hall. It was the most interesting street in Oxford. On the left-hand side was St Mary's, the university church which had been completely rebuilt since Worcestre was a student, and behind it, down Catte Street, Brazen Nose Hall, Little St Edmund's Hall, Wykeham Hall (later New College), Little University Hall, St Thomas Hall, Beresford Hall, Hart Hall (later Hertford College) and the newly completed School of Divinity. Worcestre visited all except Brazen Nose. On the other side of Catte Street, facing The High, was All Souls. Like St Mary's, it had also been rebuilt since Worcestre's student days. Further down The High was Queen's; and beyond Queen's, outside the city walls, was Magdalen Hall. It was also new – in his day it had been a Hospital of St John of Jerusalem – and workmen were still putting the finishing touches to the cloisters. The right-hand side of The High was only slightly less illustrious. There was a stretch of timber-framed houses between the street and the northern boundary wall of St Frideswide's, then came Oriel Hall, Bulkley Hall and University Hall, while behind the latter was situated Merton Hall. Beyond the city wall an open field led down towards the river.

He stayed at the Bull, in the centre of town, and there the predictable habits of the confidential secretary deserted him and the wildness broke through the lines of strain on his dark and shadowy face. He went on a drinking binge, ran out of money and, even after raising more from the local goldsmith's, still had not enough to pay the landlord, ending up owing him fourpence.

Worcestre did not spend the entire week in the taverns, however, and found time to visit the library of Merton Hall. It was an important visit, for here there were old manuscripts providing glimpses of the topography of England. He spent hours there, staring blankly through the lancet windows into Mob Quad when the strain on his single eye became too much for him. It was not an easy task, and involved much skimming, for nothing had ever been written that could be called a topographical treatise. One manuscript, by Gildas the Wise, fascinated him and the notes he took in Merton library still survive.

> Britain is an island named after a certain Brutus, a Roman Consul, but it rises from the wintery south . . . Chapter the last begins: *Arthur fought against them*, and the last word of this chapter is *The End*.

Like most notes, one can only hope they made more sense to the writer than they do to the reader.

Worcestre left Oxford on 18 August, riding out over Folly Bridge and continuing the five miles south to the Benedictine abbey at Abingdon, before turning west through Faringdon, crossing the Thames at Lechlade and coming into Cirencester. He was in the Cotswolds, hill after hill, sheep flock after sheep flock. He rode for two days through the Cotswolds, stopping for a while at Malmesbury Abbey. The abbey buildings, on the shrine of St Aldhelm, were late Norman, with a fourteenth-century square tower at the west end of the church and a crossing tower topped by a gigantic

Autumn harvesting before the Enclosures; from the illuminated Luttrell Psalter.

spire, taller than Salisbury's. You entered the church through the south porch, on which were carved medieval cartoons telling the history of the Old and New Testaments from the Creation, through the Fall, the Flood, the Burning Bush and the Crucifixion to the Resurrection. Inside, the interior was so late Norman that the arches were close to being pointed, almost Gothic. The rest of the abbey buildings lay to the north of the church, and the cloister had just been given a fan-vault. The town that had grown up around the abbey was rich from the wool trade, and on the banks of the Avon was the late twelfth-century Hospital of St John. East of the market place was the castle, by the Church of St Paul, 'in the very cemetery of the church, hardly a stone's throw', according to William of Malmesbury.

Seven miles more took Worcestre to Castle Combe. He arrived without a penny, but this was not as reckless as it might at first seem. A former confidential secretary of the local justice will always have a friend who owes him favours; and, sure enough, there was a Mister Benet, who lent him a shilling, sufficient to pay for the night's rest and take Worcestre on to Bristol.

In Bristol his pilgrimage was almost over; an old man, he had returned to the city of his birth for the last time. His friends and relatives had to keep him in cash until he was able to draw from the goldsmith's, but there is no hint that they resented the confidential secretary who suddenly, and out of character, turned up penniless at their door. From his sister he borrowed fourpence, from John Greene another fourpence, from his cousin Robert Ash three shillings and fourpence and from Thomas Bole of Lewins Head an astronomical thirteen shillings and fourpence. Then he blew the whole lot in the evening of St Bartholomew's Day and had to go through the borrowing process all over again — which must have stretched the patience and purse of at least some of his close ones. But he managed to pay all his debts and settle a lawsuit on behalf of his sister before leaving.

There was one final lap of his journey, to Glastonbury. On the way he stopped at a cave, providing us with the earliest known description of Wookey Hole.

Wookey Hole is half a league [two modern miles] from Wells and within the parish, it is a certain narrow entry where to begin with is the image of a man called the Porter. One must ask leave from the Porter, to enter the hall of Wookey, and the people carry with them *anglice* sheaves of reed sedge to light the hall. It is as big as Westminster Hall and stalactites hang from the vault which is wonderously arched over with stone.

The passage through which one enters the hall from the gate is about half a furlong in length, by my reckoning, and arched over, with stalactites hanging from the smooth surface above. Between the passage and the hall is a broad lake crossed by over 500 stone steps, each step is about 4 feet, and if a man goes off the steps he falls into the water which is 5 or 6 feet deep on every side.

The kitchen before the entry to the hall is covered with a vault of stones whose span is beyond estimation; and there is the figure of a woman clothed and spinning with *anglice* a distaff held beneath her girdle.

Thence they cross another alleyway about a hundred paces long, and a man may cross dryshod quite easily upon stepping stones.

Next comes the room called the Parlour, a round house built of great rocks, about 200 paces across; on the north side of the parlour is a well, which is beautifully arched over, full of water, and none can tell how deep it is.

He emerged into the daylight and rode the seven miles to Glastonbury. There, in the library, Dom John Murylynch showed him the chronicles of John of Glastonbury. William Worcestre sat down and copied out an extract.

There enters Avalon a party of twelve men:
Joseph, the flower of Arimathea, is chief of them;
Josophes, Joseph's son, accompanies his father
And to these with ten others the rights of Glastonbury are appropriated.
To the Britons I went after I had buried Christ,
Came to Glastonbury, taught the Britons, took my rest.

Worcestre read his copy carefully, then added a prayer at the bottom of the manuscript.

Oh Lord Jesus exceeding in perfection every creature, grant us thy servants that by the works of St Joseph done for thee at and after thy passion we may truly know on earth and find here in life his remains to receive worthy reverence.

William Worcestre was a medieval man. Yet he lived on the edge of a new era. Dom William, the librarian of St Petroc's, Bodmin, with his 'knowledge and pleasure in physics' was a sign of the times. Men were growing tired of the mystery of things, and of answers that only made the mysteries more mysterious. Worcestre did not see the new era himself: he came too early, the perpetual price paid by the pioneer.

2
BARE
RUIN'D
CHOIRS

Wherever you see a big cathedral, it's grain country.

Ernest Hemingway from *Papa Hemingway* by A. E. Hotchner

JOHN LELAND WAS a child of the new era; born in London in 1506 he belonged to the modern century. School was St Paul's under John Colet and Cambridge University. In Cambridge the architecture was Gothic (King's College Chapel had just been completed) and the teaching Renaissance. But outside the lecture halls more radical ideas of reformation, taking the ideas of the New Learning to their logical conclusions, were being spread among the revolutionary students. The focal point for the radicals was the White Horse Tavern, and it was the White Horse, and the voices of men such as Latimer, Bilney and Coverdale, that indelibly marked Leland's years at Cambridge. It was there that he first heard of Martin Luther. He threw himself into the cause. These were heady and intoxicating years: bliss it was to be alive, and to be young was very heathen. Cambridge was followed by All Souls in Oxford and the Sorbonne in Paris. They dulled in comparison.

Leland came to London, anxious to join the capital's Renaissance circles, securing a post as tutor to the younger son of Thomas Howard, Duke of Norfolk. It was only a second son, and hardly a glittering prize. Nor did Leland glitter. His manner was awkward, he lacked charm, and when he came into Renaissance circles and tried to treat men such as Polydore Vergil as his equals, they gently snubbed him.

Vergil came from Italy. For twenty years he had been working on his *Historia Anglia*. He saw Leland as a presumptuous Protestant lout. Leland was wounded and resented the snub. As he made his own way, making up in learning and diligence what he lacked in charm, he took the wound with him – to Windsor, where he was appointed Royal Librarian, and then to Henry VIII's court, where he became Royal Chaplain.

Within three years of Leland's appointment the King had divorced Catherine of Aragon, broken with Rome and married Anne Boleyn. Leland wrote the 'verses and ditties' for her coronation. It was a speedy rise, and quite naturally he expected even better things. That same year the King appointed him 'King's Antiquary'. It was a unique appointment, for which he had no predecessor and no successor. Indeed, there is no certain evidence that the appointment officially existed. Leland's orders were to search every college, cathedral, convent, abbey, priory and friary in the kingdom for rare manuscripts for the King's library at Windsor. As the Royal Chaplain he must have had some suspicion of what was behind the appointment. Henry himself was quite open about it. 'He is determined to reunite to the Crown the goods which churchmen held of it,' Chapuys, the Spanish Ambassador, reported to Madrid.

The religious houses of England were easy targets for a Renaissance prince. With the advent of the New Learning from Italy and Germany, the rediscovery of the Classics and the emergence of natural science, the monasteries had ceased being seen as beacons of learning, and were regarded rather as refuges for the comfortably-off and intellectually discredited. The younger sons of the educated middle-class no longer resorted to the monasteries as a first step to worldly success, but preferred the marginally more secular universities and the inns of court. Even Erasmus, loyal to Catholicism to the very end, found them hard to defend.

> The monastic life should not be equated with the virtuous life: it is one type of life that may be advantageous or not according to the individual's disposition of body and mind. I would no more persuade you to it than I would dissuade you from it.

The monasteries were not even counter-revolutionary; merely irrelevant.

Badly managed, inefficient, unpopular, yet possessing great wealth, they were the biggest landowner in the country after the King. In 1529 Wolsey had shown what benefits could accrue from the suppression of a mere twenty-nine houses. Henry could do better. But while the first wave of commissioners, who would value the monasteries, could be trusted to inventory gold, silver, plate and crosses, they could no more value a 300-year-old Latin manuscript than an income-tax inspector could. As for the second group of commissioners who would be visiting the monasteries, first to break the monks' will and then to break their buildings, the only written documents they were likely to value were signed confessions. Who better then for the task of salvaging from the Old Learning what could benefit the New than a resolute and bookish King's librarian with sound Protestant leanings?

Leland was not a happy man, nor an easy one; in all his life he made only one friend, John Bale, the ultra-Protestant pamphleteer. Thomas Caius, who had known Leland since his All Souls days, found him too highly strung and argumentative for friendship; Polydore Vergil just despised him.

In 1534, a few months before Leland received his commission, Vergil's *Historia Anglia* appeared in print. The introductory chapter was a description of England.

> It appeareth very champayne and plain, nevertheless it hath many hills, with most delectable valleys, wherein the most part of the inhabitants, especially the nobles, have placed their manor and dwelling houses.

The men were tall, grey-eyed, cautious and a little cold, but kind and 'well-favoured and fair in face'; the women possessed 'exquisite beauty, their whiteness not inferior to snow'; and the country was so rich from wool that the trade was called her 'Golden Fleece'. But outside the major cities and away from the main lines of communication, particularly in Wales and Scotland, the information gets scantier, and we are back in the world of monsters, magic and – that medieval raspberry – 'men whose heads did grow beneath their shoulders'.

There could have been no more avid reader than Leland to check the text for errors, nor one more socially inept at pointing them out to Vergil himself. When

Leland's commission came he saw it as the perfect opportunity to surpass Polydore Vergil, to write the definitive topographical book on England and Wales. It was a mammoth task, and Leland was a resolute man.

From 1534 until 1542 John Leland travelled the length and breadth of England and Wales:

> both by the sea coasts and the middle parts, sparing neither labour nor costs, that there is neither cape, nor bay, haven, creek or pier, river or confluence of rivers, breaches, washes, lakes, meres, fenny waters, mountains, valleys, moors, heaths, forests, woods, cities, boroughs, castles, principal manor places, monasteries and colleges, but I have seen them.

He saw more than landscapes; he saw the final days of the Middle Ages. When he began his 'laborious journey', religious houses dotted the countryside, men and women danced around maypoles and believed in miracles, and folk longed 'to goon on pilgrimages'. Within two years houses with less than twelve religious had been suppressed, and within five years all the remaining abbeys, priories, friaries, nunneries, almshouses and hospitals had joined them. A way of life that had provided the medieval world with a complete social security system for 800 years had been sold off to private hands.

*　　*　　*

He started in April 1534, the month for pilgrimages, riding north to Cambridge. There he felt at home. Unlike in Oxford, the Renaissance had already left its mark on

Laurence Nowell's 1564 map, the first 'modern' map of the British Isles.

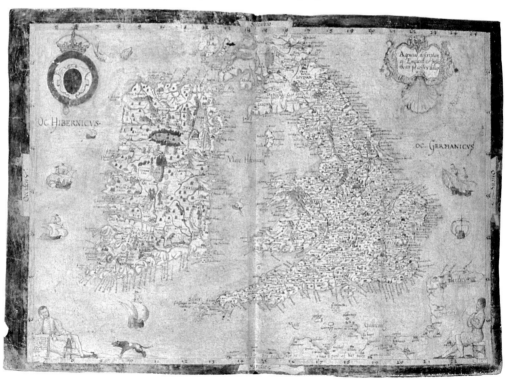

Cambridge. There were thirteen colleges, all but four of them in two rows between the High Street and the River Cam. The southernmost was the oldest, Peterhouse College, a three-sided court, and all, save the hall on the south side, built of stone and rubble. The library, Leland's primary interest, faced you as you came in; from the hall windows there were deer grazing on Coe Fen. Behind Peterhouse was Queens', set back from the High Street behind half-timbered houses and the decaying buildings of St Catherine's Hall. It had two courts. Its first one, from Queens' Lane, was all brick and had a magnificent gatehouse. The second was cloistered and half-timbered. It went all the way to the river. Beyond Queens' the Carmelite friary stretched to King's College Chapel, which from the south appeared as a spectacular rectangle, the side chapels marking its base and the buttresses and windows drawing the eyes heavenwards to the pinnacles. Inside was equally awe-inspiring. The chapel appeared to be all windows – each one portraying a different episode in the history of the Old and New Testaments – framed by the slender buttresses, so that the vaulting above appeared weightless. Leland was proud of it – it was one of the wonders of the age, and a quarter of the town centre had been demolished to give it space. The college buildings were to the north of the chapel, squashed in between Clare Hall and the School of Divinity, hidden from the south by the chapel. Behind it was Trinity Hall and Gonville Hall, where Thomas Caius's brother John was studying. They were standard Cambridge colleges, with one court each, the chapel and hall in stone, the students' accommodation (tiny cubicles with narrow windows) made of stone and rubble. North of Gonville and Trinity, Michaelhouse was equally conventional, though King's Hall next to it possessed a decidedly eccentrically shaped court. St John's, the most northerly college, was the most serene. It had two courts, and everything in them, with the exception of the old chapel of St John the Evangelist, was of brick. In its pre-1511 life it had been the Hospital of St John, and the chapel was the last memory left of its hospitaller role.

Forming a half-circle on the far side of the town were the monasteries, and the new colleges which had taken over old monasteries. The most northerly was the Benedictine Crowland Abbey, which had its own theological college, Buckingham College (now Magdalene College). Next came Jesus College, which had been the Benedictine priory of St Radegund until it turned into a college in 1496. South of Jesus was the Franciscan priory, and beyond that another modern college, Christ's. Finally there was the Blackfriars (on the site of Emmanuel College), the Dominicans' theological college, which – like the Buckingham College – was not formally part of the university, and felt increasingly isolated as Protestantism swept through Cambridge.

Leland was happy in Cambridge. When he finally left it was in dull weather, riding west through unenclosed land to the Benedictine priory at St Neots. He left St Neots a few days later and crossed the Ouse on a wooden bridge. A couple of hours on he met a farmer who had converted a ruined castle into a farmhouse and farmyard. It was a good sign. The country was peaceful and becoming prosperous. He crossed the River Nene on a stone bridge at Oundle and within an hour crossed it again on a timber one at Fotheringhay. The village had two inns and one wide street that got wider the further you went. It was all of stone. 'The glory of it standeth by the parish church, a fair building, and the college.' The west end of the church was exquisite, the fan-vaulting having been erected only five years earlier. Fotheringhay itself was a market town and river boats came up the Nene from Wisbech and Peterborough. Overlooking the town and river was the castle, recently refurbished by Catherine of Aragon, 'fair and meetly strong with double ditches and a keep very ancient', Leland noted that evening.

He retraced his steps to Oundle and struck south-west for Northampton. The road took him past Drayton ('the prettiest place in these quarters') and Wellingborough ('a good quick market town built of stone as almost all the towns be in Northampton-shire'). Northampton stood with its castle 'on the brow of a mean hill', spilling its suburbs over the walls. Beyond the suburbs stood a circle of monasteries and friaries. There was the Greyfriars, 'the best built and largest house of all the friars, a little beyond the main market place'; the Blackfriars, north-east of the castle; and the Austin friars, 'hard against St John's Hospital'. Across the river was Delapre Abbey, a Cluniac foundation.

From Northampton he rode north-east, first to Kettering, and then over rolling 'champayne ground bearing good grass and corn' and through Rockingham Forest to Leicester. The town was all timber, except for the public buildings. The walls ran round three sides, and on the fourth was the River Soar. Within the walls was the Greyfriars by Southgate, and without were the Dominicans and the Austin friars, 'the least austere and the least strictly organized of any of the religious bodies',* whose abbey was one of the biggest and richest in England. In his heyday Wolsey had tried to reform them. In his decline he came to die among them. His death marked the beginning of the end of Catholic England.

After a day's excursion to Loughborough and Lutterworth, and another night in Leicester, Leland rode due east over rolling landscape to Launde Priory, a monastic satellite to Leicester Abbey, where the Austin friars had lived, worked and prayed in solid comfort for 400 years.

Next morning he set off for Stamford. He came in from the south, along St Martin's High, passed the Church of St Martin's and went over the old stone bridge across the River Welland. Stamford was built entirely of stone, and was a natural stopping place for a Renaissance man and antiquarian. Remnants of Roman wall still separated the town from the country. It had been a Daneburgh town in the Dark Ages and a university town in the Middle Ages. Its college, Brazen Nose, founded by secessionist students from Oxford in 1333, was now in ruins. Religious houses and hospitals abounded: Browne's Hospital, with its college-like courtyard, the Whitefriars priory on the Spalding road where the Carmelites lived, St Leonard's Priory where the Benedictines overlooked the river, and half a dozen more.

Naturally restless, never staying anywhere long enough to form friendships, Leland rode north to Grimsthorpe Castle, casting his eyes over the dilapidated Vauldey Abbey and its marble quarry on the way. Most of the route was through unenclosed farmland, hilly on his left and sloping down towards the flat fenlands on his right. The castle, which he called 'an old work of stone', with a fair gatehouse, was owned by the Duke of Suffolk and had already been converted into a comfortable mansion. The duke provided him with hospitality for some three days, and he used them to make excursions into the wild and unchartered fens, whose people were 'rude' and herded cattle on stilts.

He left Grimsthorpe Castle and pressed on, with fertile pastures and 'champayne ground' on one side, and wood and fenland on the other, to Sleaford. Its castle, to the south-west of the town, was 'very well maintained' and surrounded by a moat fed from a fen stream, giving it the appearance of an island. From its high tower one could see over the undrained and unpacified Fens for miles. As for the weather, it rained almost

*David Knowles, *The Religious Orders in England*, vol. III.

every day. The winds were cold and the sky dark. It was the worst summer on record. Many blamed the King and the Protestants.

He was glad to arrive at Lincoln. The road took him straight into the city, past the Whitefriars priory on his left and the Guild of St Mary on his right, over the High Bridge – with houses and a chapel on it, like London Bridge – and through Stonebow. Then he went up High Street and Steep Hill, passing the two stone buildings called the Jews' houses, to the castle and cathedral.

> The first buildings were at the very top of the hill, the oldest of those parts inhabited since [the Ancient] Britons' time. Much Roman money was found in the north beyond this old Lincoln. After the destruction of this old Lincoln men began to fortify the southern part of the hill, newly ditching, walling and gating it, and so was new Lincoln made out of a piece of old Lincoln by the Saxons.

From Lincoln, Leland pushed through the rain to Torksey Abbey and crossed the Trent at Gainsborough, a port on the River Trent and 'a good market town'. After riding 'in low wash and somewhat fenny ground', he reached Bawtry. It was 'bare and redundant', dog-earred like some old manuscript. Ten miles on came Doncaster, a fire and a warm bed.

He liked Doncaster and noted the fine church of St George, built of stone taken from the decaying castle, and the 'right goodly house of the White Friars in the middle of the town'. The Greyfriars were at the north end of the bridge. Around the town were meadows, corn fields and woodland.

From Doncaster Leland rode through woods and farmland, 'in all places reasonably fruitful of pastures and corn', to Pontefract. It also lay on the Great North Road, and had the biggest castle in Yorkshire. West, towards Wakefield, enclosures surrounded St Oswald's Abbey, a monastery that 'hath the goodliest fountain of conduit water in this quarter of England'. From there he rode north over Castleford Bridge at the junction of the Aire and Calder Rivers, and meandered through Aberford, Towton, Ulleskelf and Tadcaster, where he crossed the River Wharfe over 'eight fair arches of stone' into York.

York stood at the confluence of two rivers, the Ouse and the Foss. Here Constantine the Great was proclaimed Emperor and King Edwin was baptized by Paulinus on Easter Sunday 627. By Leland's time the city had a population of over 10,000 and ranked after London, Bristol and Norwich as the fourth largest city in the kingdom. But, in spite of its size and its wool-wealth, it shared few of the political opinions of southern England. It was fiercely Yorkist and a devoted supporter of the monastic welfare state. It had revolted three times since Henry VII usurped the throne. Its walls were strong and, to Leland, a committed Tudor and Protestant, a little threatening.

> First a great tower with a chain of iron to cast over the Ouse: then another tower, and so to Bootham Gate: from Bootham Bar, or Gate, to Goodram Gate, or Bar, ten towers. Then four towers to Layerthorpe, a postern gate: and so by the space of two shots the blind and deep water of Foss coming out of the Forest of Galtres defendeth this part of the city without walls. Then to Walm Gate three towers, and then to Fisher Gate, stopped since the communards burnt it in the time of King Henry VII. And then over the Foss by the bridge to the castle. The area of the castle is of no very great quantity. There be five ruined towers on it.

Within the walls the minster at the northern corner and the castle at the southern corner dominated the town. Between them were half-timbered houses, nineteen churches and mazes of narrow lanes and alleys, almost closed from the sky by overhangs. The main streets were relatively wide; they had been there since Roman times. The Via Praetoria had become Stonegate and the High and Low Petergates could trace their antecedents to the Via Principalis. Half the city's churches had been built with Roman stone.

Inside and outside the walls the city was dotted with religious houses. The biggest was the Benedictine abbey of St Mary's, founded by William Rufus. It still had its Norman cloisters, but the church had been rebuilt in the late thirteenth century, and was one of the most spectacular Early English Gothic churches in England. North of the church was the abbot's house, more modern, only forty years old and built of brick; south was the Hospitium or Guest House, by the banks of the Ouse; and west was St Leonard's Hospital, 300 years old and one of the biggest hospitals in the country. The smaller houses made up in numbers what they lacked in size. There were the Austin friars by the Ouse, the Whitefriars close to Layerthorpe Gate, the Greyfriars not far from the castle, the Gilbertines at St Andrew's Priory outside Fish Gate, and the Priory of the Holy Trinity by Mickle Gate. Then there was the minster itself, the second cathedral in England after St Paul's, surrounded by its precinct of library, priests' houses, hospitals and colleges. In addition to these there were secular hospitals and charitable foundations, but no one maintained them in this hard and entrepreneurial age. 'There was a place of the Bigots, hard within Layerthorpe Gate, and by it a hospital of the Bigots' foundation. Sir Francis Bigot let both the hospital and his house fall into ruin.'

There was a month's work here, and in the surrounding hills of Yorkshire, visiting monasteries and nunneries as far away as Beverley, Kingston-upon-Hull, Scarborough, Whitby and Pickering. The moors were bleak, and it must have been a relief to return to York after each excursion. It was after one such return that Leland found out that his

Kingston-upon-Hull, on the Humber Estuary, a major port in John Leland's time.

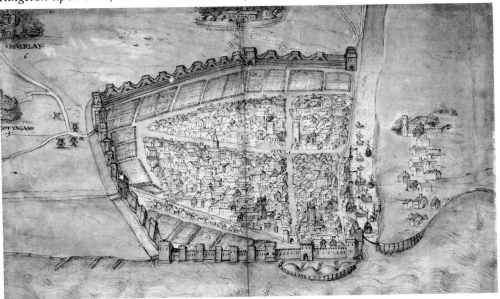

friend John Bale had been arrested for his ultra-Protestant campaigning. He wrote a letter to the King via his immediate master, Thomas Cromwell, asking for clemency. 'There is in him learning, judgement, modesty, with many other good qualities,' he begged. Bale was released. Leland was relieved – Bale was his only real friend. It was weeks before the King's Antiquary finally left the city, striking north through Darlington and Bishop Auckland for Durham.

Coming from Bishop Auckland, Durham's resolutely Norman cathedral and bishop's castle, perched on red sandstone and surrounded on three sides by water, were unforgettable. Leland came into the city across the 400-year-old Framwell Bridge, walked his horse to the market place, marked by the tower of St Nicholas and the guild hall of Corpus Christi, then turned hard right up the street where the saddlers displayed their work and climbed the red sandstone mound to the castle and cathedral. In Durham, castle and cathedral were one, 'half church of God, half castle 'gainst the Scot', and the Bishop of Durham was the last of the great prelate princes. His monastic cathedral, with its extravagant shrine to St Cuthbert, was one of the finest Norman churches in Christendom; his castle one of the strongest.

> The close itself of the Minster on the highest part of the hill is well-walled, and hath divers fair gates. The church itself and the cloister be very strong and fair. The castle standeth on the north-east side of the Minster and the Wear runneth under it. The keep standeth aloft and is stately built. The buildings of Durham town are meetly strong, but neither high nor costly. There appear some pieces of walls of the town joining to a gate of the palace wall, but the town itself within the peninsula is but a small thing in respect of the circumference of all the stately close: so that it alone may be called the walled town of Durham.

The Benedictine monastery that served the cathedral – its cloister adjoined the cathedral on the south side – was the most powerful religious house in the North. Though its revenues had declined through the fifteenth century, it was still the fourteenth richest in the country, owning fourteen manor houses, and drawing the rents from two of the city's boroughs, the grazing grounds of Beaurepaire and Elvet Moor, and the coal mines at Aldin Grange. It was also one of the most learned monasteries in the country, with its own college at Oxford, a grammar school in Durham and – most marvellous of all – a mechanical clock.

From the *Rites of Durham*, the record of a lay servant at the time of Leland's visit, we get a picture of the monastic life in its last few years. Seventy monks practised the *opus Dei* in a precinct of only four acres. The overcrowding had its price, and in the century before his visit a sub-prior had been stabbed, a monk murdered, and two others slashed in the cloisters. Yet it hardly seems the den of iniquity painted by Leland's Protestant contemporaries, and though the community constantly fell short of its ideal (what community has not?), the lay servant of Durham refers again and again to 'the goodly religious of the monastic life', praising them above all for their simplicity and humility.

Leland spent most of his time in the library, which stood between the chapter house and the south transept. In it were ten long desks. The first three were devoted to the Bible; the fourth, fifth and sixth were reserved for religious texts; the seventh was for studies in history, the lives of the saints and the Classics; the eighth and ninth were for canon and civil law; the tenth for Aristotle. All in all the library contained over 1,000 manuscripts and 500 printed books.

From Durham he went further, through Chester-le-Street ('chiefly one street of very mean buildings') to Gateshead and Newcastle, ascending 'seven miles by mountainous ground with pasture, heath, moor and firs'. There was 'a great coal pit' there. It was the furthest north he went. From there he retraced his steps to Durham and Bishop Auckland, where he turned south-west and rode the fourteen miles – past Raby Castle, owned by the Nevilles, one of the most powerful families in the North – descending into Teesdale to Barnard Castle, standing 'stately upon the Tees' between the river and the 'meetly pretty town's' market place.

He left Barnard Castle and continued south, riding for two miles along the right bank of the Tees, over Greta Bridge, and always keeping the Pennines on his right shoulder. He was in the Yorkshire Dales, with windswept pastures on the high land, corn in the valleys and woodland on the slopes between the two. The road was easy as far as Ravensworth, most of it along the old Roman road, which could still be discerned among the weeds running south-east to north-west. The road to Richmond was harder.

Richmond was quintessentially medieval: there was a castle perched on a precipice, a parish church in the market place, a Franciscan friary, and a Premonstratensian abbey dedicated to St Agatha a mile's walk along the riverside.

Twenty miles on was Ripon. The town's abbey, whose history went back to Bede, was in a sorry state. Its stones had been taken by the Cistercians to build the tower of Fountains Abbey, a few miles to the west. The cathedral was in better shape. 'The new minster is set up of the hill, a fair and big piece of work.' There were three hospitals, St John's, St Mary Magdalene (for lepers) and St Anne's (or Maison Dieu). The market place was vast, and the annual fair 'much celebrated for buying of horses'.

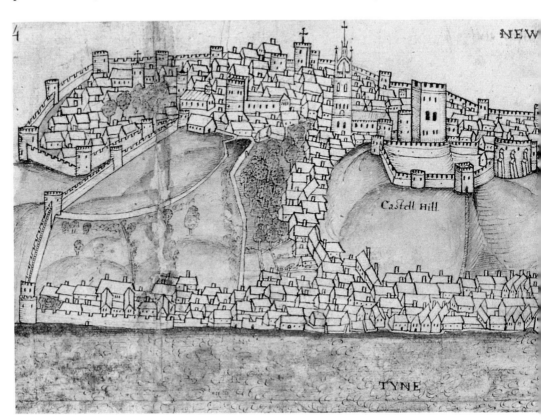

He left, crossing the River Skell by the old bridge just south of the cathedral, and rode south to Knaresborough, 'no great thing and meanly built', where there was a Redemptionist priory. From Knaresborough he continued south to Wentbridge, about a mile beyond Pontefract, where he retrod his outward route to Bawtry, branching off south-south-west to the Augustinian priory at Worksop and the Premonstratensian abbey at Welbeck, before coming into Mansfield.

Six miles out of Mansfield was Newstead Abbey, another priory founded by Henry II, and nine miles on was Nottingham, which Leland called Snottingham.

Snottingham is both a large town and well-built out of timber and plaster, and standeth stately on a climbing hill. The market place and street both from the building on the side of it, for the very wideness of the street, and the clean paving of it, is the most fairest, without exception, in all England. Southward by the waterside be great cliffs and rocks of stone, that be large and very good to build with, and many houses set on the top of them, and at the bottom of them be great caves where many stones hath been digged out for buildings in the town, and these caves be partly used for dwelling houses, and partly for cellars and store houses. The castle of Snottingham standeth on a rocky hill on the west side of the town. The base court is large and meetly strong. And a stately bridge is there with pillars bearing beasts and giants over the ditch into the second ward: the frontier of the which ward in the entering is exceeding strong with towers and portcullis. The most beautiful part and gallant building for lodgings is on the north side, where Edward IV began a right sumptuous piece of stone work.

Twelve miles on 'by low meadow and marsh ground' Leland came to Belvoir Castle. 'The castle of Belvoir standeth on the very knape of a high hill, steep up each

FLVMEN

way, partly by nature, partly by working of men's hands.' The Middle Ages were coming to an end. The roof beams had rotted and elderberry grew in the walls. Now the castle was being rebuilt by the Earl of Rutland, not as a military post but as a comfortable dwelling. The country was becoming more secure.

From the castle's battlements the view was spectacular. 'The Vale of Belvoir, barren of wood, is large and very plentiful of full corn and grass, and lyeth in three shires, Leicestershire, Lincolnshire and much of Nottinghamshire.' For once that summer the weather seems to have been clear.

Twenty miles from Belvoir was Stamford, a half-day's ride at a trot, almost a full day's at walking pace. Past Stamford the road was familiar, through the Forest of Deene to Fotheringhay and Oundle, then south over the same rolling hills and meadows, broken by streams and enclosures, to Bedford, where there were two Augustinian establishments, Newnham Priory and Caldwell Priory, and a Greyfriars house. From there he rode south through Ampthill, 'by woody ground and enclosures but after the most part by champayne ground', to Berkhamsted.

> Berkhamsted is one of the best market towns in Hertfordshire, and hath a long street meetly well built from the north to the south; and another, but somewhat lesser, from the west to the east, where the river runneth. The church is in the middle of the town. In the bottom of the river on each side be very fair meadows.

John Leland's first great journey was almost over. From Berkhamsted it was a mere day's ride through Windsor, Datchet ('where is a goodly bridge of timber') and Hampton Court, to London.

*   *   *

On his second long journey John Leland found that he was not the only visitor to the religious houses of England. A few months earlier, in January 1535, Sir Thomas Audley, Lord Chancellor, had established commissioners in each shire, to visit and value every abbey, nunnery, monastery, friary and collegiate church in the land. His commissioners were drawn from the ranks of the civil servants, the gentry and local government. Apart from the chairman, the local bishop, all were laymen owing their positions and status to the Tudor monarchy. They worked all summer, compiling their findings into the six-volume *Valor Ecclesiasticus*, to be ready for the Exchequer's accountants that winter. Suddenly the King's Antiquary found that he was no longer an honoured guest, but had become an object of fear and suspicion. Already manuscripts were disappearing from libraries and being sold for cash. Isolated and almost friendless, Leland protected himself from his isolation with an outward show of arrogance and conceit.

His journey in the summer of 1535 took him to the West Midlands, starting out on the Oxford road, then veering west about ten miles before Oxford and riding to Bicester. There was an Augustinian priory, and the brook that ran through Bicester led to the River Cherwell. It was a pleasant spot, but he stayed little time there, riding on 'by very fruitful ground, having good corn, grace and some woods, many conies, but little enclosed ground' to Banbury.

> The most part of the whole town of Banbury standeth in a valley, and is enclosed by north and east with low ground, partly meadows, partly marshes; by south and south-west the ground is somewhat hilly in respect to the site of the town. The fairest street of the town lies by west and east down the River Cherwell. And at the west part of this

street is a large area surrounded by meetly good buildings, having a good cross with many degrees about it. In this area is kept every Thursday a very celebrated market. There is another fair street from south to north; and at each end of this street is a stone gate. There is a castle on the north side of this area having two wards, and each ward a ditch. In the outer one is a terrible prison for convicted men.

From Banbury Leland rode to Warwick, 'twelve miles by champayne ground, fruitful of corn and grass, barren of woods and for two miles along some enclosed and woody ground'. Warwick stood on a rocky hill, and its two main streets crossed in the middle. Its glories were 'the magnificent and strong castle of Warwick, at the west-south-west end of the town, hard by the right ripe of the Avon', and the 'fair, large and sumptuous' Beauchamp Chapel in St Mary's: one providing the Earls of Warwick with security in this life, the other in the next.

Seven miles on in the Forest of Arden – no longer a forest and already much enclosed – was Stratford-upon-Avon. The houses had been built with the timbers of Arden.

The town of Stratford standeth upon plain ground on the right hand or ripe of Avon, as the water descendeth. It has two or three very large streets, besides backlanes. One of the principal streets leads from east to west, another from south to north. The Bishop of Worcester is lord of the town. The town is reasonably well built of timber. There is once a year a great fair at Holy-Rode Day [14 September]. The parish church is a fair large piece of work, and standeth at the south end of the town. The church is dedicated to the Trinity. There is a right goodly chapel in a fair street. This chapel was newly re-edified in living memory by one Hugh Clopton, Mayor of London. About the body of this chapel is curiously painted the Dance of Death. There is a grammar school on the south side of this chapel. Clopton aforesaid made also the great and sumptuous bridge upon Avon at the east end of the town. This bridge hath fourteen arches of stone, and a long causeway made of stone and now walled on each side, at the west end of the bridge. Before the time of Hugh Clopton there was but a very poor bridge of timber, and no causeway to come to it; whereby many poor folk and others refused to come to Stratford, when Avon was up, or coming hither stood in jeopardy of life.

From Stratford, Leland came into the Vale of Evesham, stopping at the religious houses at Evesham, Tewkesbury and Cheltenham for days at a time. From Cheltenham he descended through 'low land, corn, pasture and meadow' to Gloucester. The town was 'ancient, well-built of timber and large and strongly defended with walls'. There was a Blackfriars, a Whitefriars, a Greyfriars and an Augustinian house, but the town was dominated by the Benedictine abbey. It had been founded by the Saxons, but 'zeal and religion had grown cold many years before the coming of the Normans', according to William of Malmesbury, and it had been refounded after the Conquest. It grew rich, thanks to the grave of Edward II, whose pilgrims financed the re-facing of the Norman exterior with Perpendicular accessories and a beautifully vaulted Lady Chapel. The library, however, had been neither expanded nor modernized, and Leland searched through manuscripts under an open wooden roof, the timbers supported on exquisite Early English corbels.

Within a week of leaving the library he had crossed the Severn on a ferry and was riding north up the Wye Valley (stopping at Tintern), and through the Forest of Dean ('fruitful with iron mines') to Hereford. Its castle 'had been one of the fairest, largest and strongest castles in England'; now it was in ruins.

He stayed only a few days before riding north through the Welsh Marches, through Leominster, where the houses were still built of timber and there was a small Benedictine priory, and Ludlow, protected by a castle 'on a strong rock', to Shrewsbury.

Leland entered Shrewsbury by the Welsh Bridge over the Severn. It had:

> six great arches of stone, so called because it is the way out of the town into Wales. This bridge standeth on the west side of the town, and hath at the one end of it a great gate to enter by into the town, and at the other end towards Wales a mighty strong tower to prohibit enemies from entering onto the bridge.

The town was surrounded on three sides by the river. Its colour struck him – 'sad red earth'. Behind him, as he came over the bridge, were the mountains of Wales. He made his way to the red sandstone abbey. Wales too was on his itinerary. But it would have to wait.

From Shrewsbury he rode south-east and south along the Severn Valley to Worcester, short-cutting over 'hilly and daley' country where the river meandered, stopping at Bridgnorth and Kidderminster on the way. Worcester and its monastic cathedral looked out across the Severn at the Malvern Hills. It was a wealthy town, 'no town in England at this present time maketh so many clothes yearly'. The bridge across the river, on the road to Wales, was 'a royal piece of work, high and strong, and hath six great arches of stone'. Within the walls the houses were all of timber. The Blackfriars were close to the North Gate. Outside the gate was 'a long and fair suburb', and at the far end of it 'an ancient and fair large chapel of St Oswald. This chapel, as I learnt, was first erected by monks and then infected with leprosy. After, it was changed into a hospital, and there was a master and fellowes and poor folk.' On the other side of the lepers' cemetery was 'a place for nuns'; and in the 'low moorish ground' outside St Martin's Gate were the Greyfriars. These lesser houses were mere minnows compared to the great cathedral priory. It owned twenty-seven manors and its prior had a retinue of four gentlemen, ten yeomen, ten grooms, a huntsman and a fool. Birmingham, a day's ride away, was a total contrast.

> I came through a pretty street before I entered Birmingham town. This street, if I remember, is called Deritend, and in it dwell smiths and cutlers. There be many smiths in the town, that make knives and all manner of cutting tools. The smiths there have iron out of Staffordshire and Warwickshire and sea coal come out of Staffordshire.

He continued north-east, through 'a forest and wilderness' to Lichfield. The waters reflecting the Early English cathedral fascinated him.

> The north part of Lichfield is divided from the south part by three ponds, whereof both the first two lie by the west, there is nothing so great as the third that lieth by the east. There be divers springs in these pools, but the principal spring is the brook that entereth into them and feedeth them. It comes through a pipe for about a mile and a half west from Lichfield. The first western pool is divided from the second pool by a great main long causeway, walled on each side with stone; and in this causeway be arches of stone for the water to issue into the second pool. There also be a fair stone causeway, and an issue for the water, between the second pool and the third pool, leading out of the town hard to the south gate of the Close, and on the east side of it is a fair mill. The third pool that lyeth east is a very fair thing, and plenty full of fish and going in length of my estimation, about half a mile.

From Lichfield Leland turned sharply south-east and, passing Tamworth Castle, rode all day to Coventry. The town was walled in 'darkish deep red' stones, the streets were 'fair' and bulged with prosperity. In the centre of the town were three 'stately' churches: St Michael's, Holy Trinity and the abbey church. Elsewhere there was a Greyfriars and Whitefriars, and a hospital for ten poor men and women founded by a cloth merchant called Bond. The Carmelite house stood outside the walls.

John Leland's itinerary for the West Midlands was complete, and autumn was turning into winter. He mounted his horse and, riding south-east through the now familiar landscape he had passed on his outward journey, he returned to London.

*   *   *

The next twelve months were the most eventful of the English Reformation. Just as Leland had followed in the wake of the commissioners, so in turn Leland was followed by other visitors. They were in Evesham and Tewkesbury only a couple of months after Leland. They were the King's Visitors, harder men than the gentry and local government officials of the commissioners. They interrogated rather than asked, saw guilt in association, turned monk against monk, and used confessions of transgressions to pick at deeper sins.

On 11 March 1536 a bill for the dissolution of religious houses with less than twelve members was passed by the Commons, legitimizing the biggest privatization in English history. Friaries, nunneries and monasteries where Leland had eaten bread and salt were being turned into manor houses, their cloisters transformed into gardens or farmyards. Monastic librarians, who had proudly shown him their books and manuscripts, were taking on parishes or becoming school teachers; their older or less-educated brethren left to beg on the roadside.

In spite of his firm Protestant convictions, Leland seemed a little frightened by the speed of the revolution. His first two years' travels had been leisurely and well-thought out, as one would expect from a clerical academic. Suddenly time was no longer there. Libraries were disappearing, their books sold or bought in their entirety by the new owners. Soon he was writing to Thomas Cromwell, the King's chief minister, appealing to his xenophobia and asking for more time.

> It would be a great benefit to students and honour to this realm, whereas now the Germans, perceiving our deciduousness and neglect, do daily send young scholars hither that spoileth them and cutteth them out of libraries, returning home and putting them abroad as monuments of their own country.

He left London the following spring, setting out along Holborn, skirting Westminster and crossing the Rivers Fleet, Tyburn, Westbourne and Ravensbourne, to Hounslow, where the friars of the Holy Trinity had a hospital for the sick and a hostel for poor travellers. At Maidenhead, which he reached early that evening, 'there is great wharfage of timber and fire wood on the west end of the bridge, and this wood cometh out of Berkshire and the great woods of the Forest of Windsor'. He spent the night at Reading Abbey, built by Henry I, according to William of Malmesbury, 'in a place calculated for the reception of almost all who might have occasion to travel to the more populous cities of England'.

Next morning he set off for Oxford, over hills 'somewhat plentiful in corn but mostly laid to pasture'. At Wallingford there had been a house for Benedictines, but they had been suppressed before their time by Cardinal Wolsey, and their priory was already disappearing beneath brambles and fireweed. He arrived in Oxford a little before dusk.

The biggest of the colleges was the newest, Henry VIII College (now Christ Church). When Leland had been a postgraduate at All Souls it had been the Priory of St Frideswide. But Wolsey suppressed it, turning its buildings into Cardinal College. When he died at Leicester, he begged King Henry to save his college, which the King did, renaming it after himself. Its quad, intended by Wolsey to be a cloister, was still unfinished. Apart from Henry VIII College, Oxford was still Oxford, nothing had changed. But John Leland had changed; he had become too radical and Protestant for a university that prided itself on its resilience to change. He stayed as briefly as he could and was glad to saddle his horse, mount and leave.

He left through the south gate, crossed the Thames and trotted through good pasture and corn land to Faringdon. It stood 'in a stoney ground in the decline of a hill'. Beyond Faringdon he rode west through the 'uplandish' Cotswolds, stopping at the Augustinian abbey at Cirencester and continuing along the Foss Way, the old Roman road, turning left after about a mile on to the Malmesbury road.

'The town of Malmesbury standeth at the very top of a great slatey rock, and is wonderfully defended by nature.' It had a yearly fair, where there were regular scenes of rural violence 'at which time the town kept a band of harnessed [armed] men to keep the peace'. Saturday was market day. 'There is a right fair and costly piece of work in the market place made all of stone and curiously vaulted, for poor market folk to stand dry when rain cometh.' He spent days in the Benedictine abbey, with its gaunt Norman church on a spur over the skyline and a spire Leland called a 'mighty piramus'. Here in the abbey library were the papers of William of Malmesbury; here too were the notes and drawings of Elmer, the flying monk, who launched himself from the abbey tower in 1010 and flew 250 yards before crashing to the ground. Sitting in the library John Leland must have known its days were numbered.

He meandered on, riding south and west, through Chippenham and Corsham, coming 'down by a rocky hill' and crossing the Avon at Bath.

> The city of Bath is set both in a fruitful and pleasant bottom, which is environed on every side with great hills, out of which come many springs of pure water that be conveyed by divers ways to serve the city, many houses in the town having pipes of lead to convey water from place to place.

The Roman baths came as a great relief after so many days in the saddle.

> There be two springs of hot water in the west-south-west part of the town. Whereof the bigger is called the Cross Bath, because it hath a cross erected in the middle of it. This bath is much frequented by people diseased with leperousy, smallpox, and great aches, and is temperate and pleasant, having eleven or twelve arches of stone in the sides for men to stand under in time of rain. The other bath is called the Hot Bath; for at coming into it men think it would scald the flesh at first, but after the flesh is warmed it is more tolerable and pleasant. Both these baths be in the middle of a little street and join to St John's Hospital: so it may be that Reginald, Bishop of Bath, made this hospital near these two communal baths to succour poor people resorting to them. The King's Bath is very fair and large standing almost in the middle of the town, and at the west end of the cathedral church. The area that this bath is in is encompassed by a high stone wall. The brims of this bath hath a little wall encompassing them, and in this wall be thirty-two arches for men and women to stand separately in.

The abbey was suitably enormous. It had been there since Saxon days, but multiplied in size after the Norman occupation, with Bishop's Palace, guest houses, libraries, dormitories, schools, and – inevitably – hot baths. Its library was one of the best stocked in the country. The church had fallen into ruins after the local bishopric went to Wells, but was now being rebuilt, with new fan-vaulting by Robert and William Vertue, vaulters of Henry VII's chapel at Westminster Abbey.

From Bath John Leland's route took him to Wells. The town was large, built of stone and still rich from the cloth trade.

> The area in front of the Bishop's Palace lies east of the marketstead, and hath a fair high wall towards the marketstead, and a right goodly gatehouse in it, made of late by Bishop Beckington, as it appeareth by his arms. On the south side of this area is the Bishop's Palace broadly ditched and watered by the waters of St Andrew's stream let into it. This palace is strongly walled and embattled castlelike, and hath in the first front a goodly gatehouse in the middle, and at each end a round tower.

Five miles on was Glastonbury. The land he travelled through was 'flat and fenny', and you could see the tor, William of Malmesbury's Avalon, with the tower of St Michael on its summit, from miles around. The abbey, 'on the most magnificent complex of purely monastic buildings in England, if not in Europe',* was, after Westminster, the richest in the land. Many of the old Norman buildings had been demolished and rebuilt in splendid late Perpendicular style by the late abbot, Richard Brere, since William Worcestre's visit. But its community had never been corrupted, its monks were praised for their discipline and good works, and Leland found the new abbot, Richard Whiting, 'a most candid and friendly man'.

Glastonbury before the Reformation: a visual reconstruction by A. E. Henderson.

*David Knowles, *ibid*.

His next stop was Cadbury Castle. Some called it Camelot. It stood:

> upon a very tor or hill, wonderfully strengthened by nature, to the which be two
> enterings up by very steep way: one by north-east, and another by south-west. The
> very root of the hill whereon this fortress stood is more than a mile in circumference. In
> the upper part of the cup of the hill be four ditches or trenches, and a balky wall of
> earth between every one of them. In the very top of the hill above all the trenches is the
> *magna* area or *campus* of twenty acres or more by estimation, where in divers places
> men may see foundations and *rudera* of walls. There was much dusty blue stone that
> people of the village thereby hath carried away.

He asked the locals for more details but they could tell him nothing 'but that they had
heard it said that King Arthur much resorted to Camelot'.

Sherborne, where there was a great Benedictine fan-vaulted abbey, and Ilchester,
where Roger Bacon had been born, led him by roundabout routes over the Somerset
Levels, cut through with drainage dykes, to Bridgwater. On his way he passed through
Petherton Park, where 'there is a great number of deer, and the deer trip over these
dykes, feed all about the fens and resort to the park again'.

He could see Bridgwater Castle from a distance, 'sometime a right fair and strong
piece but now all gone to mere ruin'. There was a Greyfriars there, but that was also on
its way to ruin, and a college of St John adjoining a hospital for poor folk. Next day he
was riding over the Quantocks, their sandstone giving the earth a reddish hue. On the
other side of the hills was Dunster, its castle and priory both sandstone red, and the sea.
A few miles further along the coast he came to Minehead, where 'the fairest part of the
town standeth at the bottom of the hill' and the rest was 'exceedingly full of Irishmen'.

Next day Leland was crossing Exmoor. The landscape started as 'hilly and rocky,
full of brookes at every hill's bottom, and meetly wooded'. Then the forests faded away
and Leland was on open moorland, lined by parallel ridges, broken every so often by
thickly wooded ravines, and carpeted in bracken, heather, sedge and blue moor grass,
on which red deer grazed. A generation earlier the whole of Exmoor had been open, but
already great chunks of it had been enclosed and leased to sheep farmers.

The sheep farmers' wealth was all around him in Barnstaple, where the houses
were mostly new and built of stone, and there was a priory beside a pretty brook to the
east of the town. He left 'by hilly and moorish ground' for Torrington, rode west, and
came down the upper parts of the Tamar Valley, dividing Devon from Cornwall, into
Launceston.

> The large and ancient castle of Launceston standeth on the knap of the hill by the south
> a little way from the parish church. Much of this castle yet standeth, and the mole that
> the keep standeth on is large and terribly high, the strongest, but not the biggest, that I
> ever saw in any ancient work in England.

It was Norman. You could tell. Beneath the castle, well beneath it, was the Augustinian
priory where William Worcestre had stayed, standing 'in the west-south-west part of
the suburb of the town under the root of the hill by a fair wood'.

Cornwall was remote, the last frontier of the Old World, its people surly and
conservative, and speaking a cross between Breton and Welsh. For John Leland it must
have been like being abroad. Its politics were Catholic and anti-Tudor: it had risen in
1496 against the tin tax and in 1497 in support of the pretender Perkin Warbeck;
within a few years it was to rise again, against the *Book of Common Prayer*.

It was rich country, its wealth displayed in its late Perpendicular churches, many built within living memory. Apart from the high moorlands, the country was rapidly being enclosed. The villages were still there, their church spires protruding above the folds in the moorland, but there was something new that had not existed when William Worcestre passed through: peopleless villages side by side with rich manor houses, built in stone with slate roofs and four-sided courtyards.

He left Launceston and rode 'eight miles by moorish and hilly ground and great scarcity of wood, insomuch that all the country thereabout bringeth forth firs and heath'.

The way to Boscastle was 'by enclosed ground meetly fruitful of corn and exceedingly barren of wood, to which the bleak northern sea is not there of nature favourable'. When he arrived he found it 'a very filthy town'. So he moved on, along the coastal path via Tintagel Castle, where there had once been a Celtic monastery, to the slate mines of Port Isaac, where he cut inland over Bodmin Moor.

He came into Bodmin towards evening. It was the largest town in Cornwall, with a population of 2,000. Its Saturday market was so big that it could be mistaken for a fair. St Petroc's, where Dom William had shown William Worcestre books on physics, had become a parish church. 'There hath been monks and nuns then secular priests then monks again, and last Canons Regular in St Petroc's,' he wrote. Now they were no more. On the south side of the town, by the market place, had stood the Franciscan friary where Worcestre had stayed. That too had gone.

Two more days in the saddle took Leland to Penzance. After crossing the bay to St Michael's Mount, empty now that the tiny community of Bridgetine nuns had been dispersed, and making a fleeting visit to Land's End, he next took ship to the Isles of Scilly.

The islands depressed him. His first port of call was Hugh Town on St Mary's. In spite of the soil yielding 'exceedingly good corn, insomuch that if a man do but cast corn where hogs have rooted it will come up', the island was poor and worn by wind and rain. St Agnes was sadder. 'The whole number of almost five households that were in this isle came to a marriage or feast into St Mary's isle, and going homeward were all drowned.' Tresco was no better; its Benedictine monks had left and it too was empty. Rat island – 'in which be so many rats that if horse or other living beast be brought hither they devour him' – was best left unvisited. In spite of the corn, and the wild garlic, the islands were bleak. 'Few men be glad to inhabit these islands, in spite of all the plenty, for robbers by the sea take their cattle by force.' His only consolation was the puffins. He had never seen puffins before.

He returned to Penzance in better spirits, for from now on he would be on his way home. He left early in the morning, passing through Penryn, Falmouth and Truro, reaching Fowey that evening. The town was 'set on the north side of the haven hanging on a main rocky hill, and in length about a quarter of a mile'. The reputation of Fowey increased with the wars of Kings Edward I and III and Henry V, partly by feats of war, partly by piracy, 'and so waxing riches fell to all the merchants; and the town was haunted with ships of divers nations, and their ships went to all nations'.

Plymouth, 'a goodly road for great ships', where he stopped the next night, was Fowey's opposite, the law-abiding face of the West Country. From 'mean' beginnings as a fishing village owned by the Abbot of Plympton, it 'increaseth by little and little', always keeping on the right side of the law, until it was the biggest port in the West, with its own 16-man police force.

The mouth of the gulf wherein the ships of Plymouth lie is walled on each side and chained over in time of necessity. On the south-west side of this mouth is a block house: and on a rocky hill hard by it is a strong four-sided castle having a great round tower on each corner. It seems to be a very old piece of work.

East of Plymouth stood the Abbey of Plympton, 'the glory of the town'. The original abbey had been founded by Saxon monks. When the Normans came, bringing their own bishops, and the bishops told the monks they had to discard their concubines, the monks refused, so the monastery was dissolved and given to the Augustinians; this was ironical, since the Augustinians – laxest of all the orders – now had their own concubines.

From Plympton he continued east over wind-swept moors, crossing the River Dart near Dartington, where he watched the miners panning for tin. After a short diversion to Dartmouth, full of 'long good ships', he rode on towards Exeter, stopping at the pink sandstone buildings of Torre Abbey on the way. The landscape 'between Torquay and Exmouth both somewhat to the shore and especially inland is well enclosed, fruitful of corn and grass and meetly well wooded', he noted from Exeter that evening.

The town of Exeter is a good mile and more in circumference and is right strongly walled and maintained. There be divers fair towers in the town wall between the south and the west gate. As the walls have been newly made, so have the old towers decayed. The castle of Exeter standeth stately on high ground between the east gate and the north. There be four gates in the town, by the names of east, west, north and south. The east and west gates be now the fairest and of one fashion of building; the south gate hath been the strongest. There be divers fair streets in Exeter, but the high street that goeth from the west to the east gate is the fairest.

In the centre of the city was the cathedral, held fast by solid Norman towers and soaring flying buttresses, its precincts 'environed with many fair houses'. South-west, on the other side of the market place, stood the silent and desolate Benedictine Priory of St Nicholas; by the East Gate the abandoned Hospital of St John; the Franciscans had been 'a little without the South Gate'; the Blackfriars to the north of the cathedral cemetery. The only foundation left was 'a poor hospital in the town wherein yet six men be kept' outside the walls on the Honiton road.

Leland left the city through the South Gate, taking the coast road to Lyme Regis, 'a pretty market town set in the roots of a fine hill down to the hard shore'. From Lyme Regis he meandered eastwards, touching the sea at Weymouth, Lulworth and Poole; before turning up the Avon Valley for the 25-mile ride to Salisbury. It had the best inland fish market in southern England, he had been told.

'There are many fair streets in the city of Salisbury, especially the High Street and Castle Street, so called because it lies as a way to the castle of Old Sarum.' Where the town was not defended by the Avon, a large ditch had been dug. There had been a Blackfriars and a Greyfriars, and a Hospital of St Nicholas for eight poor women and four poor men at Harnham Bridge. The Early English cathedral, at which William Worcestre had marvelled through his single eye, stood apart from the town. Its cloisters on the south side were 'one of the largest and most magnificent in England'.

Later he visited Old Sarum, saw its Ancient British fort, Roman antiquities and crumbling medieval castle and cathedral, which had been cannibalized for the building of New Sarum or Salisbury. It was a city of the dead. 'There hath been houses in time out of mind inhabited in the east suburb of Old Sarum, but now there is not one house.'

Twenty-four miles, an easy day's ride over clay and chalk, 'all by champayne ground barren of wood', took him to Winchester. He came through the West Gate along the High Street, with the cathedral and abbey to his right. Facing the High Street, in front of the cathedral, was the Norman church of St Maurice. Running off it to the left was Jewry Street, 'called Jewry because Jews did inhabit it and had their synagogue there'. The 'fair Hospital of St John where poor sick people be kept' had been on the other side of the Itchen. Beyond the North Gate was Hyde Abbey, still functioning and performing the *opus Dei* as the monastic order around it crumbled, and beyond the South Gate the Hospital of St Cross, close to the Austin friars. There had been 'a hospital for poor folks a little without the King's Gate'; but the monks who maintained it had been dispersed and it had closed down.

There were only two places left to visit on his West Country itinerary – Southampton and Portsmouth, which he covered in a 60-mile loop taking two days. Back in Winchester he prepared for his final two-day ride to London. All in all, adding in the diversions, he had travelled more than 1,000 miles. It had taken over four months. But he was hardly relieved that the journey was over. All he could think of was the work yet to be done. The destruction of a whole way of life – which a few years earlier he would have welcomed – had left him sick of heart. The obsession with completing this great survey left him sick of mind.

*   *   *

The lesser houses had already gone, and within a couple of years the larger houses went the same way, without protest, the abbots and priors exchanging their guardianship for pensions and preferments. Events had outstripped John Leland. As his role as King's Antiquary became redundant, so he became more and more obsessed with completing his great topographical project. In between his long journeys he squeezed in shorter ones, through the Cotswolds, South Wales, East Anglia, Kent and the Sussex coast, leaving nowhere out, hardly stopping between excursions, adding some to previous narratives, keeping others separate. One month he was in Canterbury, the next Norwich. There seemed no method to it all. His papers became a jumble, 'utterly mangled, defaced with wet and weather and finally imperfect for want of sundry volumes', according to the Elizabethan William Harrison.

By the early 1540s he was back in Shrewsbury, using it as a base for explorations of Cheshire and North Wales. By now all the monasteries had disappeared. Richard Whiting, Abbot of Glastonbury, 'a most friendly and candid man', had been hanged on Glastonbury Tor, but from the other great religious houses – with a few noble exceptions – the Catholic world ended not with a martyr but with a whimper. By the time Leland came to Shrewsbury there were neither monks nor libraries left.

One journey took him north through Oswestry, Wrexham, Chester and Denbigh. Another led along the north coast of Wales to 'Bangor where the great abbey was', and down the west coast, past the Straits of Menai, Caernarfon, Dolgellau, Aberystwyth and Cardigan, to St David's Head. In a third he completed the coastal tour, riding through Pembrokeshire, Carmarthenshire, Glamorganshire and Monmouthshire. A fourth took him south-west from Shrewsbury, up the final stages of the Severn Valley, through Welshpool, Montgomery, Newton ('meetly well-built after the Welsh fashion'), to Llanidloes at the head of the Severn. Hardly pausing he went on, crossing the upper stages of the Wye, ascending and descending one range and valley after another, through Tregaron to Carmarthen Castle.

Monks at study, following the Rule of St Benedict in the last days of the monasteries.

Then, in 1542, he set off from Shrewsbury on the last of his great epic journeys: up through Lancashire, Westmorland and Cumberland, across the Pennines, along Hadrian's Wall, then down the east side of England and back to London. By now his notebooks had become chaotic: 'moth-eaten, mouldy and rotten' was how the London antiquarian, John Stow, described them.

Riding north from Shrewsbury, through Northwich ('a pretty market town') and the Forest of Delamere, where he saw grazing deer, Leland crossed the Mersey and rode into Manchester, 'the fairest, best built, quickest and most populous town in all Lancashire'. It had its own colony of Flemish weavers. Beyond Manchester he crossed the Ribble at Preston and, after looking over the empty Premonstratensian Cockersand Abbey, 'standing very bleakly and object to all the winds', he came into Lancaster. It lay in good farming country, 'plentiful of wood, pasture, meadow and corn'. The castle was well constructed and, at the bottom of the hill, where the new town was being built after a disastrous fire, was a fine parish church, St Mary's.

He rode on. 'About the borders of Westmorland and Lancashire be many dales. And in every one of them a brook giving name to the dale.' Kendal he found to be a 'good market town', but he skirted the Lake District as much as he could, as did any sensible Renaissance traveller. Its people were rude and crude, cut off by their lakes and mountains from civilized society. Sticking to the coast he passed the ghost of the Cistercian Calder Abbey and, swinging inland at Workington and up the Derwent Valley, pushed up through Cockermouth, with Bassenthwaite Lake on his left, to Penrith and Carlisle. Until the Dissolution, Carlisle had the only cathedral in England served by Augustinian monks. Now the abbot had become the dean, and the educated Austin friars were kept on as canons and prebendaries. The rest made do on the outside as best they could.

From Carlisle he rode the seventy miles along Hadrian's Wall, the necklace of Britain: passing the still and empty Lanercost Priory, a silent mix of grey limestone and red sandstone; the crumbling signal towers on which the rain was always falling; the stables converted into castle sheds; and the forts converted into farms. At Vindolanda and Housesteads he looked over ruined Roman barracks, and at Chesters Fort he crossed the North Tyne on what was left of a Roman bridge. On the bridge abutment was a lucky charm, a stone phallus.

He left the Wall at Newcastle, and after a week's excursion north to Alnwick and Berwick made his way south through York, Pontefract, Southwell ('where the Minster of Our Lady is a large but unpleasant building') and Sherwood Forest. He was still manically writing up his notes.

> To Thurgarton village and priory of Black Cannons, lately suppressed, two miles by corn land. And then on a good mile to Hoveringham ferry, where my horse passed over the Trent *per vadum* and I *per cymbam*. I never saw fairer meadows than there on both sides of the Trent.

But already he must have known that his work as King's Antiquary had become meaningless, and that his work on the topography of England and Wales would never be completed. It could have no ending for a man as obsessed as Leland. There would always be more details to add. Riding back towards London, through Rockingham Forest and Bedford, he must have realized that his mind was going.

*   *   *

It was his last journey. He returned to London, renting rooms by the Church of St Michael-le-Quern at the west end of Cheapside, opposite St Paul's Cross, to write his great work. It was never finished. In between venomous quarrels with more successful scholars, and campaigns to keep the Protestant revolution on its correct course, papers got mislaid, manuscripts thrown away, and unnumbered pages piled up in disorder. Parts emerge out of the chaos in narrative form; other parts never got further than notes. In the late 1540s Leland was asking a fellow-scholar in Louvain to find him 'a forward young man about twenty years of age, learned in the Latin tongue and able *sine cortice nare* in Greek' to make sense of it all. Nothing came of it. John Bale, whom Leland had got out of prison a decade earlier, looked after him through the depressions, recriminations and manic optimism, until inevitably 'by a most pitiful occasion he fell besides his wits'. Two years later, in 1552, Leland died. Among the jumble of papers found in his rooms, one fragment of one sentence stood out. 'I trust so to open this window that the light shall be seen so long, that is to say, by the space of a whole thousand years.'

3
THE CLOWN, THREE HOORAYS AND THE WATER CABBIE

WHEN LELAND DIED in 1552, his project died with him. But the idea of a great topographical survey of the kingdom did not die. Indeed, the more maps and travel books on the New World appeared, the greater the awareness of the blank spaces on the maps of Britain became. Between 1577 and 1587 William Harrison wrote the first sociological treatise on the English, complimenting them on their gardens and complaining that market traders and middle-men could not be trusted. In 1579 Christopher Saxton completed the first series of properly surveyed maps of the counties of England and Wales. And before the century was out William Camden was plodding through his *Brittania; or a Geographical Description of the Kingdoms of England, Scotland and Ireland*, Richard Carew was surveying Cornwall, William Lambard was perambulating Kent and John Stow was writing his monumental history of London.

By the turn of the century England and Wales had been mapped, surveyed, sketched, categorized and flattered – and very worthy it all was. The mood was for something else, however, something less serious. The new century wanted to be entertained, and to entertain. Travel had become fun.

It was still difficult, though. In fact, by 1600 travel had become *more* difficult than in Leland's time. Travel, *travail*, to everyone it meant labour. Before the Reformation the upkeep of the roads had been the responsibility of the parishes and monasteries, and rarely did they carry anything heavier than pack-horses. In Queen Elizabeth's reign roads became the sole responsibility of the parishes, but few of them could afford to maintain them, and less had the inclination. Besides, the coach with its narrow wheel rims and the lumbering ten-horse wagon had appeared, churning up the roads and scoring deep ruts in them until they degenerated into quagmires. The best roads were still the Roman roads, and sensible travellers went by riverboat.

Bridges were no better. Today we see only the survivors from the period, the exceptions made of stone. At the time most bridges were built of wood, liable to be swept away in floods and to collapse from rotting timbers. They too were the responsibility of the parish, but since rivers frequently acted as parish boundaries, neither side did anything about them. 'Women and bridges always lack mending,' people said.

*   *   *

It was in these conditions that William Kempe set out to morris-dance from London to Norwich in 1600. Kempe was the most famous comic actor of his day, and had received accolades for his Dogberry in *Much Ado About Nothing* at the Globe a couple of years earlier. His motives were obvious. He was over forty, his interpretation of Dogberry had been lauded as the summit of his career, and his best scriptwriter had gone over to tragedies. It was a publicity stunt, to stay in the public eye while still resting.

Always an optimist and never one to back out of the limelight, he set off from Aldgate, accompanied by a vast crowd, a little before 7 a.m. on 11 February, with Thomas Slye, his drummer, William Bee, his servant, and George Sprat, his manager. The manager was important; people had paid money to sponsor Kempe. 'My tabourer struck up merrily, and as fast as kind people thronging together would give me leave, through London I leapt.'

Whitechapel and Mile End were lined with people. 'Many a thousand brought me to Bow, where I rested awhile from dancing: but had small rest with those, that would have urged me to drinking.' At Bow Bridge his fans, knowing how much he enjoyed bear-baiting, had prepared a baiting, 'but so unreasonable were the multitudes of people, that I could only hear the bear roar and the dogs howl'.

Kemps nine daies vvonder.

Performed in a daunce from
London to Norwich.

Containing the pleasure, paines and kinde entertainment
of *William Kemp* betweene *London* and that Citty
in his late Morrice.

Wherein is somewhat set downe worth note; to reprooue
the slaunders spred of him: many things merry,
nothing hurtfull.

Written by himselfe to satisfie his friends.

LONDON
Printed by *E. A.* for *Nicholas Ling*, and are to be
solde at his shop at the westdoore of Saint
Paules Church. 1600.

He danced on through Ilford to Romford, where he stayed two days 'to rest my well-laboured limbs'. Coming out of Romford on his second day's dancing he strained a hip, but the old pro would not leave the stage and 'endured exceeding pain' as he danced on. Stopping for a break at Brentwood, he could hardly get into the inn, the people were so many. Two London pickpockets who had fed on the crowds for days were arrested and taken into the inn by the local constable to be identified by Kempe. After a dance at the town's whipping post they were sent back to the place they had come from.

It was the same leaving Brentwood as leaving Romford. The crowds followed. It was not until Kempe reached Ingerstone in the evening that he managed to shake them off. When he left for Chelmsford next morning a mere 200 came in his wake. In Chelmsford he locked himself in his inn to escape from his admirers. 'To deal plainly, I was so weary that I could dance no more.' But he did dance more. A 14-year-old serving girl, playing on his vanity, persuaded him to dance with her for a whole hour before she collapsed in exhaustion.

The road from Chelmsford was thick with mud, clasping his boots and slowing him down. 'This foul way I could find no ease in, thick woods being on either side, the lane likewise being full of deep holes, sometimes I skipped up to the waist.' At Sudbury a butcher announced that he would dance with Kempe all the way to Bury St Edmunds, but after half a mile he collapsed.

'Faint-hearted lout!' a fat girl shouted. 'If I had begun to dance, I would have held out one mile.'

Many laughed but the girl was not daunted.

'Nay, if the dancer will lend me a leash of his bells, I'll venture to tread one mile with him myself.'

Kempe fitted her with bells, she tucked in her skirts, 'shook her fat sides and footed it merrily to Melford'.

> A country lass (brown as a berry,
> Blithe of blee, in heart as merry;
> Checks well fed, and sides well lared;
> Every bone with fat flesh guarded)
> Meeting merry Kempe by chance
> Was Marian in his Morris dance.
> Her stump legs, with bells were garnished;
> Her brown brows, with sweating varnished;
> Her brown hips, when she was lag,
> To win her ground, went swig-a-swag:
> Which to see, all that came after
> Were replete with mirthful laughter.

Kempe made a short (and very muddy) excursion along the Stour Valley to Clare Castle, and the local squire's jester accompanied him out of Long Melford for a mile or so through the mud. 'Leaving me, two fools parted fair in a foul way.' A few miles on from Clare a kind widow gave him food and rest. 'Her behaviour being very modest and friendly, argued her bringing up not to be rude. She was a woman of good presence; and, if a Fool may judge, of no small discretion.'

From there he danced to Bury St Edmunds. As he came in from the south the Lord Chief Justice arrived from the north. It was to the south that the crowds flocked. Kempe was pleased; he had just upstaged the Lord Chief Justice.

From Bury he danced the twelve miles to Thetford in three hours, the country people gawping at him along the way and urging him to go through their own villages, claiming that the way would be easier.

On the ninth day he came to Norwich. But the crowds had expected him the day before and had left the city. So the mayor persuaded him to delay his entry for a couple of days so that they could come back. Never one to play before an empty house, Kempe readily agreed.

> Passing by the Market Place, the press still increasing by the number of boys, girls, men and women, thronging more and more before me, to see the end; it was the mischance of a homely maid that coming unluckily in my way, as I was fetching a leap, it fell out, that I set my foot on her skirts. The point either breaking or stretching, off fell her petticoat from her waist! But, as chance was, though her smock was course, it was cleanly.

A fitting end to another great performance.

*　　*　　*

It was from Norwich in 1634, thirty-four years later, that three very different travellers left on an 11-week journey through 'twenty-six famous shires, fifteen fair and strong cities, forty neat and ancient corporations and thirteen ancient, rich and magnificent cathedrals'. The three were a captain, a lieutenant and an ancient, and they had no motive other than to have a jolly good time. They were members of the Military Company of Norwich, not that different from today's Territorial Army; at their happiest growing moustaches and milking military metaphors, and no nearer a battlefield than a bread-roll fight. But the three weekend soldiers were not entirely unattractive. At ease with people, they also found people were at ease with them, and though they may have been hoorays they were never snobs.

'Mustering their triple fore', they left Norwich on Monday 11 August, riding forty miles to King's Lynn on the first day. King's Lynn was a boom town, with wealth coming in from the farmers in the newly drained stretches of the Fens, and from the navvies employed in draining the rest of the Fens. After a night of beer and wine, they left the following morning, making a half-circle to the south, the Fens 'being neither firm nor safe for travellers, especially now of late, by reason of the newly made sluices and devices for turning the natural course of the waters', according to the lieutenant, the narrator. They crossed the Ouse and rode to Wisbech, then north, 'over rich flat level ground for Spalding', where 600 navvies were engaged in drainage work.

Next day they rode to Lincoln. 'We cannot forget what brave, uniform, fair churches and steeples with towering spires' stood out on the flat landscape. 'When we first espied the high towers of the Cathedral, we thought it near, but it proved to our pains and patience a full jury of miles.'

They stayed at the Antelope on the top of Steep Hill, but they never saw the landlord that day. 'It seems he had boozed it so, as he was wearier than we, for he was bedded at our first approach, and we saw him not.' Morning came and the innkeeper still had not come down, so they visited first the castle and then the cathedral. He finally appeared and 'gave us a free welcome at an easy rate which made us sing, loath to depart, but our time would in no wise permit us to stay longer'. So they leisurely discussed over their wine and ale whether to go north-east to Beverley and Hull, or south-west to Newark-upon-Trent.

They opted for Newark and reached it early in the morning. They liked the church, St Mary Magdalene, with its Early English tower, and the castle where King John had died, and went to the 'neat market place' where there were two inns, the White Hart and the Saracen's Head, to find beds for the night. That evening they wandered around the market place looking at the local girls, but 'our supper stayed for us, so we were forced to leave all those sweet objects, to hasten to that: at which our jovial host did so play us with mirth, merry tales, and true jests, as made all our weariness clean forgotten'.

They left in the morning, crossed the Trent, passed through Southwell, 'where there is a fair minster', and 'went through a little part of Sherwood Forest' to Doncaster.

As they approached Doncaster they came upon 'some Scotch gentlemen'. 'We joined our forces, English and Scottish together that night, and being well aired, and dried, we had good free mirth.' Next morning the 'Scotch blades' just could not cope with the booze and the heartiness, so the captain, lieutenant and ancient went on without them.

Pontefract, which they reached that evening, was equally exhausting, so at York the next night:

we most happily and fortunately lodged our Colours in Coney Street and victualled the camp at the house of a loving and gentle widow, who freely and cheerfully extended her bountious entertainment to us; for no sooner heard she her wet and weary benighted guests, but she came to us and welcomed us with a good glass of sack [dry white wine] and a dish of hot fresh salmon, she herself presenting both, in that kind and modest family phrase of the Northern speech, 'May God thank thee, for making her house our harbour'; and likewise took such care of us, both at board and bed, as if she had been a mother rather than a hostess.

They spent most of the following day, a Sunday, at York Minster, 'which we found to be stately, large and ancient, richly adorned and of excellent uniformity, with a rich rare library in it'. On the roof, 270 steps up, 'we took view of the city and suburbs, which are situated in a sweet and fertile soil, the meadows, pastures, cornfields and wolds near twenty miles about'. They counted the church spires – there were twenty-eight of them.

A couple of days later they set off for Durham, reaching Darlington by dinner, 'where we were entertained by a hideous noise of bagpipes'. They liked Durham, with its castle and cathedral and long, arched bridge across the Wear; and they liked the 'large and sumptuous table' of the Dean of Durham, who plied them with venison, sweet salmon and fine wine. After recovering from the lunch they pressed on to Newcastle, a 'seacoal' town, where they arrived late at night and lodged in Pilgrim Street. From Newcastle they crossed the neck of Great Britain, passing the 'Pict's Wall which the Roman emperor first made', and came to Carlisle, surrounded by a stout wall against 'the fiercest of the bordering Scots'. They stayed at the Angel in the market place. The cathedral did not impress them. The monuments were of little note, the organ sounded as if it had been tuned by a bagpipe enthusiast, the sermon was incomprehensible and communion 'was administered and received in a wild and irreverent manner'.

From Carlisle they rode south, alternating long days (about forty miles) and short days (about twenty miles) so as not to tire their horses, a leisurely pace for leisurely people. But that did not necessarily make it easy. Their road through the Lake District took them on 'such ways as we hope we shall never see again, being no other but climbing and stony, nothing but bogs and mires, or the tops of those high hills, so we were enforced to keep these narrow loose stoney base ways'. The people were 'rude, rustical and ill-bred. We could not understand them, nor they understand us that had we not happily lighted on a good old man (having lost our way in this day's travel upon the Fells) we had been laid up irrecoverably, without help or hope'. The old man showed them the way to Kendal, where the taverns provided what was expected of them, and the three continued on through Lancashire to Chester.

In Chester they found the innkeeper a hospitable fellow, and next morning they went straight from the inn to the cathedral. Alas, it proved as disappointing as Carlisle. But they cheered up in the afternoon when the innkeeper gave them a guided tour, marching them round the two miles of red sandstone city walls, from where they had a view of Chester's celebrated bridge over the Dee, which led to the road to Wales, and 'saw many of her huge high mountaintops'. Then the innkeeper showed them Chester's new waterworks, which provided water piped through hollowed-out elm trunks throughout the city. They returned to their inn via the Rows, the medieval timbered, first-floor galleries in the middle of the city. 'In the Market Place and heart of the City, you may walk dry in any wet weather on the Gallery on either side of the streets by all the shops, under arches,' the lieutenant wrote. 'The form is rare, the buildings but indifferent.'

In Derby they admired the Tudor Gothic spire of All Hallows, but were in such a hurry they did not even stop for beer. In Lichfield they inspected the cathedral, and in Nottingham the castle and Mortimer's Hole. The fifth week began in Coventry, where an old acquaintance of the captain, poor but generous, gave them lunch and as much to drink as they could take. They lurched on to Kenilworth Castle, a couple of miles away, refurbished by Essex for Elizabeth I at vast expense. It was spectacular.

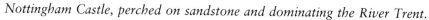

Nottingham Castle, perched on sandstone and dominating the River Trent.

We were ushered up a fair ascent, into a large and stately hall, of twenty paces in length, the roof whereof is all of Irish wood, neatly and handsomely framed: in it is five spacious chimneys, answerable to so great a room; we next viewed the Presence Chamber of the Guard, the Chamber of Presence, the Privy Chamber, fretted about richly with coats of arms, and all adorned with fair and rich chimney-pieces of alabaster, black marble and of joiner's work in curious carved wood; and all these fair and rich rooms, and lodgings in that spacious tower not long since built, and repaired at a great cost by the great favourite of late days.

A few miles on was Warwick Castle and its magnificent grounds, landscaped since Leland's time and 'furnished with beech, birch and several sorts of plum trees'. It was 'tiresome to ascend, yet it is so finely and artificially constructed, with winding walks, that no man can be weary at all'. Here was an enchanted garden, 'adorned with all kinds of delightful and shady walks, and arbors, pleasant groves and wildernesses, fruitful trees, delicious bowers, odorous herbs, and many rare and curious fish ponds'.

Next day they came into Stratford-upon-Avon, where the lieutenant noted, among the tombs and monuments in the Church of the Holy Trinity, 'a neat monument to that famous English poet, Mr William Shakespeare, who was born here'. In Worcester they spent their time visiting the cathedral, when they were not drinking and making merry at the Talbot. They left after a long lunch, riding through the Forest of Dean and arriving at Gloucester in the evening. It was another inn, another cathedral, another town. Three days later they were in Bristol.

The city was 'sweet and clean', and on a patch of ground called the Marsh there was 'a bowling green and other recreations for the rich merchants and gentle citizens, adorned with many fair trees, wherein constantly the City Companies drill and muster'. After visiting the nearby lead mines they rode on to Wells. The town was poor and the Bishop's Palace, where they drank exceptionally good wine and strong beer, was rich; they saw nothing unusual in that. They set off for Glastonbury in the morning, the lieutenant mistaking the tower of St Michael's on Glastonbury Tor for the ruins of the abbey; but it hardly mattered and great fun was had by all investigating the stalactites and stalagmites of Wokey Hole.

We passed many vast and strange places; one was like a spacious high church; another was a long passage like an arched cellar, some were like butteries, some like kitchens, and some like halls: some rooms were very strong and like we know not what, and with the continual dropping and distilling of the waters, such strange shapes, and several forms were congealed as there did palpably appear to our fancies, men, women and other creatures, in that glittering diamond-sparkling hollowness, as made us gaze and wonder.

After we had tried and tired our legs more than a furlong in an uncouth stoney and desperate march, and gone the furthest period of our rock journey the way likely enough to Purgatory, we there rested ourselves, being (as our guide affirmed, and as it partly appeared to us afterwards) eighty fathoms deep, if not more.

Many sweet pools, little springs and clear shallow standing pools we passed by and over, and of some tasted, and here at the furthest of our underground travail, being weary, we sat down and rested, by a murmouring deep and spacious river.

Music doth sound and re-echo most sweetly and melodiously in these hollow caverns and passages, and we had a full trial thereof by a recorder, which was tunable, sweet and pleasant to our ears.

A couple of days later they were in Bath, where, under the direction of the ancient, they dived into:

> those admired unparalleled, medicinal, sulphorous hot bathes. There we met all kinds of persons, of all shapes and forms, of all degrees, of all countries, of all diseases, of both sexes; for to see young and old, rich and poor, blind and lame, diseased and sound, English and French, men and women, boys and girls, one with another, peep up in their caps and appear so nakedly and fearfully in their uncouth naked postures, would astonish, and put in mind of the Resurrection.

At Bath they split up, the captain and ancient making their way to Salisbury and the lieutenant to Malmesbury, where he looked over the ruins of the great abbey. Continuing across the Cotswolds, he rode through Burford, where he stayed a night, and Woodstock, where he made a quick tour of the palace, and came into Oxford. There the three – the captain, the lieutenant and the ancient – met up again and inevitably spent the evening celebrating their reunion. Next morning, touring the colleges, 'the organs, voices, monuments and windows of both the cathedral and every other college church and chapel, were so fair, sweet, rich and glorious, as which exceeded each other, we were not able to judge'.

Two days later, after riding through Bicester, Buckingham, Bedford and Cambridge, they were back in Norwich. They had travelled 800 miles, and a jolly good time had been had by all.

*   *   *

A year later the lieutenant and the ancient, leaving the captain behind, made another tour, through southern England. Leaving Norwich on 4 August, they rode down the coast, stopping at Aldeburgh, Harwich and Colchester, which they found 'not unfurnished with handsome creatures', on their way to Tilbury, where they crossed the Thames, landing at Gravesend. They continued on, taking the Dover road to Rochester. Neither castle nor cathedral was large, but it did not matter. 'As I found this city little and sweet, so I found her chief and best structures correspondent to her smallness, which was neat and handsome and neither great nor sumptuous.'

On the way to Canterbury they joined a party of French travellers riding to Dover. At the head of the party was 'a light and sprightly Mademoiselle, who, being well mounted, would be sure always to be at the Front and a File Leader, and to leave a whole cloud of choking dust behind her'. They lodged that night at the Flower de Luce:

> and had free mirth and good content from them: they were all weary as well as I, especially that pretty She Rider who at that time held it no nicity, nor point of incivility, to disrobe and bed her little tender wearied corpse in our presence.

When morning came the French continued on to Dover and the lieutenant and ancient, noting the large numbers of French people in Canterbury, made a tour of the town, visiting the cathedral, chapter house and cloisters, 'sad relics of their goodly monastery'.

Two days on, part by horse and part by coaster, they came to a busy port flanked by white cliffs.

> I hastened to Dover and thither I descended a steep rocky and high hill, close by that famous castle. I found the town situated in a deep bottom, close upon the main ocean. She needs no walls, for what with the high over-topping cliffs, all along on one side of her, the Castle Hills, as high and higher, and the haven on the other side, the forts and

Canterbury Cathedral, bounded on three sides by open country.

bulwarks almost on every part of her, these may well serve for to lock her up safely, being the chief Cinque Port, lock and key of this kingdom.

They continued west, through Hythe and Dymchurch, across Romney Marsh and Walland Marsh, and through Rye, 'a pretty island maritime town', to Hastings; then along the South Downs to Arundel, Chichester and Petworth. They loved Petworth. They would.

> To set out the glory whereof suiting its stateliness, were a labour above my perform-ance to decipher; or to set forth the brave parks replenished with deer; the walks, gardens, orchards, bowling ground, stables and fishponds without; the sumptuous chambers, parlours, galleries, chapel, hall, cellars and kitchens within, with all their rich furniture, adornments, delights and appurtenances, were too long a task, they being so magnificent and complete.

Havant and Portsmouth came next on the itinerary, and at Portsmouth they stayed at the Red Lion, where they found the landlady 'brisk, blithe and merry, a handsome sprightly lass fit for the company of brave commanders'. After inspecting the Fleet they came 'over the Downs, till I tumbled down a steepy hill a whole mile together, into that old and ancient city of Winchester'. The town was 'in a rich valley, environed round with great hills, a sweet and pleasant river gliding in, by, and through her'. The cathedral was magnificent, but the ruins of Hyde Abbey were 'lamentable to behold'.

After a night in Southampton and a miserable visit to the Isle of Wight, they rode north through the New Forest to Salisbury, where they marvelled at the Early English cathedral and the rivulets running through the streets.

> The city abounds in the happiness of enjoying the full fruition and plenitude of two of the four elements which are so commodious for pleasure and profit, to wit, Air and Water; for the first it is as pleasant, sweet and healthful as the heart of Man can desire, for the latter it is as commodious and useful as the bounty of nature, or the art of man can make it; for every street in her is supplied therewith by pleasant little rivulets, which are knee deep, gliding sweetly through her bowels, to wash and cleanse them, in four main streets, east and west, and four more north and south, so that thereby are made sixteen chequers in this neat city.

From Salisbury they made a short excursion over Salisbury Plain to Stonehenge, 'those admired, strange, confused, huge, fixed, astonishing stones' forming a circle, 'some in a hanging and tumbling posture and some entwined together on the top like a hideous pair of gallows'. They returned to Salisbury via the Elizabethan pile of the Earl of Pembroke's at Wilton, not yet restored by Inigo Jones. 'The rooms, chambers and other delights within, and the pleasant gardens, orchards and walks without, renders it indeed the only grace and glory of the town.' The next day they rode south-west, 'over topped hills and deep dales', to Weymouth and Portland, and in the days that followed they passed through Lyme Regis and Axminster and arrived at Exeter. The cathedral, to which they made their obligatory visit, was 'wide, fair and lofty', and in the cathedral library, looking out on to the cloisters:

> there is a rarity, which is a real anatomy of a man, who (for his delinquency) ended his life at the heavy tree: all his several bones, two hundred and forty-eight, his teeth, twenty-eight, etcetera, all fixed and placed in their proper places, which was dissected by a skillful Italian doctor.

At Exeter the lieutenant and the ancient decided to go no further west, so away they trooped to Taunton, thirty-five miles north-east, and continued to Glastonbury, where they saw 'a sight at full of the stately ruins and the demolished downfalls of that ancient, rare and unparalleled abbey'.

The final week took them through Bath, Banbury and Northampton to Fotheringhay, Mary, Queen of Scots' last prison, 'a sickly and dying castle not able to hold up her head'.

> I entered over a bridge through a strong gatehouse. In her I found many large and goodly rooms, chambers, galleries, chapel, kitchens, butteries and cellars.
> Her stately hall I found spacious, large and answerable to the other princelike rooms, but drooping and desolate, for that there was the altar where that great queen's head was sacrificed; as all the rest of those precious sweet buildings do sympathize, decay, fall, perish and go to wreck, for that unlucky and fateful blow.

Peterborough was less than half a day away, but it hardly raised their spirits: 'the buildings and her inhabitants much alike, poor and mean,' noted the lieutenant. The cathedral was the only decent thing in the 'beastly nasty town'. As for the locals, the Fen Slodgers, they were even worse.

> They be half fish and half flesh, for they drink like fish and sleep like hogs; and if the men be such creatures, judge what their women are, such as are neither worth

meddling with nor inserting. But how both men and women are able to subsist in winter exceeds my reach; their climate is so infinitely cold and watery; their habitations so poor and mean; their means so small and scant; their diet so coarse and sluttish; and their bodies so lazy and intemperate.

Ely was no relief. The people stank; and 'time and age had much defaced' the cathedral. After a brief visit to Wisbech, they returned to Norwich. They had travelled 700 miles through seven counties, seven cities, seven boroughs and seven ports; visiting seven cathedrals, seven stately mansions and seven castles. It had taken seven weeks.

Nothing more is known of the trio, except two of their names. The lieutenant was called Hammond and the captain Dehumas, a Dutch name. With their reverence for authority, High Church attitudes and Royalist sympathies, we can be sure that at least two of the weekend soldiers did finally get on to a battlefield. What became of them we have no idea: with any luck the ancient – at least – would have been too old to fight.

*   *   *

Equally High Church, Royalist and at ease with the world, but hardly as conventional, was John Taylor: sailor, waterman, tavern-keeper, working-class Tory, hater of wheels and self-styled 'Water Poet'. Born in Gloucester in 1580, he joined the navy at the age of sixteen, fought at the siege of Cadiz under the Earl of Essex and made sixteen voyages as an able seaman before leaving the navy and becoming a Thames waterman – the Jacobean equivalent of a London cabbie. Watermen did not only take customers across the river, they took them up and down too; but with 40,000 watermen, and the fashion of the upper classes for coaches, it was difficult to make a living, so he cultivated his image as a character, supplementing his income with doggerel verse.

Carrouches, coaches, jades and Flanders mares
Do rob us of our shares, our wares, our fares:
Against the ground we stand and knock our heels
Whilst all our profits run away on wheels.

It hardly made his fortune, but it made him influential friends among the rich and the talented, and he was happy to have his drinks paid for by the likes of Sir Fulke Greville and Ben Jonson.

When it became known in the taverns that Ben Jonson was planning a trip to Scotland, Taylor announced that he too would go to Scotland but, unlike Jonson, 'not carrying any money to or fro, neither begging, borrowing, or asking meat, drink or lodgings'. He was told it was impossible; so he set out on Tuesday 14 July 1618 from the Bell Tavern in the Barbican with a pack-horse 'well-rigged and ballasted both with beer and wind' to prove the impossible.

Sir Richard Burton has said that there are three starts to every journey in Africa, the short start, the long start and the real start. Taylor had the same problem. His short start began at the Bell, and his long start next morning after a night's drinking in Islington. It was not until the Thursday, on the Dunstable road, with his friends and drinking companions far behind him, that John Taylor experienced the real start.

I speak not of the tide, for understand,
My legs I made my oars, and rowed by land.

It still took a week to reach Lichfield, though he rarely appears to have been in a hurry, except at the end of a line.

For all that day, nor yet the night that followed,
One drop of drink I'm sure my gullet swallowed.
At night I came to a stoney town called Stone,
Where I knew none, nor was I known to none:
I therefore through the streets held on my pace,
Some two miles farther to some resting place:
At last I spied a meadow newly mowed,
The hay was rotten, the ground half o'erflowed:
We made a breach, and entered horse and man,
There our pavilion, we to pitch began,
Which we erected with green broom and hay,
To expel the cold, and keep the rain away;
The sky all muffled in a cloud 'gan lower,
And presently there fell a mighty shower,
Which without intermission did we pour,
From ten a night, until the morning's four.

In Manchester he drank his way from the south end of the town to the north, sampling ale of hyssop, ale of sage, ale of malt, ale of wormwood, and ale of rosemary. The final ale was the roughest of all, it was called scurvy ale. He finally found a bed at the Eagle-and-Child where the innkeeper, 'a good and ancient woman', washed his clothes, fed him on bacon, and mothered him through his hangover.

Taylor's fame had gone before him. At Prestwich he was provided with a horse and guide, and at Preston, where it rained all day, he found refuge at the Hind, where the bill was footed by the local mayor.

> There, as if I had been a noted thief,
> The mayor delivered me to the sheriff.
> The sheriff's authority did much prevail,
> He sent me unto one that kept the jail.
> This I perambuling, poor John Taylor,
> Was given from mayor to sheriff, from sheriff to jailor.
> The jailor kept an inn, good beds, good cheer,
> Where paying nothing I found nothing dear.

The jailor provided him with food, money and a guide to Carlisle. They rode side by side, with the Lakes on their left and the Pennines on their right. Eight miles north of Carlisle, accompanied by another guide, he came into Scotland.

> I being come to this long-looked-for land,
> Did mark, remark, note, renote, viewed, and scanned:
> And I saw nothing that could change my will,
> But that I thought myself in England still.

It was an anti-climax, in fact such an anti-climax that Scotland seemed unworthy of poetry, which comes as a relief to the exhausted reader.

> So much in verse, and now I'll change my style,
> And seriously I'll write in prose awhile.

He spent his first night in Scotland at Moffat, thirty Scottish miles from Carlisle – 'indeed the Scots do allow almost as large measure for their miles, as they do for their drink'. Next day 'since I was born, I never was so weary or so near being dead from extreme travail'. At Blyth Bridge there was nowhere to sleep, so Water Poet and guide ended up in the shack of a woman in labour, abandoned by her man and alone but for a maidservant. Even there Taylor made a point of eating and drinking for nothing. 'At last to bed I went, my man lying on the floor by me, where in the night there the pigeons did very bountifully mute [shit] in his face.'

Fifteen miles on they hobbled 'through a fertile country for corn and cattle' to 'the wished, long expected, ancient, famous city of Edinburgh, which I entered penniless, altogether moneyless, but, I thank God, not friendless'.

Using well-tried methods he struck up a conversation with the most affluent-looking person in the street, one John Maxwell, whom he charmed into stabling his nag, buying Taylor 'a pint of Spanish', lending him ten shillings and showing him the best of the city. The castle, when they reached it, brought forth a typical Tayloresque response: 'Strongly grounded, bounded and founded, that by force of man it can never be confounded; the foundation and walls are unpenetrable, the ramparts impregnable, the bulwarks invincible.' There he saw Mons Meg, the giant cannon, its diameter so large 'a child was once begotten there'. Not the slimmest of men, he crawled inside – 'there was room enough for spare'.

From there he 'descended lower to the city, wherein I observed the fairest and goodliest street that ever mine eyes beheld'. It was the High Street:

> the buildings on each side of the way being all squared stone, five, six and seven storeys high, and many by-lanes and closes on each side of the way, wherein are gentlemen's houses, much fairer than the buildings in the High Street, for in the High Street merchants and tradesmen do dwell, but the gentlemen's mansions and goodliest houses are obscurely founded in the aforesaid lanes.

Like most men who have to sing for their supper, John Taylor was a terrible snob. At the end of the High Street was Cannongate, and at the end of Cannongate Holyroodhouse Palace. The palace, particularly the chapel, was sumptuous, and over a door in the inner courtyard he saw written in Latin, 'One hundred and six forefathers have left this to us unconquered'.

Edinburgh had its drawbacks, however. 'The worst was that wine and ale was so scarce, and the people were such misers with it, that every night before I went to bed, if any man had asked me a civil question, all the wit in my head could not have made him a sober answer.'

It was hardly a place he would call home, definitely unworthy of his verse, and from Leith, Edinburgh's port, Taylor crossed the Firth of Forth by ferry to the medicinal springs at Kinghorn, where he found the water as sweet as milk. He rode along the north coastline of the Forth Estuary to Culross, where he was entertained by the local coal magnate, Sir George Bruce, who took the Water Poet down his *subaqua* coalmine.

> The mine hath two ways into it, the one by sea and the other by land. Now men may object, how can a man go into a mine by sea, but that the sea will follow him and so drown the mine? To which objection thus I answer, that in low water, the sea being ebbed away, and a great part of the sand bare; upon this same sand (being mixed with rocks and crags) did the master of this great work build a round circular frame of stone, very thick, strong, and joined together with glutinous and bityumous matter, so high withall, that the sea at the highest flood, or the greatest rage of storm or tempest, can neither dissolve the stones so well compacted in the building, or yet overflow the height of it. Within this round frame (at all adventures) he did set workmen to dig with mattocks, pick-axes, and other instruments fit for such purposes. They did dig forty foot down right into and through a rock. At last they found that which they expected, which was sea-coal, they followed the vein of the mine, did dig forward still: so that in the space of eight and twenty, or nine and twenty, years, they have digged more than an English mile under the sea, that when men are at work below, a hundred of the greatest ships in Britain may sail over their heads. Besides, the mine is most artificially cut like an arch or a vault, all that great length, with many nooks and by-ways; and it is so made, that a man may walk upright in most places, both in and out. Many poor men are there set to work, which otherwise through the want of employment would perish. The sea at certain places doth leak, or soak into the mine, which, by the industry of Sir George Bruce, is all conveyed to one well near the land, where he hath a device like a horse-mill, that with three horses and a great chain of iron, going down many fathoms, with 36 buckets fastened to the chain: of the which 18 go down still to be filled, and 18 ascend up to be emptied, which do empty themselves (without any man's labour) into a trough that conveys the water into the sea again.

His next stop, still travelling on the north bank of the Forth, was Stirling. The castle stood on a crag and looked impregnable. The new Renaissance palace, started in 1496, was still incomplete, but the old castle's magnificent late Gothic Great Hall, with hammerbeam roof and minstrels' gallery, impressed him so much that he compared it to Westminster Hall.

From Stirling he rode north-east, across the Ochil Hills and through Perth, to Brechin on the edge of the Grampians. His quarry was the Earl of Marr and Sir William Murray, whom he knew would be only too glad to provide food and ale. But they were hunting in the Grampians, and the next week was spent trying to catch up with them. 'The way was rocky, and not above a yard broad in some places, so fearful and horrid it was to look down at the bottom.' The people spoke Gaelic, which Taylor called Irish, and the houses were hovels and breeding-grounds for bugs. He hated them. Soon he was on the edge of the Cairngorm Mountains, shrouded in a thick mist that dampened him to the skin. He was so cold that his teeth danced like the keys on a pianoforte.

> Thus with extreme travail, ascending and descending, mounting and alighting, I came at night to the place where I would be, in the Brea of Marr, which is a large country, all composed of such mountains, that Shooter's Hill, Highgate Hill, Hampstead Hill or the Malvern Hills, are but mole-hills by comparison, or like a gizzard under a capon's wing, in respect to the altitude of their tops, or perpendiculars of their bottoms. There I saw Mount Ben Avon, with a furried mist on his snowy head instead of a nightcap: for you must understand that the oldest man alive never saw but the snow was on the top of divers of those hills, both in summer as well as in winter.

Here, he found what he was looking for, Sir William Murray, the Earls of Marr, Murray and Enzie, and 100 knights and landowners.

> For once in the year, which is the whole month of August, and sometimes part of September, many of the nobility and gentry do come into these Highland countries to hunt, where they do conform themselves to the habit of Highland men; shoes with but one sole apiece; stockings (which they call short hose) made of a warm stuff of divers colours, which they call Tartans: as for breeches, many of them, nor their forefathers, never wore any, but a jerkin of the same stuff that their hose is of, their garters being bands or wreathes of hay and straw, with a pleat about the shoulders, which is a mantle of divers colours much finer and lighter stuff than their hose, with blue flat caps on their heads, a handkerchief knit with two knots about their neck.

Soon Taylor himself was dressed in the same attire.

Twelve days' hunting in the mountains followed, hunting deer, wild horses and wolves; while the nights were spent in lodges furnished with kitchens and cellars providing 'venison bak'd, sodden, roasted, and stewed beef, mutton, goats, kid, hare, fresh salmon, pigeons, hens, capons, chickens, partridge, moorcoots, heathcocks, good ale, sack, white and claret', which the Water Poet appreciated far more than the actual hunting. Yet the sight of 400 deers' antlers coming over the ridge like a moving forest was spectacular.

> Then all the valley on each side being way-laid with a hundred couple of strong Irish greyhounds, they are let loose as occasion serves upon the head of the deer, that with dogs, guns, arrows, dirks and daggers, in the space of two hours, fourscore fat deer were slain.

There were four days spent hunting on the Earl of Enzie's estates. More followed at Castle Grant, 'a fair and stately house', where there were banquets every night. From there Taylor went to Darnaway Castle, 'a goodly house of the Earl of Murray, where that right honourable Lord and his Lady did welcome us four days more'. Close by was Elgin, 'an ancient city where there stood a fair and beautiful church with three steeples'. This was Elgin cathedral, one of the most beautiful in Scotland, but it stood in ruins, a victim of the Reformation, when 'Knox knock'd down churches'.

From Elgin, after a flying visit to the Bishop of Murray, Taylor moved on to Gordon Castle, seat of the Marquis of Huntley. In all he had spent thirty-five days hunting in the most agreeable surroundings, and it had not cost him a penny.

He then set off on his return to London, spending his first night at Brechin.

There a wench that was born deaf and dumb came into my chamber at midnight (I being asleep), and she opened the bed, would fain have lodged with me: but I think that either the great travail over the mountains had tamed me: or if not, her beauty could never have moved me. The best parts of her were, that her breath was as sweet as sugar-candy. But howsoever, she made such a hideous noise, that I started out of my sleep, and thought that the devil had been there: but I no sooner knew who it was, but I arose, and thrust my dumb beast out of my chamber: and for want of a lock or a latch, I staked up my door with a great chair.

Next morning he was on the road for Dundee, and within a few days across the Forth and back in Edinburgh, bumping into none other than his old friend Ben Jonson, who 'gave me a piece of gold of two and twenty shillings to drink his health in England'.

There was still a lot of drinking to do. In Dunbar he consumed ten Scottish pints of wine, all paid for by somebody else. Two days and many pints later, he crossed the Tweed at Berwick into England. It was 12 September. At Newcastle, after being entertained by his old captain from the siege of Cadiz, Sir Henry Witherington, he picked up several aquaintances from his time in Scotland, and they all rode south together through Durham and Darlington into Yorkshire. At York the Scottish fellow-travellers must have got fed up with paying the tavern bills, for 'I took my leave of them, and would needs try my penniless fortune by myself'. One day's ride from York took him to Doncaster, 'where my horses were well-fed at the Bear' and its rider even better fed at the house of the High Sheriff of Yorkshire, Sir Robert Swift. Newark proved equally rewarding; at Stamford, too, where he was staying at a tavern called The Virginity, he managed to get bed and board for nothing, while in Huntingdon, staying at the Crown, he got 'a gentleman who was with me' to foot the bill. Two days later:

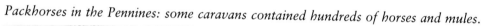

Packhorses in the Pennines: some caravans contained hundreds of horses and mules.

I came into London, and obscurely coming within Moorgate, I went to a house and borrowed money: and so I stole back again to Islington, to the sign of the Maidenhead, staying till Wednesday, that my friends came to meet me, who knew no other but that Wednesday was my first coming: where with all love I was entertained with much good cheer.

*   *   *

Four years later in 1622 Taylor published his first fictional work, his own Book of Nonsense, a 'translation' of *Sir Gregory Nonsense's News from Noplace*, preceding Edward Lear by 250 years. But it was not the success he had hoped for, so to supplement his waterman's income he returned to the well-tried formula of travel-writing in verse. He called his epic *A Very Merry Wherry Ferry Voyage*, a narrative of a journey by rowing boat from London to York with a crew of three. They set out in July.

> About the waist or naval of the day,
> Not being dry or drunk, I went my way.
> Our wherry somewhat old, or stuck in age,
> That had endur'd near four years pilgrimage,
> And carried honest people, whores and thieves,
> Some sergeants, bailiffs, and some under-sheriffs,
> And now at last it was her lot to be
> Th' adventurous bonny barque to carry me.
> But as an old whore's beauty being gone
> Hides Nature's wreck, with art-like painting on:
> So I with colours finely did repair
> My boat's defaults, and made her fresh and fair.

After many delays in the waterside taverns, they sailed down the Thames Estuary, passing their first night at Gravesend and their second at Harwich, where they got drenched. Next morning they rowed through calm waters past Aldeburgh and Lowestoft to Yarmouth. They set off from Yarmouth the following morning, skirting the East Anglia flatlands and salt marshes, but hit a storm just before evening as they came up to Cromer.

> Thus on the lee-shore darkness began to come,
> The sea grew high, the winds 'gan hiss and hum:
> The foaming curled waves the shore did beat,
> (As if the ocean would all Norfolk eat)
> To keep at sea was dangerous I did think,
> To go to land I stood in no doubt to sink:
> Thus landing, or not landing (I suppos'd)
> We were in peril round about enclosed;
> At last to row to shore I thought it best,
> 'Mongst many evils, thinking that the least:
> My men all pleas'd to do as I command,
> Did turn the boat's head opposite to land,
> And with the highest wave that I could spy,
> I bade them to row to shore immediately.
> And thus half sous'd, half stewed, with sea and sweat,
> We land at Cromer Town, half dry, half wet.

As they dragged their boat ashore they were seen by some women and children who, thinking them pirates, fled back to the town in terror. The bedraggled wherry crew trudged off to the nearest house for shelter, little knowing that it was the only house in the district owned by a Roman Catholic. As they tried to warm themselves, they were suddenly manhandled and dragged outside by the Town Watch, forty men carrying rusty bill-hooks and 'armed with ale', led by Cromer's four constables, Masters Pescod, Wiseman, Kimble and Clarke, who escorted their prisoners to the nearest ale house for interrogation.

Taylor explained who he was, and appeared genuinely upset that no one knew of him. His letters of introduction to such eminences as the Archbishop of York were treated as forgeries, and his wherry was damaged by the Watch searching for concealed arms. Most painful of all for Taylor, the entire male population of Cromer appeared to have forced themselves into the saloon and were all drinking ale at his expense. The prisoners were locked up and it was not until the following day, when a brace of Justices of the Peace rode over to see what the commotion was about, that they were released.

> So farewell Pescod, Wiseman, Kimble, Clarke,
> Four sons of ignorance (or much more dark)
> You made me lose a day of brave calm weather,
> So once again farewell, fare ill together.

They continued rowing along the Norfolk coast to Blakeney and Cley, and set off again next morning, sailing past Wells-next-the-Sea and across the Wash, where they were almost swept away by the currents, then up the estuary of the River Witham to Boston in Lincolnshire. They arrived at Lincoln, fifty miles up the Witham, that evening.

> A brave cathedral church there now doth stand,
> That scarcely hath a fellow in this land:
> 'Tis for a Godly use, a goodly frame,
> And bears the Blessed Virgin Mary's name.
> The town is ancient, and by course of fate,
> Through wars, and Time, defac'd and ruinate,
> But monarchies and empires, kingdoms, crowns,
> Have rose and fell, as Fortune smiles or frowns:
> And towns and cities have their portions had
> Of time-tossed variations, good and bad.
> There is a proverb, part of which is this,
> They say that Lincoln was, and London is.

From Lincoln they took the old Roman dyke linking the Witham to the Trent. Soon they wished they hadn't. It was choked with weeds and brambles, more mud than water, and looked as if it had not been dredged since the Romans left.

> 'Tis 8 miles long, and there our pains were such.
> As all our travel did not seem so much,
> My men did wade and draw the boat like horses,
> And scarce could tug her on with all our forces:
> Moil'd, toil'd, mir'd, tir'd, still labr'ing, ever doing,
> Yet were 9 long hours that 8 miles going.

They came to Gainsborough. A day's drifting down the Trent brought them to the Humber Estuary. But they were unable to cross it to the Yorkshire Ouse, and were blown off-course down the estuary to Hull, where they stayed for a long-winded diversion, before continuing up the Ouse to York. There Taylor was welcomed and dined by the Lord Mayor and the Archbishop. His return to London must have disappointed the good citizens of York. It was by horse.

*   *   *

Undaunted by his experiences, the Water Poet was back in a wherry a year later, sailing from London to Salisbury, via the English Channel. 'Thousands gaz'd', according to Taylor when the five men in a boat launched themselves, a little upstream from London Bridge. They passed under the bridge without mishap, sailed past Cuckold's Point, Deptford, Greenwich Palace and Gravesend.

> And as our oars thus down the river pull'd,
> Oft with a fowling piece the gulls we cull'd
> For why, the Master Gunner of our ship
> Let no occasion or advantage slip,
> But charg'd and discharged, shot, and shot again,
> And scarce in twenty times shot once in vain,
> Foul was the weather, yet thus much I'll say.
> If't had been fair, fowl was our food that day.

They continued down the Thames Estuary, as it got wider and wider, and off Sandwich they were grounded on a sandbank almost four miles out to sea. The experience was not dangerous, merely ridiculous.

> At last unlook'd for on our starboard side
> A thing turmoiling in the sea we spied,
> Like to a Merman; wading as he did
> All in the sea his nether parts were hid,
> Whose brawny limbs, and rough neglected beard,
> And grim aspect, made half of us afear'd.
> Quoth he, kind Sir, I am a fisherman,
> Who many years my living thus have won
> By wading in these sandy troublesome waters
> For shrimps, whelks, cockles, and such useful matters,
> And I will lead you, (with a course I'll keep)
> From out these dangerous shallows to the deep.
> Then (by the nose) along he led our boat,
> Till (past the flats), our barque did bravely float.

An hour and a half later they disembarked at Deal, where they gorged themselves on their dead fowl.

The next morning, a Wednesday, they sailed on to Dover, where they inspected the castle, 'saw a gun thrice eight foot long of brass', and drank water from a hundred-fathom well, the water drawn by a donkey in a wheel, and so cold it made Taylor's teeth chatter.

They pushed on and, rowing past Romney Marsh, the weather worsened. It hardly abated for the rest of the voyage.

Toss'd and retoss'd, retoss'd and toss'd again:
With rumbling, tumbling, on the rolling main,
The boist'rous breaking billows curled locks
Impetuously did beat against the rocks,
The wind much like a horse whose wind is broke,
Blew thick and short, that we were like to choke:
As so outrageously the billows shaves,
The gusts (like dust) blown from the briny waves,
And thus the winds and seas robustious gods
Fell by the ears stark mad at furious odds.
Our slender ship, turmoil'd, 'twixt land and seas,
Aloft or low, as storms and flaws did please:
Sometimes upon a foaming mountain's top,
Whose height did seem the heav'ns to underprop,
When straight to such profundity she fell,
As if she div'd into the deepest Hell.

They came ashore at Dungeness, stripped off their soaking clothes and skipped around the beach naked, trying to get dry. Nearby was a cluster of cottages. They were empty. Taylor, now clothed, set off two miles inland to the 'ragged town' of Lydd, where the local innkeeper and his wife proved a fair match for Taylor.

Mine hostess did account it no trouble,
For single fare to make me pay double:
Yet did her mind and mine agree together:
That (I once gone) would never more come hither.

They stayed two days, occasionally resting from the food and drink to repair their wherry.

When we (like tenants) beggarly and poor,
Decreed to leave the key beneath the door,
But that the landlord did that shift prevent,
Who came in pudding time and took his rent.

Back on board they sailed past Rye and Winchelsea, but the seas foamed up again and they came ashore a little to the east of Hastings, where they waited for three days for the waves to calm, and the mayor picked up the bill. They got as far as Newhaven before the storms forced them to stop again. Goring, near Worthing, their next haven, was hardly a refuge. As in Cromer, they were promptly arrested by the local Watch, though this time they were taken for aristocrats fleeing the country. The constable told them to stay exactly where they were until he fetched a Justice of the Peace from six miles away. They happily acquiesced, waited for the constable to disappear out of sight, then relaunched their wherry, only to find that they had underestimated the constable's intelligence – he had taken their oars. A friendly ploughman found them in a nearby field and the five-men-in-a-boat left Goring, sailed past Littlehampton, Bognor Regis and Selsey Bill, and landed for the night at Selsey.

Five hours of rowing through a rough sea took them to Chichester Harbour, where they stayed a night. Next morning they came into Portsmouth, where they were entertained by the Admiral of the Fleet, an improvement on Goring. Fully bloated by the admiral's hospitality, they crossed to the Isle of Wight, visited Cowes Castle and, after a night of eating and drinking, set off from Yarmouth. It was their last day at sea. After facing flats, depths, ragged rocks and village constables, they came into Christchurch at five o'clock.

The River Avon, lacking the waves and tides of verse and worse, deserved only prose. Indeed, it was so cluttered with rubbish that it hardly deserved that. After writing a dozen very long pages extolling the economic prosperity that comes from navigable rivers, Taylor slowly pushed up the Avon towards Salisbury, escorted – so he claims – by 2,000 swans. On Friday night they arrived in Salisbury.

*   *   *

The two decades that followed, when the country was dividing between Royalists and Parliamentarians, were busy times for John Taylor. He managed to make a journey from London to Queenborough in a boat made out of brown paper, with two stockfish tied to bamboos as oars, compile a guide to London taverns, write a verse epic about a voyage by rowing boat down the Thames and publish an attack on coaches.

The year 1639 saw Taylor travelling through the Midlands, at the age of fifty-nine. He left London in July, passing through Mimms on his first day. Twenty-four hours later he was in Northampton and the day after that in Leicester. There he stayed at the Blue Boar, where his brother was the landlord. He liked the town. The streets were so well-paved that a man could walk in slippers through the foulest weather and not get his feet wet. The inhabitants were so peaceful that the only lawsuit in the town was over three geese which, grazing on the common, had been impounded by the local authorities and held with their necks in the stocks. The stocks strangled the geese and the court had to decide whether they had been unlawfully killed in custody, or had committed suicide.

Coventry bored Taylor ('I have little to say, but that it is a fair, famous, sweet, and ancient city, so walled about in strength and neatness, as no city in England may compare to it.'), but Nottingham fared better in his estimation.

> The town of Nottingham is seated on a hill, which hill is almost of one stoney rock, or a soft kind of penetrable sandy stone; it hath very fair buildings, many large streets, and a spacious marketplace; a great number of inhabitants (especially the poorer sort) do dwell in vaults, holes, or caves, which are cut and digged out of the rock: so that if a man be destitute of a house, it is but to go to Nottingham, and with a mattock, a shovel, a crow of iron, a chisel, a mallet, and such instruments, he may play the mole.

Two days later, after a night at Derby, he was in the Peak District, 'stoney, craggy with inaccessible hills and mountains', and dotted with lead mines. He returned to his brother's tavern in Leicester on 16 August.

Four days later he set off eastwards to King's Lynn, then made a half-circle around the Fens and struck out north to Boston and up through Lincolnshire to York, stopping by at the archbishop's on the way. At a 'poor alehouse' on the road to Leeds he found himself in the company of a tinker 'who made pretty music with his Banbury kettle-drum', and two drovers taking thirty-five hogs to Leeds market. The four travelled to Leeds together.

Leeds, a vast town for its time with 12,000 inhabitants, had only one church until John Harrison built the very Jacobean and High Church St John the Evangelist, about five years before Taylor's visit. Though classed as a chapel, it was sufficiently large for a congregation of 4,000 and was graced with:

exquisite art of carving and masonry, with painting, gilding, polishing, embellishing and adorning, with a most stately roof, a fair lofty tower or steeple, a sweet ring of bells.

Close by the church were twenty-one almshouses, a grammar school 'and a fine street built on both sides in a uniform and fair manner with houses: the rents whereof are for the maintenance of the alms-houses, the school, and reparations of the church to the end of the world'.

On 4 September Taylor was back in the Peaks, riding 'over rocks and cloud-kissing mountains', one of them so high that on a clear day you could see Lincoln Cathedral and York Minster. On his second day in the Peaks he hired a guide to take him to Halifax. It was sixteen miles away but so mountainous that the sixteen miles took all day. There he saw the town's guillotine or 'fatal engine', as he called it. Halifax was a cloth town, and treated cloth had to be left in the sun to dry. Only the town's unique privilege, which proscribed death for cloth stealing, was thought sufficient to deter thieves. Characteristically, Taylor approved. For the executions had to be carried out by the thief's victim, and most, understandably, shrank from the act.

He spent two days there before riding south-west through Rochdale and Manchester to Chester, where the Earl of Derby paid for the drinks. 'For the reverend respect which I do owe and bear to nobility, it did me good to see so grave and honourable a peer.' On 10 September he was in Lichfield where 'there is a fair and curious old cathedral', and four days later was back at his brother's in Leicester.

*   *   *

When civil war broke out in 1642, Taylor – Royalist, Loyalist and Tory – moved to Oxford, where the King had his headquarters. He lodged at Oriel College, becoming jester and propagandist for the Royalist cause. A surreal woodcut on the title page of one of his pamphlets gives us some idea of his feelings during these 'distracted times'.

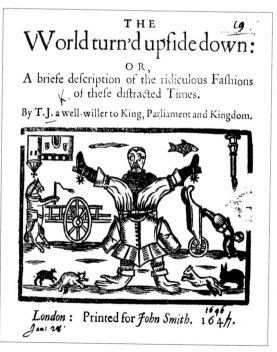

This monstrous picture plainly doth declare
This land (quite out of order) out of square
His breeches on his shoulders doth appear,
His doublet on his lower parts doth wear;
His boots and spurs upon his arms and hands,
His gloves upon his feet (whereon he stands)
The church o'erturned (a lamentable show)
The candlestick above, the light below,
The coney hunts the dog, the rat the cat,
The horse doth whip the cart (I pray mark that)
The wheelbarrow doth drive the man (oh base)
And eels and gudgeons fly a mighty pace.

In 1649, the Royalist cause lost and the King executed, John Taylor, 'a youth of threescore and ten, with a lame leg and a half', embittered by defeat, made one of his longest journeys, to Land's End and back.

'Tis a mad world (my masters) and in sadness
I travelled madly in these days of madness:
Eight years a frenzy did this land molest,
The ninth year seemed to be much like the rest,
Myself (with age, grief, wrongs, and wants oppressed,
With troubles more than patience could digest)
Amongst those ills, I chose the least and best,
Which was to take this journey to the West.

He left London on 21 June, riding through Brentford, Colnbrook, Maidenhead and Henley to Abingdon, where he stayed with a nephew, John. After four days in Abingdon he paid '2/6 d for the hire of a skeleton or anatomy of a beast to carry me ten miles to Faringdon'. Faringdon was depressing, half the town having been burnt by the Royalists, the other half by the Parliamentarians, 'so between them there was a good market town turned into ashes and rubble'. Travelling on almost the same route as John Leland, he went on, riding and 'footing it' to Malmesbury, where he 'found an ancient town, an old castle and new ale'. His next stop was Bath, where he tried the baths, but found the local mayor strangely reluctant to pay the bills. Fifteen miles further on lay Wells, which he reached on 30 June and where 'these holy, profane days, and blessed execrable times of troublesome tranquility, have spoilt and defaced one of the goodliest and magnificent cathedral churches in the Christian world'. He continued to Glastonbury, where 'I saw the ruins of an abbey, which was one of the stateliest and most sumptuous in England or Europe.' Thanks to a Mr Brooke and his sister, Taylor was fed and given a bed for two days, 'so that the town of Glastonbury was not one penny the richer for any expense of mine'.

On 2 July – 'a mad, sad, glad, auspicious, unlucky day' – he was in Bridgwater. For John Taylor, Bridgwater was the scene of a serious disaster. It all happened when he was crossing a stile:

a splinter off a stile took hold of my one and only breeches, and tore them in that extreme unmerciful, unmannerly manner, that for shame and modesty's sake I was feign to put them off and go breechless into the town, where I found a botching threepenny tailor, who did patch me up.

He continued five miles to a 'ragged market town called Nether Stowey'. He stayed at the local inn, and wished he had stayed at Bridgwater.

> Mine host was very sufficiently drunk, the house most delicately decked with exquisite artificial and natural sluttery, the room besprinkled and strewed with the excrements of pigs and children: the walls and ceilings were adorned and hanged with rare spider's tapestry, or cobweb lawn: the smoke was so palpable and perspicuous, that I could scarce see anything else, and I could scarce see that, it so blinded me with weeping.

Taylor's host announced that dinner would be beef and carrots, but three hours later there was neither beef nor carrots, nor even the serving maid, who had gone to feed the hogs. He woke his host, who told him to be content with fried eggs and parsley, but two hours later there were neither fried eggs nor even parsley. He lay down to sleep, only to be attacked by 'an Ethiopian army of fleas so plump and mellow that they would squash to pieces like young boiled peas. For my further delight, my chamber pot seemed to be lined within with crimson plush.' He finally got to sleep, only to be woken by screaming children. When the children stopped, the dogs started; the dogs stopped and 'the hogs began to cry out for their breakfast'. The hogs had more luck than Taylor, and he was relieved to arrive breakfastless at Dunster, all red sandstone, ten miles away on the other side of the Brendon Hills.

> From excrements, and all bad scents,
> From children's bawling and caterwauling,
> From grunting hogs and barking dogs,
> And from biting fleas, there I found ease.

On 4 July he was crossing Exmoor, a 'tedious weary way for a crazy old, lame, bad, foundered footman'. Next day he was in Barnstaple, 'a very fine sweet town, so clean and neat, that in the worst of weather, a man may walk the streets, and never foul shoe or boot', and where there was 'fiddlers fare, meat, drink and money'. A boat down the Taw Estuary took him to Appledore. Two days later he was in Cornwall.

Most of Cornwall he approved of, and there were no complaints about the natives not understanding him – their language was disappearing. But at a village called Blisland on Bodmin Moor he was mistaken for a server of writs and beaten up. Dusting himself down with all the dignity he could muster, he left Blisland and came to Bodmin, continuing on to Truro the next day.

Two days later he reached St Michael's Mount. The empty nunnery that William Worcestre had known had been demolished and rebuilt, and was now occupied by the Godolphin family. The church had been turned into an ammunition store. Fourteen miles on was Land's End, where he cut his name in the rock, 'and there I saw the Island of Scilly, with other smaller islands'. It was still held by the Royalists, whose privateers took any ship within range, 'whereby they have great riches, with all necessities' – the last redoubt of his defeated cause.

From Land's End there was nowhere to go but back the way he had come, keeping to the South Cornwall coastline after Penzance. The quiet fishing village of Mevagissey, which made its money out of the pilchard business, had two taverns and six ale houses, but no one would take him in and he was gawped at as if he was 'some strange beast or monster brought out of Africa'. In the end he lost his temper and became just an angry old man. Another old man – a Justice of the Peace – took him into his own house, where he 'found more Protestant religion in two days than I had in five years before'.

St Michael's Mount: a holy place in Worcestre's time, an arsenal in Taylor's.

Three days later Taylor was in Plymouth, which had a strong Parliamentarian garrison. Already he had been obliged to reschedule his itinerary to avoid Parliamentarian posts that might ask him too many awkward questions; but here, in a typical Taylorian gesture, he provocatively visited the Royalist prisoner, held in the Guildhall, Colonel William Legge, wishing him 'health and liberty'. Realizing that he had gone too far, that 'the town was too full of suspicions to hold me', he left in a hurry. At Plympton, just outside Plymouth, he hired a horse for the 40-mile journey across Dartmoor to Exeter, where, to his intense chagrin, 'I was two days entertained at mine own cost'.

Seventeen miles on foot took him to Honiton, where he hired a horse, 'which turned out to be a blind mare' with more bones than flesh, and he ended up walking with the horse on a leading rope to Axminster. From there, alternatively walking and riding on hired nags, he passed through Sherborne, Salisbury and Andover, arriving back in London on 3 August, six weeks after he had set out.

*　　*　　*

Three years later, at the age of seventy-three, John Taylor took to the road again, travelling this time through the West Midlands and Wales.

> For he that wants legs, feet, brains and wit,
> To be a traveller is most unfit:
> And such am I by age of strength bereft
> With one right leg, and one lame left leg left.

He left London on 13 July, riding an inadequate beast through Stockenchurch, Abingdon, Warwick, Coventry and Lichfield to Chester, where an Italian physician,

Vincent Lancelles, who 'cured the rich for as much as he could get, healed the meaner sort for what they could spare, and cured the poor for God's sake', treated him for his leg, charged him God's rate and paid for his lodgings.

On 30 July he was in Flint, but 'war hath made it miserable' and its castle was 'almost buried in its own ruins'. He could find 'neither saddler, tailor, weaver, brewer, baker, butcher or button-maker' and there was not one ale house. Leaving Flint, he rode and walked west, 'ascending and descending almost impassable mountains', sometimes touching the coast, sometimes passing inland, going through Bangor to Caernarfon.

> I thought to have seen a town and a castle, or a castle and a town; but I saw both to be one, and one to be both; for indeed a man can hardly divide them in judgement or appreciation; and I have seen many gallant fabrics and fortifications, but for compactness and completeness of Caernarfon I never yet saw a parallel.

He had hardly left Caernarfon when he was arrested by a trooper as a suspicious person, and taken back. When the castle governor, Colonel Mason, found out who he was, he 'used me most respectfully', buying Taylor dinner, furnishing him with a bed for the night and providing a guide for a week. His guide took him to Harlech, 'almost uninhabitable by the late lamented troubles', then the two rode down the coast of Cardigan Bay, through 'a miserable market town called Aberystwyth', where the castle was in ruins and many fair houses had been turned into rubble. There were silver mines four miles away, but they were as neglected as the town.

At Aberystwyth Taylor turned inland, through 'many miles, with too many turning and winding mountains, stoney turning ways, backward, sideways, circular and semi-circular'. Each day he was forced to hire guides, 'for I knew neither the intricate ways, nor could speak any of the language'. It was harvest time and guides were expensive, sometimes as much as three shillings a day, not to mention the cost of the guide's meat, drink and lodging. His destination was Carmarthen, and the country was so mountainous that he was forced to dismount and walk thirty times in one day. By evening he was lost and, seeking a 'field-chamber' to lie down in, he ended up in a bog. He was rescued by a passing traveller who spoke some English and took him into Carmarthen. It was a large town with a good harbour, and the agricultural produce was the cheapest Taylor had come across. The only thing the town did not run to was a tobacco pipe.

Pembrokeshire, where the people spoke English, was even better. As for Pembroke, the shire town, its castle was strong but the town itself had known better days, and many of the houses were deserted. Milford Haven, a few miles away, had no equal; 'for it is of such length, breadth and depth that a thousand ships may ride safely in it in all weathers'. But St David's Cathedral, eighteen miles away, had suffered its roof to be stripped of its 'dull and heavy coat of peaceful lead, which was metamorphosized into warlike bullets'.

On 18 August he hired a guide to take him to Swansea, 'sixteen well-stretched Welsh mountain miles' away, where the local notable took him in and provided him with a letter of introduction to his son. But when Taylor reached the son's house, he found that the son was away and the servant, 'with her posterior or but end towards me', would have nothing to do with him. He rode off in a fury, followed by a dozen yelping dogs, 'when luckily a gentleman overtook me, and after a little talk of my distress and travel, he bade me be of good cheer, for he would bring me to a lodging and entertainment'.

The Water Poet continued east along the coast of Wales, through Cardiff and across the River Usk to Monmouth. He crossed the border and, passing through Gloucester, spent his first night in England at Barnsley, near Cirencester. It was a Sunday. Two women were in the stocks for flaunting the Lord's Day. They had been:

> at church both before and after noon, did but walk in the fields for their recreation. They were put to their choice, either to pay sixpence apiece (for profane walking), or to be laid an hour in the stocks; and the peevish wilful women (though they were able enough to pay), to save their money and jest out the matter, lay both by their heels merrily one hour.

He thought back to Wales, where 'they have neither service, prayer, sermon, minister, or preacher, nor any church door opened at all, so that people do exercise and edify in the churchyard at the lawful and laudable games of trap, cat, stool-ball, racket, *etcetera*, on Sundays.'

Taylor arrived in London, 'where I brought both ends together on Tuesday 7 September'. It was almost the end of his travels. There the new regime treated him with the same tolerance as Colonel Mason – a tolerance Taylor would never have given them if his side had won. They gave him the licence of the Poet's Head (formerly the King's Head, but that sign had become a little tactless) in Long Acre, where he finally made a profession of getting other people to pay for the drinks. He made one last journey, a short trip through Kent and Sussex the following year, by now old, lame, alcoholic and bitter: bitter of the laws that would not suffer children to play games on Sundays, bitter at the execution of his King, and bitter at the Commonwealth for treating him so patronizingly, marginalizing him as a harmless eccentric. A few months later he was dead. His epitaph was written in his own style.

> Here lies the Water Poet, honest John,
> Who rowed in the streams of Helicon;
> Where having many rocks and dangers past,
> He at the haven of Heaven arrived at last.

4
THE
WEEKEND
GUEST

TEN YEARS AFTER John Taylor's death William Fiennes, Lord Saye and Sele, was attending the christening of his granddaughter, Cecilia. Saye and Sele had been one of the leaders of the Parliamentary cause in its early pre-revolutionary phase and ended his political career as a Royal Counsellor to Charles II. 'Old Subtlety', as his enemies called him, was one of the winners in the civil war. Celia (as her name was shortened to) received little formal education, as her spelling and grammar show, but, at ease with herself and with other classes, she was self-confident, sensible (she took her own bed linen on her travels) and a strict Nonconformist. Occasionally hectoring, possessing a limitless curiosity about everything and everybody, she liked her food and her beer and was a passionate enthusiast of modern architecture.

Travel in England was no easier in the last decades of the seventeenth century than it had been in the first decades. The roads were still layered in adhesive mud, discharged soldiers had become highwaymen, and inns varied in quality from five-star hotels with impeccable service to wayside whorehouses. A *Book of Roads*, giving details of mileage between different towns, the exact definition of the length of a mile, and a strip-map of England's and Wales's major roads, had been published by John Ogilby in 1675, but it was far too bulky to carry on a journey. It was not until 1721 that a pocket edition was published. Travel was still tedious, dangerous, extremely uncomfortable, and never the sort of thing that young girls did without the maximum of artificial comforts and an armed escort. Celia travelled escortless for the pure pleasure of travelling; but then Celia had been born into an élite to whom all things were possible.

*   *   *

She was practically brought up on a horse, and made several journeys in her youth riding sidesaddle from her home at Newton Toney near Salisbury, regularly visiting her older brother's house, Broughton Castle, the fourteenth-century family pile where Pym, Warwick, Hampden and Old Subtlety plotted the downfall of absolute monarchy. She did not like the place, and dismissed it as 'an old house, moated round, and a park and gardens, but much left to decay and ruin'.

The medieval sewers of Old Sarum impressed her, and Stonehenge, which she called Stoneage, she reckoned 'one of the wonders of England how such prodigeous

Stonehenge: originally Stanhengist *(hanging stones), but to Celia Fiennes* Stoneage.

stones should be brought there'. Somerset was rich in fruit, but its people wasteful, particularly in making cider – pressing good and bad apples indiscriminately into enormous presses. 'They pound their apples then lay fresh straw on the press, and on that a good lay of pulp of the apples, then turn in the ends of the straw over it all round, and lay fresh straw, and more apples up to the top.'

In her mid-twenties she was visiting Bath by coach, a mode of transport about as comfortable as an unsprung Volvo. 'The houses are indifferent, the streets are a good size well-pitched, there are several good houses built for lodgings that are new and adorned with good furniture, the baths in my opinion make the town unpleasant, the air thick and hot.'

There were five baths in all. The hottest was quite small and enclosed, which made it hotter. From there the water ran into the 'Lepours Bath', gradually cooling before dropping down into the Cross Bath, where it joined the water from the hot springs bubbling up from beneath. There were underwater stone seats, for the men on the cross of the Cross Bath and for the women under the arches that ran round the outside. They were extremely comfortable. 'The water bears you up so that the seat seems as easy as a down cushion.' The last two baths were the King's Bath and the Queen's Bath. The King's was as large as all the others put together, while the water in the Queen's was so hot 'it tasted like water taken from the pan in which an egg had been boiled'.

She made several visits to Tunbridge Wells, where the waters were so wholesome that they were bottled up and sold in London. The wells were surrounded by inns and dance halls, and the Walk, which ran from the town to the wells, was lined with 'shops full of all sorts of toys, silver, china, millinery, curious wooden ware', a casino, two coffee-houses and several apothecaries, their overhanging floors supported on pillars, like a piazza. Its proximity to London, and patronage by the late Queen Henrietta

Marie, had made it into one of the most fashionable spots in the Home Counties. There was an orchestra at the wells every afternoon, dancing every night and endless titillation about the unsatisfactory love affairs of others.

Ten years later in 1693, aged thirty-one, she was in Oxford. She found the town pleasant and compact, Wren's Sheldonian Theatre 'a noble pile of building, paved with black and white marble and exceedingly large and lofty, built round and full of galleries', rising above the skyline. In the alcoves were the printing presses of the Oxford University Press, and she could not resist printing her name in all the different typefaces before she left.

Of the colleges Trinity 'had a fine neat chapel new made finely painted'; the courts and ranges at Christ Church, which Henry VIII College had finally become, were 'large and lofty': Magdalen had 'a very large and good cloister'; and St John's 'fine gardens and walks but I did not just look into it'; but the ultra-modern library at Queen's College did not impress her, for it was really just a copy of Wren's library at Trinity, Cambridge. On more practical matters, the beer at Corpus Christi was utterly marvellous.

*   *   *

Short as they were, these light excursions gave her a taste for travel. The manor house at Newton Toney must have seemed boring by comparison. She wanted more, more than Newton Toney had to offer her, and since she came from a class to whom nothing was impossible, there was nothing to stop her finding it. So she left her London home with a single maidservant in May 1697 and, picking up a cousin at Amwell, twenty-four miles north of London, set off on an 800-mile journey through the north of England, making her first stop at Audley End.

0   50   100 miles

GLASGOW
Edinburgh

Newcastle
Carlisle   Durham
Keswick
Windermere   Richmond
Ripon
Lancaster   York
Halifax   Beverley
Preston   Kingston upon Hull
LEEDS
Liverpool   Doncaster
MANCHESTER   Lincoln
Chester
Snowdon
Nottingham   Grantham
Shrewsbury   Derby   Stamford   Norwich
Lichfield   Peterborough
Leicester   Ely   Thetford
BIRMINGHAM   Bury St Edmunds
Ludlow   Coventry   Huntingdon   Ipswich
Worcester   Warwick   Cambridge
Stratford-on-Avon   Colchester
St David's   Gloucester   St Albans
Cardiff   Bristol   Oxford   Canterbury
Bath   LONDON   Tunbridge
Wells   Wells   Dover
Glastonbury
Salisbury   Winchester
Taunton   Southampton
Launceston   Exeter
Plymouth   Dorchester

Penzance
Falmouth
St Michael's
Mount

—·—·— Journeys in 1697

············ The Great Journey of 1698

– – – –

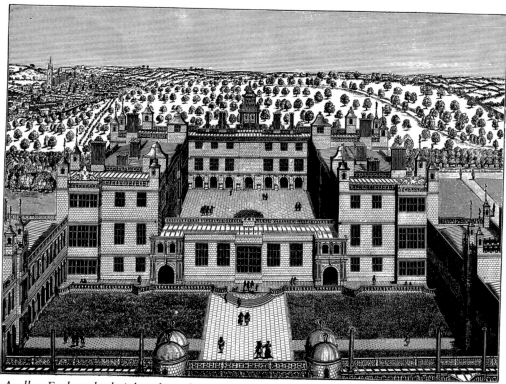

Audley End at the height of its glory in 1688, ten years before Celia Fiennes's visit.

The house, she wrote in her journal five years later, 'makes a noble appearance like a town, so many towers and buildings of stone within the park, which is walled round, a good river runs through it'. She crossed the river and saw the house in front of them, 'too large for a king, but might do for a Royal Treasurer', according to James I, who later imprisoned its owner, a Lord Treasurer, for embezzlement. Charles II bought it in a fit of extravagance, restored it with equal extravagance, and it stood in all its Jacobean splendour with 'thirty great and little towers on the top and a great Cupid in the middle'. Inside were over 750 rooms, 'large and lofty with good rich old furniture and tapistries, altogether a stately palace'.

They rode on through a series of 'neat villages with rows of trees about them' – Great Chesterford, Sawston, Great Shelford, Trumpington – towards Cambridge, which they reached that evening.

Cambridge was in the middle of a great building era. It was the age of Grumbold, whose grandfather had completed the tower of St Mary's Church, whose father had rebuilt Clare College, and who himself had been Wren's master mason on Trinity College library. Robert Grumbold dominated the post-Restoration architecture of the university's colleges. His north range for Clare completed his father's work, his extensions to Pembroke were by now well over a decade old and his *magnum opus*, St Catherine's College, was half-built.

Of the colleges Trinity was Celia's favourite.

Trinity College is the finest, yet not so large as Christ Church Oxford. In the first court is a very fine fountain in the middle of the quadrangle with a carved top and dials around; there are large cloisters in the Second Court and the Library runs all the range of the building at the end and stands on three rows of stone pillars; it opens into the gardens and walk with three large gates or doors of iron carved very fine with flowers and leaves. The Library fair exceeds that at Oxford, the stairs are wainscoted and very large and easy ascent, all of cedar wood. The room is spacious and lofty, paved with black and white marble, the sides wainscoted and decked with all curious books of learning; there are two large globes at each end with telescopes and microscopes, and the finest carvings in wood in flowers, birds, leaves, figures of all sorts as I ever saw.

She also loved King's College Chapel – 'the finest building I have ever heard of,' she enthused between breaths. She ascended the 120 steps, walked over the vaulting and climbed on to the roof, from where she could see the lantern of Ely Cathedral fifteen miles away.

She stayed a night in Cambridge and left for Huntingdon after a morning's sightseeing. It was summer. The roads were easy riding and the prospects delightful, as the little party of unescorted females rode through woodland, enclosures, open country and little villages. At Huntingdon they stayed at Lord Sandwich's house, Hitching-brooke, and Celia was shocked to find a nude Venus in her bedroom. They left the next morning after inspecting Lord Sandwich's Dutch Garden, riding up the Great North Road to Stamford, where the countryside reminded her of Oxfordshire.

Stamford she liked, in spite of its unfashionable Gothic ambience, 'as fine a built town all of stone as may be seen'. On the south edge of the town lay Burghley House, its skyline broken by towers, chimneys, cupolas and castellation. 'The situation is the finest I ever saw,' she exclaimed. 'It stands in a fine park which is full of deer and very fine trees.' The wrought-iron gateway by Tijou was spectacular, with 'leaves, flowers, figures, birds, beasts, wheat'. It led to a magnificent courtyard. The interior of the house was being modernized, with splendidly vulgar baroque ceilings by Verrio almost completed. For two hours Celia dragged her exhausted cousin around the house. One awe-inspiring ceiling followed another: 'Fortune blindfolded and tied to a wheel', 'Rewards of Virtue', 'Reunion of Cupid and Psyche', 'Feast of the Gods' and –

Cambridge: King's College chapel dominating the skyline.

completed only a year earlier – 'Assembly of the Gods'. She approved of them, but she disapproved of the 'immodesty of the pictures' in the private apartments. Like the Venus in the Hitchingbrooke bedroom the night before, they were *not* in the best of taste.

Rutland was woody and the church at Grantham had a high steeple (the third highest in the country, in fact). Celia did not really like the place. She passed through without stopping and followed the River Brant to Lincoln.

> Lincoln opens to view at least six miles off, it stands on a very high hill and looks very fine at the entrance, the houses stand compact together, the streets are but little, but it is a vast hill to ascend into the town where the Minster stands.

She climbed up the cathedral tower to Great Tom's Nest and inspected the bell, so large that eight people could stand in it with ease, she announced. But the rest of Lincoln was a disappointment. 'The houses are small but not lofty, nor the streets of any breadth.'

Newark was better, 'a very neat stone built town', its walls pockmarked by three sieges since the captain, the lieutenant and the ancient had made their visit. The castle was another casualty of the war, the great edifice on the Trent where King John died having been shorn of towers and battlements.

She followed the Trent upstream to Nottingham. 'It looked very pleasant to ride by its banks for so many miles.' She liked Nottingham, where the ale was 'pale but exceedingly clear'; the town reminded her of Holborn. Like Leland she looked out from the parapet of Nottingham Castle and could see Belvoir Castle sixteen miles away. Nottingham Castle had changed since Leland's time, though. It was now an Italianate palace, and one of the most sumptuous she had visited. She stayed at the Blackamoor's Head (now the Trip to Jerusalem), at the bottom of Castle Hill. It had excavated beer cellars in the sandstone, which accounted for the excellence of the beer. Next morning, before she left Nottingham, she visited a glass works. The craftsmen were turning the blobs of melted glass into birds and beasts. Always ready to have a go, 'I spun some of the glass' with the help of one of the glassblowers, 'and saw him make a swan presently'.

The little party rode north through Sherwood Forest to Mansfield, then on to Worksop. It was Bess of Hardwick country. She had left her mark on Worksop, Hardwick, Chatsworth, Bolsover and Welbeck Abbey. But they faded beside the glory of Blyth Abbey, recently rebuilt by a very successful London merchant, all symmetrical, with brick dressing and sashed windows. The gardens were 'after the London mode', gravel walks and lawns adorned 'with dwarfs and Cyprus fir and all sorts of greens and fruit trees'. The orchard was out of this world – everything she tasted in it was superb. 'It is just by the church, so that a large arch which did belong to the church is now made a shady seat to the garden, with greens over it, under which is a sepulchre for the family.'

She continued on to Doncaster, where she stayed at the Angel, crossed the Don and pressed on, across the Aire and the Wharfe, 'which on great rains are not to be passed', to York, which had a 'mean appearance' in spite of its size and importance.

> It looks better at the approach, because you see the towers of the gates and several churches encompassing the Minster, and all the windmills round the town. There are a great many pretty churches, sixteen in number, but the Minster is a noble building, very large and fine of stone, carved all the outside.

It was the biggest church Celia had ever been inside. She climbed one of the three towers, counting 'those very steep steps', 262 in all. Then she walked around in the clerestory 'and looked down into the body of the church and that was so great a distance that the men and ladies that were walking below looked like pygmies'.

Outside, in the precincts, the chapter house had been temporarily turned into a mint. 'I saw them at work and stamped one half crown myself,' she gushed. That night Celia and her cousin ate 'a very good codfish and salmon, and that at a pretty cheap rate, though we were not in the best inn: the Angel is the best'.

From York she passed on to Knaresborough, where she visited a chapel cut out of the rock. It had been a shrine before the Reformation.

> There was a Papist lodged where we did, and our landlady at the inn where we were treated civilly told us she went with this lady among the ruins where the lady would say her prayers, and one day some had been digging and brought up the bone of a man's arm and the hand and the ligature of the elbow held the bone together, which by striking came asunder, and in the hollow part of the joint was a jelly-like blood that was moist, this lady dipped the end of her handkerchief in it.

They bade goodbye to their landlady and continued through wet and marshy land to the spa waters at Harrogate. After Bath and Tunbridge, Celia Fiennes was something of an expert on spas, a sincere believer, and here were four different springs within a two-mile compass. One was full of sulphur, 'the smell being so strong and offensive that I could not force my horse near the well'. The second was covered in white scum. At the third, which turned copper in colour as the water came out of the ground, 'I drank a quart in the morning for two days, and hold them to be a good sort of purge, if you can hold your breath so as to drink them down.' A quarter of a mile away she found a fourth, very ordinary 'sweet spring of common water, very good to wash eyes and pleasant to drink'. It must have come as a relief after the purge.

There was another spring at Copgrove about six miles away. It was called St Mungo's Well, and had also been a shrine before the Reformation. The water was cold and you could spot the Papists because they knelt in the water. 'Some of the Papists I saw had so much zeal as to continue a quarter of an hour on their knees.'

> Setting aside the Papist fancies of it, I cannot but think it is a very good spring, being remarkably cold, and just at the head of the spring so it is fresh which must needs be very strengthening, it shuts up the pores of the body immediately so fortifies from cold, you cannot bear the coldness of it above two or three minutes, and then you come out and walk round the pavement and then in again, and so three or four or six or seven, as many times as you please; you go in and out in flannel, I used my Bath garments and dipped my head quite over every time I went in and found it eased a great pain I used to have in my head, and I was not so apt to catch cold so much as before.

Their next stop was Ripon, 'a pretty little market town mostly built of stones'. It was market day, meat and vegetables were plentiful and cheap. But the town made up for this with the bill for the inn. It was outrageous. Always busy, Celia found time to visit the minster and liked the *trompe-l'oeil* behind the altar. 'It looks so natural, just like real crimson satin with gold fringe-like hangings and several rows of pillars in aisles on either side.'

Three miles away was Newby Hall, a Queen Anne house, built by Sir Edward Blanket, who had made his fortune taking coal from Newcastle and had married into the aristocracy. It was very modern, made of brick with stone dressing, and had a flat roof and a lead cupola in the centre, while the wrought-iron railings were topped with gold paint and formed a crescent. But there was an air of tragedy about the house.

> Over the door at the entrance is a fine carving of stone with leaves and flowers with fine stone pillars and the arms cut finely, there is a fine dial and clock above it; the hall you enter is of a very good size and height, two dining rooms and drawing rooms, one for the summer with a marble hall, six or seven chamber of a good size and lofty, so that most of the beds were two foot too low which was a pity there being good beds, one was crimson figured velvet, two damask beds, the rest mohair and camlet. The rooms are mostly wainscoated and painted, the best room was painted just like marble, few rooms were hung, the furniture was very neatly kept, and so was the whole house. The roof of the stairs was finely painted, there were several pictures but not set up, the house being in mourning for his lady and her mother, the Lady York, which died in a month or two of each other.

Newby Hall stood in the middle of a park with a river running through it and had two gardens on either side, with gravel walks, lawns, statues and flowerbeds, laid out so symmetrically that they would have needed a draughtsman's contract. Behind the gardens were the coach house, estate offices and cellars, 'and there I drank beer four years old'.

They returned to York but passed straight through, continuing on to Beverley, Hull and Scarborough. Beverley was preferable to any town she had been through save Nottingham. The main streets were much bigger than in York and there were three separate markets, one for meat, a second for corn and a third for fish.

'The Minster has a fine building all of stone, carved on the outside with figures and images, and more than a hundred pedestals that remain where statues have stood, of angels and the like.' Once inside, she inspected the fourth Earl of Northumberland's tomb in the Percy Chapel. The stone floor in the chapel had subsided and the tomb cracked open. She resisted the impulse to stick her hand in, but she still had quite a close look. 'Of the bones, the skull was whole and the teeth firm'.

Six miles on lay Hull, standing between two rivers in flat meadowland. They rode into the town over two drawbridges. It was well fortified, she noted, but the defences 'seemed to run a great length and would require many soldiers to defend the half-moons and works'. There was an almshouse, Trinity House, for seamen's widows, and in the almshouse chapel were the pathetic effects of an eskimo captured in 1613.

> In the middle of this room there hangs a canoe just big enough for one man to sit in, and an effigy of a man that was taken with it, all his clothes, his cap and a large bag behind wherein his fish and provisions were, these were all made of the skin of fishes and were the same that he wore when taken. He would not speak any language or word to them that took him, nor would he eat, so in a few days died.

From Hull the tiny party rode north across flatlands to Scarborough, stopping at a cousin's in Burton Agnes on the way. At Brandesburton, where they spent the night, there were no lodgings at the inns, but a Quaker family took them in and 'did enterain us kindly, made two good beds for us, and also for our servants, and good bread and cheese, bacon and eggs'.

Scarborough was a pretty seaport with the ruins of a castle, and fields where cattle grazed within the city walls. From the seawall Celia watched a convoy of colliers, protected from French privateers by warships, sail down the coast towards London. 'The town had no lodgings either, but there was an 'abundance of Quakers' who took in travellers, at so much a meal, though 'ale everyone finds themselves'. The Quakers' genuine hospitality and simple goodness touched her, but she was left cold by their religion. 'I was at a Quakers' meeting in the town where four men and two women spoke, one after another had done, but it seemed such a confusion and so incoherent.'

From Scarborough, the furthest north they went, the two cousins and their maidservants turned south-west, passing through York again *en route* to Pontefract. It was tiring. 'These miles are long, and I observe the ordinary people both in these parts of Yorkshire and in the northern parts can scarce tell you how far it is to the next place, and do not esteem it uphill unless so steep as a house or a precipice.'

What struck her most about Pontefract were its gardens and orchards, which lined the hill in terraces. The town specialized in the cultivation of the liquorice plant. The leaves were like rose leaves, she noted, but longer and yellower.

They meandered southwards into Derbyshire, and at Chesterfield they saw their first coal mine. The shafts reminded her of wells. There was even a bucket and pulley, hauling coal and coal miners up and down.

Soon she was in the Peak District, feeling dwarfed by the rocks. The way was 'steep which makes travelling tedious and the miles long; you see neither hedge nor tree but only low dry stone walls round some ground, else it's only hills and dales as thick as you can imagine'. Never one to judge by appearances, she found the geology quite inspiring.

> Though the surface of the earth looks barren, yet those hills are impregnated with rich marbles, stones, metals, iron and copper and coal mines in their bowels, from whence we may see the wisdom and benignity of our great Creator to make up the deficiency of a place by an equivalent.

Their next destination was Chatsworth, which the first Duke of Devonshire had almost completed rebuilding. They made their way towards the west front over the simple unadorned bridge spanning the River Derwent, 'which runs all along the front of the house and by a little fall made in the water, which makes a pretty murmuring noise'. The wrought-iron gate through which they passed was by Jean Tijou, which was just about as original as a Giacometti.

> Before the gate there is a large park and several fine gardens, one without another, with gravel walks, and squares of grass with stone statues in them, and in the middle of each garden is a large fountain full of images of sea gods and dolphins and sea horses which spout water in the basin and all about the gardens.

There were other gardens with fountains, one in an artificial wilderness; and in a grove stood 'a fine willow tree, the leaves, and bark look very natural; and all of a sudden, by turning a sluice it rains from each leaf and from the branches like a shower, it being made of brass and pipes'.

The original house was opulent Elizabethan, a suitable pile for a Queen of Scots to be held hostage in. The first Duke's rebuilding campaign was virtually finished. Already the south range had been pulled down and replaced by William Talman's late Renaissance Classicism. The rest of the exterior was still as Bess of Hardwick had left it 140 years before. In front of the entrance was a court with 'piazzas supported with stone pillars under which you pass from one place to another'. Inside, the chapel was galleried and paved in black and white veined marble. The paintings on the walls and

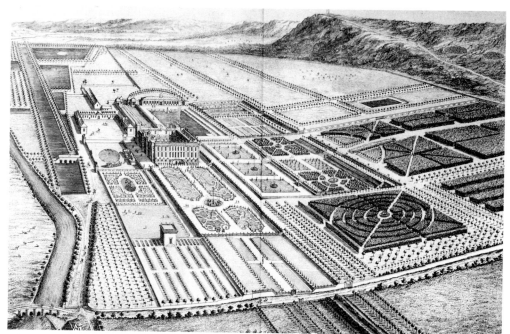

Chatsworth, its waterworks and gardens, as they were after the first Duke's rebuilding.

ceiling by Verrio and Laguerre, depicting scenes from the New Testament, were a technicoloured dreamland, and she marvelled at the stone carvings of cherubs and a dove by Caius Gabriel Cibber, and the limewood fruit and vegetables by Samuel Watson. The baroque ceilings went on and on, one great epic following another. In the hall was the 'Life of Julius Caesar'. Upstairs the ceilings were still being painted, Laguerre and his assistants lying flat on scaffolding boards, smothered beneath a profusion of baroque bosoms of their own making – the 'Assembly of the Gods' in the dining room, 'Phaeton praying to Apollo' in the music room, 'Aurora chasing Diana' in the state bedroom and 'Mercury' in the dressing room. Undeterred by the pink bits, Celia was soon poking around the back of the house.

> There is a fine grotto all stone pavement roof and sides. This is designed to supply all the house with water besides several fancies to make diversion; within this is a bathing room, the walls all with blue and white marble, the pavement mixed one stone white, another black, another of red rance marble; the bath is one entire marble, all white, finely veined with blue and is made smooth, but had it been as finely polished as some, it would have been the finest marble that could be seen; you went down steps into the bath big enough for two people.

They left Chatsworth and rode on through the Peaks, led by a guide, for 'the common people know not above two or three miles from their home'. It was a rough ride. 'Indeed all Derbyshire is but a world of peaked hills which from some of the highest you discover the rest like steeples.'

Their next stop was Haddon Hall, a castle on a hill overlooking the River Wye. It left her cold. 'It is a good old house, all built of stone on a hill and behind it is a fine grove of high trees and good gardens, but nothing very curious as the mode now is.'

They rode on to Buxton, another spa surrounded by hills. It was appalling.

So much for your dinners and suppers and so much for your servants; all your ale and wine is to be paid besides, the beer they allow at the meals is so bad that very little can be drank. Two beds in a room, some three and some four, so that if you have not company enough of your own to fill a room they will be ready to put others in the same chamber, and sometimes they are so crowded that three must lie in a bed; we stayed two nights by reason one of our company was ill, but it was sore against our wills.

Like every other visitor to Buxton, Celia explored the limestone cavern called Poole's Hole. Sounds echoed to the continual drip of water, and the centuries of drips had worn the rocks into strange shapes, one resembling a lion, another a throne with a canopy, glittering like diamonds. St Anne's Needle, which she saw by the light of burning torches, appeared to be made of crystals and shaped like candy. 'We had some broken off which looked like the insides of oystershells or mother of pearl.'

From Buxton she rode south along Dove Dale, passing Charles Cotton's classical fishing house built in memory of Isaak Walton and dedicated to friendship, to the copper mines at Ashbourne, and on to Uttoxeter and Lichfield, staying with an uncle, Sir Charles Wolseley, on the way. She liked Lichfield, particularly the artificial pools between the cathedral close and the town which Leland wrote about, and in which only the magistrate had the right to fish. She liked the close too, with its modern houses for the bishop, dean and prebendaries. Above all, she liked the cathedral, with its Gothic sugar-coating on the west front.

Her next stop was Coventry, some twenty-seven miles away, where she admired the steeple of St Michael's, but thought the sixteenth-century market cross resembled the Tower of Babel. The houses were timber-made and very old, but the streets were wide, which gave it a modern look. Coventry was a centre for both Presbyterians and Independents, but they lived easily together. 'Though they differ in some small things, in the main they agree, and seem to love one another which is no small satisfaction to me.' One statue there fascinated her.

Coventry has one thing remains remarkable not to be omitted, the statue of a man looking out of a window with his eyes out, a monument as history tells us of some priviledges obtained by a lady, wife to the nobleman who was lord of the town. She was to purchase them by passing on horseback through the town naked, which he thought she would not do, but out of zeal to relieve the town of some hard bondage she did, and commanded all windows and doors to be shut and none to appear in the street on pain of death, which was obeyed by all, but one man would open a window and look out and for his impudence had this judgement on him to be struck blind, this statue is his resemblance and one day in a year they remember the good lady by some rejoicing.

From Coventry they passed the red sandstone ruins of Kenilworth. The civil war had left it a stately wreck. Three miles on came Warwick. Most of the town had been gutted in a fire three years earlier. The church of St Mary's was almost a shell, and restoration work had only just started. But the exquisite late Gothic stone carvings in the Beauchamp Chapel had survived, and so had the tomb of Sir Fulke Greville. From St Mary's, Celia and her cousin rode slowly out of the town, passed Lord Leycester's Hospital, one of the few timber-framed buildings to survive the fire, and went up the hill to the castle. Warwick Castle was 'stately' and the wall hangings 'so curious all of silk that the very postures and faces look extremely lively and natural, and the groves, streams and rivers look very well in it'.

From there the road was easy, through Daventry, 'a pretty large market town', to Woburn Abbey, where she ate too many gooseberries. The abbey was still in its old form, just recognizable for what it had once been, and untouched by Flintcroft, who so transformed it in the next century. It stood:

in a fine park full of deer and wood, and some of the trees are kept cut in the shape of several beasts. The house is an old building, low, there are very good stables and out-offices, laundry, yard etc; the gardens are fine, there is a large bowling green with eight arbours kept cut neatly, and seats in each, there is a seat up in a high tree that ascends from the green fifty steps, that commands the whole park round to see the deer hunted.

From there they passed through Dunstable to St Albans, 'where the handsome church dedicated to St Alban is much out of repair; so worn away that it mourns for some charitable person to help repair it'. It was the last night of their journey. Next morning they rode slowly through Barnet to London, less than a day away.

*　　*　　*

The journey had taken seven weeks; now it was over, but it had hardly put Celia off travel. Within a couple of months she was touring Kent. Once more she set off from her cousin's at Amwell, riding 'through lanes and much wood', to Tilbury. There she took a ferry across the Thames to Gravesend, 'which lies over against it, a little snug town under a hill, the houses little and thick together, fit only for seamen and soldiers'.

The Medway was 'the finest river I ever saw' and the bridge at Rochester 'the finest in England, said to equal any in the world'. Rochester and its suburbs were bigger than she expected, and from the hill above the town she had a prospect of the castle, 'several good churches', the docks and the ships at anchor in the estuary.

Sixteen miles on lay Canterbury, the road flanked by hop fields.

The cathedral is the finest sight there, the carving of stone is very fine from the outside, as also within; it has a square tower, no spire running up from it, but small ones at each corner of the tower. The windows of the Choir are most delicately painted as ever I saw, an art which now is lost amongst us.

Canterbury was the centre of the silk-weaving industry, developed by the Huguenot refugees whom the lieutenant and ancient had noticed sixty years earlier. 'I met them every night going home in great companies, but then some of them were employed in the hopping, it being the season for pulling them.'

I saw twenty looms in one house, with several fine flowered silks, very good ones, and it is a very ingenious art to fix the warps and chain in their looms to cast their work into such figures and flowers. There stands a boy at every loom and pulls up and down the threads, which are fastened to the weaving and so pulls the chain to the exact form for the shuttle to work through.

It was a centre for paper-making too, a trade which had also been brought over by Huguenot refugees, whose paper mills lined the banks of the Stour.

They were then making brown paper when I saw it; the mill is set a-going by the water and at the same time it pounded the rags to mortar for the paper. When the substance for the paper is pounded enough, they take it in a great tub and so with a frame just of the size of the sheets of paper, made all of small wire just as I have seen fine screens to screen corn in, only this is much closer wrought, and they clap a frame of wood round the edge, and so dip it into the tub and what is too thin runs through; then they turn this frame down on a piece of course woollen just of the size of the paper and so give a knock to it and it falls off, on which they clap another such a piece of woollen cloth which is ready to lay the next frame of paper, and so till they have made a large heap which they by a board at the bottom move to a press, and so lay a board on the top and so let down a great screw and weight on it, which they force together into such a narrow compass as they know so many sheets of paper will be reduced, and press out all the thinner part and leave the paper so firm as it may be taken up sheet by sheet, and laid together to be more thoroughly dried by the wind. They told me white paper was made in the same manner only they must have white woollen to put between.

It was a good road to Dover, through 'champion country'. Celia arrived at the castle and saw the 60-fathom well, its bucket drawn up by a horse, which Taylor had seen; and also a dry well, used to identify the sound of mining under the castle during sieges, which Taylor had not seen. His visit had coincided with the Protectorate, and he had not been thought politically reliable enough.

After a seven-mile ride along the Downs to Deal, she started out on her return to Amwell. Her route took her through Maidstone, 'a very neat market town; its buildings are mostly of timber work, the streets are large, and the Market Cross runs down in the middle of the great street'. It was a Thursday, market day, and the streets were crowded. There were three parts of the market, one for fruit, one for corn 'and another for all sorts of things'.

She skirted London, riding over Shooters Hill ('a noted robbing place'), from where 'you see a vast prospect', taking in Deptford, Blackheath, Greenwich Palace and the Thames estuary. She descended down the hill to Greenwich, where she took a ferry across the river, and rode through Hackney and Tottenham to her cousin's at Amwell.

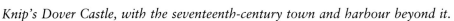

*   *   *

Knip's Dover Castle, with the seventeenth-century town and harbour beyond it.

The following year, 1698, Celia Fiennes made her longest journey, her 'Great Journey', a gigantic figure of eight that took her from one end of England to the other. She left London and stopped for a while at Amwell, but this time Celia travelled as a lady alone, accompanied only by two maidservants and a greyhound. Her long-suffering cousin had had enough.

From Amwell she rode east to Colchester. Much of the town was still in ruins after the 1648 siege. Still, the streets were broad enough for two coaches to go abreast and the pavements were secured from coaches by wooden bollards. 'The whole town is employed in spinning, weaving, washing, drying and dressing their baize,' she exclaimed. It was Colchester's main industry.

Their buildings are of timber, of loam and lathes and much tiling, the fashion of the country runs much in long roofs and great cantilevers and peaks; out of these great streets runs many little streets but not very narrow, mostly old buildings except a few houses built by some Quakers that are brick and of the London mode.

She crossed the Stour at Dedham 'over a wooden bridge pretty large with timber rails' and rode on to Ipswich, where, because of 'pride and sloth, the ships that bring their coal goes light away'. There was only one reasonable house, Christchurch Manor, owned by the Earl of Hereford. A broad gravel walk lined with stone balls, and two walled courts enclosed by wrought-iron railings, led to a third court, of which the house and its two wings took up three sides. The ground floor was still original Tudor, but the upper floors had been damaged in a fire and recently rebuilt in red brick. You entered through the central porch that gave the house its classic Tudor E-plan. Inside was 'a good hall parlour and drawing room and large closet, two or three other rooms left answering it and a billiard room; above were as many rooms of state, all furnished with good old things; a pretty staircase but it is too little'. The rest of Ipswich was painful to recall, 'and so to Norwich'.

Norwich opens to view a mile distant by the help of a hill whereon is a little village; as I observe most of the great towns and cities have about them little villages as attendants or appendixes to them, which are a sort of suburb, there being straggling houses for the most part all the way between that and the gates. You pass over a high bridge that leads on over a high causeway of a pretty length which looks somewhat dangerous. Then you proceed to the City which is walled round full of towers, except on the river side, which serves for the wall. They seem the best in repair of any walled city I know, though in some places there are little breaches, but the carving and battlements and towers look well. I entered through the west gate, there are twelve gates in all and thirty-six churches which is to be seen in a clear day altogether on the city walls, I told [counted] thirty myself; there they are built all of flints well-headed or cut which makes them look blackish and shining.

The cathedral was 'nothing remarkable' and 'all their buildings are of an old form, mostly in deep points'. The acquaintance she had come to see had died ten days before she arrived. She did not stay long.

From Norwich she meandered through East Anglia – still rich from the wool industry – via Thetford, Bury St Edmunds and Newmarket; 'mostly through lanes where you meet the ordinary people knitting, four or five in a company under the hedge'.

Soon she was in the Fens, 'full of water and mud', while the road was:

on each side defended by fen dykes, which are deep ditches with drains. On each side they plant willows, so there is two rows run along the ground which looks very finely to see, a flat of many miles so planted, but it must be ill to live there; all this while Ely Minster is in one's view.

Celia hated Ely. The town was quite 'the dirtiest place I ever saw, a perfect quagmire' and 'a harbour to breed and nest vermin in'. As if that was not enough, she was obliged to share her bedchamber with frogs, slow-worms and snails.

Ely Minster is a curious pile of building all of stone, the outside full of carvings and great arches and fine pillars in the front, and the inside has the greatest variety and neatness in the works; there are two chapels [the Bishop Alcock and Bishop West chantries] most exactly carved in stone, all sorts of figures, cherubims and gilt and painted in some parts; the roof of one chapel was entirely stone most delicately carved and hung down in great points all about the church; the pillars are carved and painted with the history of the Bible, especially the New Testament and description of Christ's miracles, the lanthorn in the choir is vastly high and delicately painted, and fine carved work, all of wood, in it.

She climbed into the octagonal lanthorn. 'I could see Cambridge and a great prospect of the country which by reason of the great rains just before laid under water, all the feny grounds being overflowed which I could see for a huge tract of ground being all on a flat.'

As for the people, the 'Fen Slodgers' who herded cattle on stilts, she did not think much of them. 'They are all a lazy sort of people and are afraid to do too much', and they lived on the government subsidies given to them to drain the land. The only beautiful things were the swans, 'some were with their cygnets, three or four in a troop, with their dames hovering over them for their security'.

Peterborough, washed on three sides by the River Nene, looked 'like a very industrious thriving town, spinning and knitting amongst the ordinary people'. The buildings were mostly timber, the streets were wide and there was a spacious market. The cathedral was 'a magnificent building standing in the midst on advanced ground, all stone the walls very neatly wrought', while in the precincts the bishop's palace looked 'very neat, and the Doctor's houses, all in the space called the College, very neat but nothing curious'.

From Peterborough Celia rode due west, through the Forest of Rockingham to Leicester.

As I passed the road I saw upon the walls of the ordinary people's houses and walls of their outhouses the cow dung plastered up to dry in caking which are used for firing – it is a very offensive fuel but the country people use little else in these parts.

It was also a sign of the effect of enclosures, and of the power of the new squirearchy. This was, after all, a forest.

On the other side of the River Welland the houses changed as the landscape became hillier, frequently scarred by stone quarries. Even the meanest dwellings were built of stone.

Leicestershire is a very rich country, red land, good corn of all sorts and grass, both fields and enclosures; you see a great way upon their hills the bottoms full of enclosed woods and different sorts of manuring and herbage, amongst which are placed many little towns, which gives great pleasure of the travellers to view.

But a few miles further on, the road was 'most tiresome, being full of sloughs, clay deep way, that I was near eleven hours going but twenty-five miles'. It was quite true what Charles Cotton had written in *The Compleat Angler*. 'There is good land where there is foul way.'

Leicester was nothing special. The churches were 'none very big and none fine', there were a couple of very worthy almshouses, but apart from in the Newark, the oldest quarter of the town, the buildings were uninteresting. So, after inspecting the nearby battlefields of Bosworth and Naseby, she passed through Lichfield on her way once again to the half-timbered and moated house of her uncle, Sir Charles Wolseley, on the River Trent. There she stayed six weeks, enjoying the orchards and the deer park, and making a short excursion to Derby.

Derby she approved of, except for its prices. Her evening meal of mutton, bread and beer cost her five shillings and eightpence. The town was built of brick, and had a water wheel on the Derwent that both ground corn and supplied the town with piped water. The tower of All Saint's, which the captain, lieutenant and ancient had visited, was 'finely carved full of niches and pedestals whereon statues had been set', and inside was the tomb of the redoubtable Bess of Hardwick.

On her return to her uncle's she stopped off at the thoroughly modern church in Ingestre. It was glorious, and not unlike the new churches being built in the City of London by the King's Surveyor, Christopher Wren.

> The church is new and very handsome, good fretwork, on the top the woodwork well carved, its seats good wainscoting and with locks. In the chancel are two monuments of marble, one all white, the other white with a black border and white pillars, the middle at the bottom is alabaster; the pillars of the church are made of red stone, which is plenty in this country, and they are all polished over, the font is all white marble, the stem the same, veined blue, the cover is wood carved very well; the porch is very high on which is a dial, it almost breaks one's neck to look up at it.

She left her uncle's and rode north to Newcastle-under-Lyme, keeping to the high ground 'below which the River Trent ran and turned its silver stream forward and backward into "S"s, which look very pleasant, circling about the fine meadows in their flourishing time, bedecked with hay almost ripe and flowers'.

At Newcastle-under-Lyme she saw the beginning of the Stoke pottery industry – 'fine tea pots, cups and saucers of the fine red earth, in imitation and as curious as that which comes from China' – before going on to Chester. The Roman city she found altogether too old, spoilt by the Rows, the first-floor medieval arcades in the town centre, which 'does darken the streets and hinder the light of the houses in many places'.

On the other side of the River Dee, at Holywell, she visited St Winifred's Well, another spa which had once been a shrine to a saint. It combined two of her fundamental interests, spas and religion.

> They tell of many lamenesses and arches and distempers which are cured by it. It is a cold water and clear and runs very quick, so that it would be a pleasant refreshment in the summer to wash one's self in it, but I think I could not have been persuaded to have gone in unless I might have had curtains to have drawn about some part of it to have sheltered from the street, for the wet garments are no covering to the body; but there I saw abundance of the devout Papists on their knees all round the well; the poor people are deluded into an ignorant blind zeal and are to be pitied by us that have the advantage of knowing better and ought to be better.

As for the locals, she disapproved of them more than she did the Papists. 'At Holywell they speak Welsh, and the inhabitants go barefoot and barelegged, a nasty sort of people.'

She forded the sands of the Dee estuary at low tide with two guides and took a ferry across the Mersey to Liverpool. Unlike Chester, Liverpool was modern, very modern.

> It is a very rich trading town, the houses of brick and stone built high and even, that a street quite through looks very handsome, the streets well-pitched; there are an abundance of persons you see very well dressed and of good fashion; the streets are fair and long, it's London in miniature as much as I ever saw anything.

She then rode north through Wigan, 'a pretty market town built of stone and brick', to Lancaster, 'old and much decayed'. Amid the ruins of the abbey, where Leland had read manuscripts, there were wild strawberries. Her next stop was Kendal, on the edge of the Lake District, where the roads were so narrow that you could not even take a carriage on them. She stayed at the King's Arms, where Mrs Rowlandson, the landlady, made the best potted char in Westmorland.

The first lake she caught sight of was Windermere.

> This great water seems to flow and wave about with the wind or in one motion but it does not ebb and flow like the sea with the tide, neither does it run so as to be perceivable, though at the end of it a little rivulet trills from it into the sea, but it seems to be a standing lake encompassed with vast high hills that are perfect rocks and barren ground of a vast height from which many little springs trickle down their sides, and as

Liverpool when Celia Fiennes visited it: 'London in miniature'.

they meet with stones and rocks in the way when something obstructs their passage and so they come with more violence that gives a pleasing sound and murmuring noises.

Like the captain, lieutenant and ancient, when she first saw the 'said little huts made up of dry walls' where the natives lived, she thought they were barns. The people were so poor that they could offer nothing but beer, butter, cheese and the local bread. She approved of the bread, which was unleavened and waifer-thin, 'as we say of all sorts of bread there is a vast deal of difference in what is housewifely made and what is ill-made'. Then, recalling a passage from the Bible, she added, 'I cannot but think it was after this manner they made their bread in the old times, especially those Eastern countries, where their bread might be soon dry and spoilt.'

She rode north through Kirkstone Pass to Ullswater, with Harter Fell on her right and Helvellyn on her left, taking the path along the water's edge and 'through a fine forest or park where was deer skipping about and hares, which by means of a good greyhound I had a little course', but they lost their quarry, being unfamiliar with the land. Half a dozen miles on, past Pooley Bridge, was Penrith. It was a Tuesday, market day. The stones of the buildings were so red that Celia thought the houses were made of brick when she first saw them.

She was glad to leave 'those desert and barren rocky hills' and arrive at Lowther Castle, which was thoroughly modern and built of red stone slabs. It stood at the end of a stretch of woodland, its front facing the road. You rode through the outer yard flanked by stables and through a Dutch-inspired symmetrical garden, divided by gravel walks into four lawns with statues of Cupid in the middle of each. Inside, she ascended the staircase, 'very wainscoted and carved at the top', into a 'noble hall', its ceiling painted in the latest exuberant style by Antonio Verrio, 'the best hand in England'. There were 'gods and goddesses sitting at some great feast and a great tribunal before them, each corner a season of the year with the variety of weather, rains and rainbows, stormy winds, sunshine, snow and frost'.

Carlisle, twenty 'pretty long' miles away, was 'all walled in and built all of stone. The cathedral stands high and very eminent to be seen above the town; you enter over a bridge and iron gates'. There were only a couple of decent houses, but far worse, the inn in which Celia lodged turned out to be a whore-house where you rented rooms by the hour.

My landlady notwithstanding ran me up the largest reckoning for almost nothing; it was the dearest lodging I met with. A young giddy landlady that could only dress fine and entertain the soldiers.

From Carlisle she made a short trip into the Border regions of Scotland. Like Taylor, 'the more I travelled northwards the longer I found the miles'; and though she had the luck to see an eagle, her experience of the people only confirmed her English prejudices. The habitations were filthy, pigs and cattle slept with humans, and the people were totally uneducated. She put it down to their sloth, but then she would. Smug English prig.

I took them for people which were sick, seeing two or three great wenches as tall and big as any woman sat hovering between their bed and chimney corner all idle doing nothing, or at least not settled to any work, though it was nine o'clock when I came hither, having gone seven miles that morning.

Riding east she caught a glimpse of Hadrian's Wall, 'the walls and towers of which was mostly standing'. At Haltwhistle the village's only inn would not take her and she was forced on to the charity of a poor peasant's family. She must have been a difficult, though impeccable, guest.

> The landlady brought out her best sheets which served to secure my own sheets from her dirty blankets, and indeed I had her fine sheet with hook seams to spread over the top of the clothes, but no sleep could I get, they burning turf, and their chimneys are sorts of flues or open tunnels, so that the smoke does annoy the rooms.

Next morning, tired and bad-tempered, she followed the River Tyne to Hexham, 'one of the best towns in Northumberland except Newcastle', and continued along the river and past the coal pits to Newcastle itself. 'As I drew nearer and nearer to Newcastle I met with and saw abundance of little carriages with a yoke of oxen and a pair of horses together, which is to convey the coal from the pits to the barges on the river.'

She approved of Newcastle. Its buildings were of brick, its streets wide, it was rich from the coal industry and everybody looked gainfully employed. 'Their shops are good and are of distinct trades,' she added, 'not selling many things in one shop as is the custom in most country towns and cities.'

The following morning, a Sunday, she rode south to Durham, 'along a most pleasant gravel road on the ridge of the hill and had the whole country in view'. She could see the steep hill and its crown of battlements, with castle and cathedral atop, from four miles away.

Next day she was in the Pennines. On the way to Darlington her guide lost the bundle with her nightclothes in it, and at Richmond Celia looked down from the walls at the foaming waters of the River Swale, 'full of stones and rocks, the water falling over the rocks with great force'. Stretching across the river were weirs 'which is great convenient for catching salmon by spear when they leap over'.

There was a parliamentary election campaign going on as she meandered down through Harrogate to Leeds, and the towns were rowdy and the ale houses full, which must have made the lives of an unescorted lady and her two maidservants difficult, though you would hardly realize it from the lady's memoirs. Ignoring the *hoi polloi*, she pressed on to Leeds regardless. It was large, clean and wealthy from the cloth industry; and when you paid for your ale, which was very strong, 'you may have a slice of meat either hot or cold according to the time of day you call, or else butter and cheese *gratis* into the bargain'. Equally rewarding for the *cognoscenti* at the Bush Tavern on market days:

> anybody that will go and call for one tankard of ale and a pint of wine and pay for these only, shall be set to a table to eat with two or three dishes of good meat and a dish of sweetmeats after. Had I known this, and the day that was their market, I would have come then, but I happened to come a day after the market, however I did only pay for three tankards of ale and what I ate, and my servants were *gratis*.

Halifax she avoided on principle. The town was 'almost ruined and the engine that the town was famous for, to behead their criminals at one stroke with a pulley', had been destroyed, since the town had been deprived of its charter, according to Ms Fiennes, for 'barbariously and rigorously acting with an absolute power'. Taylor would have been disgusted at her naivity.

In Manchester, where Celia did stop, 'the houses are not very lofty but mostly of brick and stone, the old houses are timber work'. She visited Cheetham Hospital, built in 1422 and turned into a Bluecoat School in 1653. In the library where Doctor Dee, the Elizabethan astrologer, had worked, she noted globes, maps, a long, whispering trumpet, two walls of books, the skin of a rattlesnake and the jaw of a shark.

The three women rode on unescorted towards Shrewsbury. The day was coming to an end. Suddenly, a few miles before Whitchurch, their horses started.

> Two fellows all of a sudden from the wood fell into the road, they looked trussed up with greatcoats and as it were bundles about them which I believe were pistols. They dogged me, one before, the other behind, and would often look back to each other and frequently jostle my horse out of the way to get between one of my servant's horses and mine. But the Providence of God so ordered it as there was men at work in the fields hay-making, and it being market day at Whitchurch as I drew near to that in three or four miles was continually meeting with some of the market people, so they at last called each other off and so left us and turned back.

Relieved by Providence, she came into Whitchurch and bedded for the night at the Crown Inn. Next morning she was admiring the inn's garden, 'exceedingly neat with orange and lemon trees and fine flowers, all things almost in a little tract of garden ground'.

Her destination was Shrewsbury, where she wanted to arrive by evening. 'The miles were long and the wind blew very cold,' she recalled four years later. The town's roofline was low, broken only by the spires of two churches, a dilapidated castle, and the town walls which she walked round. Most of the houses were old and built of timber, and there were 'some remains of a great abbey and just by it the great church, but nothing fine or worth notice save the Abbey gardens, with gravel walks set full of all sorts of greens, orange and lemon trees'. Adjoining the abbey garden was a second garden:

> much larger, with several fine grass walks kept exactly cut and rolled for Company to walk in; every Wednesday most of the town, the ladies and gentlemen, walk there, as in St James' Park, and there are abundance of people of quality living in Shrewsbury, more than in any town except Nottingham.

It was not all promenading, though, and there was a school for the daughters of the townspeople 'for learning work and behaviour and music'. She approved of that.

From Shrewsbury Celia rode east, past The Wrekin, which looked paltry besides some of the peaks she had seen in Derbyshire, the Lakes and the Pennines, visiting the very *à la mode* gardens of Patshull Park on the way.

> Before you come to the house for a quarter of a mile you ride between fine cut hedges and the nearer the approach the finer still, they are very high and cut smooth and of each side beyond are woods, some regular rows, some in its native rudeness, with ponds beyond in grounds beneath it; the end of this walk you enter a large gate. In this outward court you may see the house and court full of statues in grass plots with a broad paved walk to the house; in the middle on the one side are flower gardens and the park, the other side other grounds with rows of trees by it very handsome stables and coach houses and then in the front is a large opening to this garden where is a fountain always playing. Just the side of the house, into which it opens with glass doors, and just over against it, is a large aviary of birds with branches of trees stuck

into the ground. Beyond is another garden with a broad gravel walk, quite round, in the middle is a long as well as large fountain. There two large images stand in the midst, four sea horses all casting out water.

From there it was only a day's ride to her uncle's house at Wolseley, where she spent a very social week before leaving for Worcester. It was election day.

All the way the road was full of the electors of the Parliament men coming from the choice of the Knights of the Shire, some for one, some for another, telling their reason much according to the good liquors operating; and of these people all the public houses were filled that it was a hard matter to get lodging or entertainment.

She finally found lodgings in Worcester. There were a few new houses, particularly the Guildhall, 'which stands on pillars of stone', but the majority were half-timbered. The cathedral was magnificent; in the middle of the choir was the tomb of King John and to its left lay Prince Arthur, elder brother of Henry VIII, under 'plain marble in a fine chapel which is made all of stone finely carved'.

She rode south-west to a cousin's at Stretton Grandison, then south-east to Gloucester with the cousin's family. The road was awful. Her only consolation was that she was travelling in August. In winter it was worse. Gloucester was 'like a very huge place being stretched out in length'. The Benedictine abbey, once rich from the pilgrims who flocked to the grave of Edward II, was now a cathedral.

Bristol and its spires: left to right, *(2) Cathedral, (3) St Austin's, (4) St Mary's Redcliffe, (6) St Michael's, (11) St Nicholas's, (12) Christ Church, (18) Temple.*

The cathedral or minster is large, lofty and very neat. There are twelve chapels, all stone finely carved on the walls and roofs. There is a large window just over the altar, but between it and the altar is a hollow walled in on each side, which is a whispering place, speak so low just in the wall at one end, the person at the other end shall hear it plain, though those which stand by you shall not hear you speak, it is the walls carry the voice.

She passed through Bath and came to Bristol. The cathedral 'had nothing fine or curious about it', and the timber-framed houses with their overhangs made the narrow streets 'somewhat darkish'. Sailing ships, slave ships and coal barges lined the quays. The river had its own bridge 'built over with houses, just as London Bridge is, but is not so big or long'.

She rode on, past St Vincent's Rock on the River Avon, where 'they dig the Bristol diamonds which look very bright and sparkling and in their native rudeness have a great lustre and are pointed', to Wookey Hole in the Mendips, where the stalagmites looked like candy.

They fancy many resemblances in the rocks, as in one place an organ, in another two little babies, and in another part a head which they call the Porter's Head, and another a shape like a dog; they fancy one of the rocks resembles a woman with a great belly which the country people call the Witch which made this cavity underground for her enchantment.

A couple of miles down the lane was Wells, crowded with country people. It was Assizes week. She did not think much of the bishop's palace, but 'the cathedral has the greatest curiosity for carved work in stone, the West Front is full of all sorts of figures, the twelve apostles, the King and Queen with angels and figures of all forms as thick one to another as can be'.

Five more miles took her to Glastonbury, where the tower of St Michael's on the tor 'remains like a beacon'. The town, when she descended to it, she found 'a ragged poor place', where the ruins of the abbey church's nave and transepts, the kitchen, abbey walls and the odd cellar and vault were all that was left to recall its former glory.

It rained that night and the 22-mile journey to Taunton next day was through a quagmire. Crossing the River Parrett, she watched the haulers loading pack-horses with coal from barges that had sailed up from Bristol.

The following day took Celia to Exeter. The River Exe, which washed the south side of the town, was unnavigable, but already there were plans for a ship canal from the town to the sea. An earlier Tudor attempt had become clogged up and soon the canal's terminus would be lined with quays and warehouses.

> The whole town and country is employed for at least twenty miles around in spinning, weaving, dressing and scouring, fulling and drying of the serges, it turns the most money in a week of anything in England.

She observed the process. The best serge, she was told, was soaked in urine.

Of the public buildings, only the very modern brick and stone customs house, with an arcade on the ground floor and sash windows in the offices above, received her unconditional admiration; apart from the west front, the cathedral hardly excited her; the fourteenth-century guildhall was simply 'a large place set on pillars', and the 'water engine' reminded her of the New River pump at Islington in London. Across the River Exe were weirs providing the water power for the mills that pressed the serge into felt, and where, as in Richmond, the locals speared the salmon as they leapt the weirs.

The mills fascinated her. She had to have a closer look.

> It's a pretty diversion to see it, sort of huge notched timbers like great teeth, one would think it should injure the serges but it does not, though the mills draw in with such violence that if one stands near it, and it catches a bit of your garments it would be ready to draw in a person ever at a trice.

She crossed the River Exe and rode to Chudleigh, over hills, through marshland and over hills again. Trees and hedges grew up on either side of the road, 'so close the sun and wind cannot come at them', and the mud never dried. She was on the edge of Dartmoor, and continued along its southern edge from Chudleigh to Ashburton, where the old north–south pack-horse track across the moor started. It was a poor town, and 'bad was the best inn'.

Next day she rode on towards Plymouth. The moors rose up on her right: cold, bleak and inhospitable.

> I passed through several little places and over some stone bridges; the running of the waters is with a huge rushing by reason of the stones which lie in the water, some of them great rocks which gives some interruption to the current which finding another way either by its sides or mounting over part of it, causes the frothing of the water and the noise, the rivers being full of stones bigger or less.

She passed through Plympton – 'all built of stone and the tiling is all slate' – and came into Plymouth. The slate roofs glistened in the sun. Plymouth in close-up, however, proved a disappointment. Most of the houses were small and shoddy, inhabited by soldiers and dockers. The sole building she liked was the citadel, only a few years old. From there she could see as far as Henry Winstanley's Eddystone Lighthouse, itself only two years old. It was 'a good reflection on the great care and provision the wise God makes for all persons and things in his Creation'.

She also saw Mount Edgcumbe across the Sound, 'on the side of a hill, all bedecked in woods which are divided into several rows of trees in walks' and 'built like a court so the four sides are alike'.

Leaving Plymouth, she was soaked on the ferry across the Tamar, but rode on, keeping to the seashore and galloping over the flat sands. But at Fowey estuary she had to strike deep inland:

The Eddystone Lighthouse, designed by Henry Winstanley.

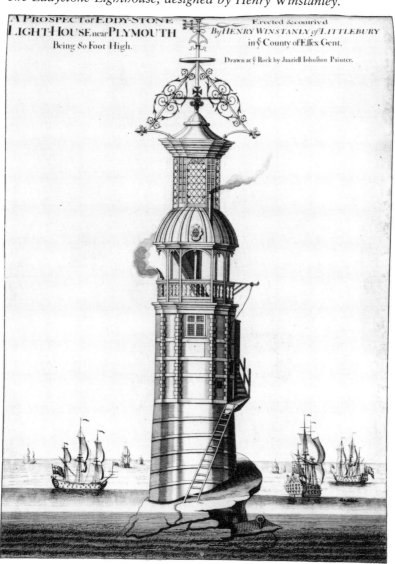

which by the rain the night before had made it very dirty and full of water; in many places in the road there are many holes and sloughs wherever there is clay ground, and when by rains they are filled with water it is difficult to shun danger; here my horse was quite down in one of these holes full of water but by the good hand of God's Providence, he flounced up again.

She ended the day at St Austell, where she had her first taste of Devonshire cream. 'They scald their cream and milk so it is a sort of clotted cream as we call it, with a little sugar, put on top of the apple pie.' She was less pleased with her landlady's habit of smoking. 'Men, women and children all have their pipes of tobacco in their mouths, which was not delightful to me when I went down to talk with my landlady for information of any matter and custom amongst them.'

She pressed on next morning through Cornwall. The hills were dotted with tin mines and nothing could keep Ms Fiennes away from them. Boys and men worked 'digging and carrying the ore to the little buckets which conveys it up, or else are draining the water and looking to the engines that are draining it, and those above are attending and drawing up the ore in a sort of windlass as is to a well'. Riding to Tregony she passed a hundred shafts, some working, others drowned and abandoned. When the day came to an end she was glad of the hospitality of a cousin, Hugh Boscawen, at Tregothnan, a splendid white-faced mansion built by the Earl of Falmouth 'with several rows of trees and woods beyond it'.

It was raining when she awoke, so she delayed her final journey to Land's End. A day later, 'finding it fair weather on the change of the moon', she set off. The way was bleak and the heathland pockmarked with iron and copper mines. It was market day when she passed through Redruth and she admired the Cornish ponies that 'are well-made and strong and will trip along as light on the stoney road without injury to themselves, whereas my horses went so heavy that they wore their shoes immediately thin and off'. She touched Hayle on the north coast, saw St Gwithian's Chapel 'which was almost stuck in the sands', and after complaining about the guides, who 'know but little from home', came within sight of St Michael's Mount on the south coast.

Penzance, 'so snug and warm' to look at, had no coal as a result of the French blockade, and wood was so scarce that the townspeople had to cook with firs; but the harbour and quayside were good and you could see across Mount's Bay to the Lizard.

Land's End, ten miles further on, was so bleak that she compared it to a desert.

> The Land's End terminates in a point or peak of great rocks which runs a good way into the sea, I clambered over them as far as safety permitted me, there are abundance of rocks and shoals of stones stands up in the sea, a mile off some, and so here and there are some quite to the shore, which they name by several names of knights and ladies rolled up in mantles from some old tradition or fiction the poets advance.

She looked out across the sea for a while, 'and being at the end of the land, my horse's legs could not carry me through the deep, and so returned again to Penzance'.

Her journey back took her through Hayle and Redruth. The north coast of Cornwall was even starker than the south, and so windy that the locals stretched plaited straw rigging over their hay ricks and thatched roofs, while the roads were so narrow and uneven that the people used their Cornish ponies as pack-horses. 'I had the advantage of seeing their harvest brought in, which is on a horse's back with sort of crooks of wood like yokes on either side, two or three on a side stands up in which they stow the corn and so tie it with cords.'

Truro was pretty, surrounded by copper mines. Her landlady was a Dissenter, like herself, 'an ordinary plain woman but she was as understanding in the best things as most, the experience of real religion and her quiet submission and self resignation to the will of God'.

Next day she was back with her cousins in Tregothnan. They wanted her to stay, 'but the season of the year inclined to rain, and the day's declining, I was afraid to delay my return'. So she rode to Camelford over hills and moors. The lanes were full of holes and had steep banks of stones on either side. That night the rains came down and did not stop until ten o'clock next morning, delaying her usual early-morning departure. Hardly had she started when they came down again. She rode inland through non-stop rain to Launceston, 'the chief town in Cornwall' with a good strong castle.

> The town is encompassed with walls and gates, it is pretty large, though you cannot discover the whole town, being up and down in so many hills; the streets themselves are very steep unless it be at the Market Place where is a long and handsome space set on stone pillars with the town hall on the top.

The next day 'was the wettest day I had in my summer travels'. The roads became rivulets and the rivers floods. She abandoned the day's journey at Okehampton. It was 5 p.m., 'so I had good time to take off my wet clothes and be well-dried and warm to eat my supper'.

Keeping to the high ground, avoiding the swollen rivers that threatened to carry their bridges with them, Celia skirted the northern edge of Dartmoor and came into Exeter again. 'This was the basest way you can go, and made much worse by these rains, narrow lanes full of stones and loose ground clay, and now exceedingly slippery.' She rode on to Honiton next morning and, crossing the River Axe at Axminster, came into Somerset. Forde Abbey, a Cistercian monastery going back to the twelfth century, which Leland had visited, was now 'a fine old house and well-furnished'. But the owner, a Mr Prideaux, did not permit members of the public to make visits, and his servants closed the doors in Celia's face. So Celia continued on to yet another cousin's house a few miles away, hiding her wounded pride behind a haughty exterior. Next day she rode across Salisbury Plain and came to her childhood home at Newton Toney.

She did not stay there long. She was still travelling. The last stretch of her Great Tour took her through Farnham and Windsor.

> About a mile off Windsor Castle appears standing on a hill much after the manner of Durham, with the walls and battlements round, only that is all stone, and this is but partly so, and the rest brick, plastered over in imitation of stone, which does not look so well.

She inspected St George's Chapel and admired the late Perpendicular vaulting on the roof, the stained-glass east window and the painting of the Passover behind the altar. Then she strode across the lower ward to the keep, marched up the stairs and had 'a great prospect of the whole town and Windsor Forest, the country around Kensington; I could see Lord Holland's house and rows of trees, and to Harrow-on-the-Hill and to Shooters Hill beyond London'. The quadrangle reminded her of Christ Church, Oxford, and Trinity College, Cambridge; while she pronounced the royal apartments, completely overhauled by Charles I, the finest in the country. She looked over the armour collected by Prince Rupert in the Queen's guard chamber, and the hall, 'which has very fine paintings' and an inevitable over-the-top celestial ceiling by Verrio.

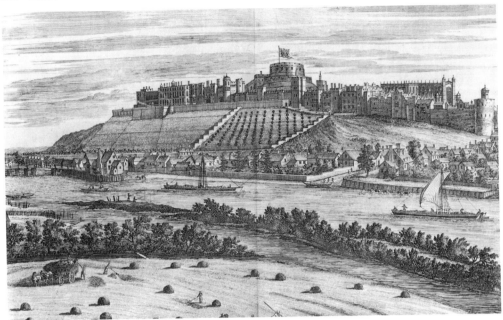

Windsor Castle astride its chalk cliff: Knip's view from across the River Thames.

The King's private chapel, which led off the hall, was painted all over with scenes from the life of Christ. There was another fantastic Verrio ceiling in the state dining room, 'thence into a gallery full of pictures with a large looking glass at the end'. The Queen's presence-chamber was 'all Indian embroidery on white satin' and Gobelin tapestries, and her audience chamber was 'noble indeed', its ceiling painted by Verrio and its walls again decked in Gobelin tapestries. The throne in the garter room was set against a background of green velvet 'richly embroidered with silver and gold'. But Celia came from good Parliamentary stock and in spite of the glamour remained eminently sensible. 'These fooleries are requisite sometimes to create admiration and regard to keep up the state of a kingdom or nation.'

After a short stop at Eton she rode east along the Thames Valley, through Hounslow to London. Her journey had covered 1,500 miles, 'in all which way and time I desire with thankfullness to own the good providence of God protecting me from all hazard or dangerous accident'.

Four years later, a little after her fortieth birthday, Celia set down an account of her travels. It was not designed for publication, but for 'my near relations'; yet even to those near relations she could not resist a little lecturing.

> If all persons, both ladies and, much more, gentlemen, would spend some of their time in journeys to visit their native land, and be curious to inform themselves and make observations of the pleasant prospects, good buildings, different produces and manufactures of each place, with the variety of sports and recreations they are adapt to, would be a sovereign remedy to cure or preserve from these epidemic diseases of vapours, should I add laziness? It would also form such an idea of England, add much to its glory and esteem in our minds and cure the evil itch of overvaluing foreign parts.

She lived to the age of seventy-nine. Her will, to which one of the witnesses was a man named Daniel Defoe, instructed that she should be buried 'without ostentation'.

5
A WANDERING DISPOSITION

The fate of things gives a new face to things, produces changes in low life, and innumerable incidents; plants and supplants families, raises and sinks towns, removes manufactures, and trades; great towns decay, and small towns rise; new towns, new palaces, new seats are built every day; great rivers and good harbours dry up and grow useless; again, new ports are opened, brooks are made rivers, small rivers navigable, ports and harbours are made where none were before.

Daniel Defoe, *A Tour through the Whole Island of Great Britain*

IT IS NOT difficult to picture Daniel Defoe riding into an English town, any town; making his way through the late afternoon crowds on his horse, sometimes alone, sometimes with others; the rainwater dripping from the overhangs of the half-timbered houses and leaving a damp patch on the back of his wig. Going into an inn, he had a familiar way with both landlord and stablehand, so that both felt he had been going there for years, though neither had set eyes on him before. Inside, the inn was crowded, but the dapper little man with a mole on his right cheek took up little space, and he was a good listener. When morning came he did not leave before dawn, as other travellers did, to get ahead of the pack-horse trains so impossible to overtake on the narrow roads, but stayed for several days. He could be seen in the High Street with the merchants and shopkeepers, in the Moot Hall with the mayor and local worthies, in the gentlemen's mansions outside the town, and in the ducal home, after which the town was named. He fitted in everywhere, a listener rather than a talker, all things to all people. No one saw him late at night, when the inn's guests were all asleep and the last drunk had sung himself home, sitting by his bedside table with a Bible, the intellectual furniture of a dissenter, beside him, writing his reports on the political opinions of his hosts to his master, Robert Harley, the Tory minister.

He was born Daniel Foe in Cripplegate, London, in 1660, just three months after the Restoration, and remembered playing in the streets of pre-Fire London. Educated at a college for dissenting clergymen, he remained totally ignorant of Greek and Latin his whole life. The memory of that college was an awful burden. 'It was my disaster first to be set apart for, and then to be set apart from, the honour of that sacred employ.' Unsuitable for the cloth, he turned to trade, marrying Mary Tuffles and setting himself up in Freeman's Yard, just off Cornhill. Like most writers' wives, Mary put up with a lot.

The London Defoe was living in was the biggest city in the world after Paris, fifteen times the size of its nearest national rivals, Bristol and Norwich, and with a population – if you included the suburbs and surrounding villages, such as Kensington, Chelsea, Hampstead and Hackney, growing 'in a most straggling, confused manner, out of shape, uncompact and unequal' – of nearly 1 million people. Its heart, the City, was one of the most densely populated square miles in the country.

Since the Great Fire, the entire City had been rebuilt and its streets paved. Throughout his boyhood and adolescence he watched it being reconstructed. The new squares were noble, and Wren's churches were nobler still, and most noble 'of all the Protestant churches in the world' was St Paul's, shrouded, like the rest of the City, in a perpetual cloud of smog.

There was still only one bridge over the Thames, and the river was still the City's main thoroughfare, with thirty landing places between Westminster and London Bridge. The Thames provided the lifeblood of London. 'The whole river, from London Bridge to Blackwall, is one great arsenal, nothing in the world can be like it.'

Then there were the markets: first Smithfield for living cattle, 'the greatest in the world'; then Billingsgate for fish and coal; Covent Garden and the Stocks Market for fruit, herbs and vegetables; Three Cranes Wharf for cherries and apples; Queenhythe and Bear Key for corn; Hungerford and Whitecross Street for cereals; Whitechapel, Southwark and Haymarket for hay; Leadenhall for leather; and Blackwell Hall for broad cloth.

The whole city was one enormous market, and from his base in Freeman's Court Daniel Defoe tried to play the market as a merchant, buying and selling, first in London and then all over the country. He was an awful businessman, too impetuous to build up capital, possessing 'a wandering disposition' and hardly able to earn a living. Until the success of *Robinson Crusoe* he spent half his life fleeing from creditors, and the other half trying to pay them back.

He became a failed rebel, riding west in 1685 and joining Monmouth's uprising, a Protestant crusade led by an amoral rake, a 'cause I never doubted of'. It was a débâcle, and Defoe, avoiding Judge Jeffreys by discreetly slipping abroad, made a precarious living as a merchant in Europe before returning to England in time to see the Glorious Revolution. The Protestant revolution had a profound effect on him – age could not wither it – and he remained an unrecanting radical until his death. Even as a radical he fitted no mould: a Whig employed as a secret agent by a Tory minister, a Dissenter who preached toleration of Catholics, a Londoner who belonged nowhere. 'A man that has no residence, no place that has a magnetic influence upon his affections, is in one of the most odd, most uneasy conditions in the world.'

He may have worked for a Tory, and written for money, and lived beyond his means, but Defoe was never a coward, and he was prepared to suffer for what he believed in. He did. Between 20 and 22 July 1703, long after the Glorious Revolution had been forgotten by all but a few balding *enfants terribles*, he stood for three mornings in the pillory, the first morning outside the Royal Exchange, the second in Cheapside, the third by Temple Bar. His crime was to have published a 'treasonable' satire, *The Shortest Way with Dissenters*, which mocked the intolerance of the day. Dissenters, unaware that it was a satire, were horrified by his 'intolerance'; High Churchmen and Tories, who approved of its arguments advocating the hanging of all dissenters, were furious to discover that it was a hoax and disgusted by his tolerance. Faced with a Tory government lacking tolerance and humour, Defoe went into hiding. The Wanted posters published in the *London Gazette* described him as 'a middle sized spare man, about forty years old, with a brown complexion and dark brown hair, but wears a wig, a hooked nose, a sharp chin, grey eyes, and a large mole near his mouth'. He remained in hiding for four months, then an informer betrayed him for £50 and he was arrested in Spitalfields. His sentence was prison and the pillory.

He looked out from the pillory frame at the crowd witnessing his punishment and humiliation. He watched them bend back their arms to throw things at him. But what they threw were not turds, but flowers. For a whole hour the crowd heaped flowers on him. The embarrassed soldiers guarding him did nothing to stop them. Then the crowd 'hallowed him down from his wooden punishment, as if he had been a Cicero', according to a hostile eye-witness, and the soldiers took him back to prison. Eventually it was the Tory minister Lord Harley who secured his release – for which Defoe remained perpetually in his debt.

Harley was a powerful man, rapidly becoming the most powerful man in the country, and he used Defoe ruthlessly. But Harley was of use to Defoe too; for not only did Harley pay Defoe's debts, but he developed a reliance on his informer that gave Defoe great, if discreet, political influence. Besides, though Defoe provided information, he never betrayed. His aim was to strengthen the moderate Tories led by Harley against the extremists in the High Church, and to this end he devoted thirteen years of his life. He played his own game and, if he appeared disloyal to his obvious beliefs, he never betrayed his higher loyalty, religious toleration.

He knew much of Britain from his earlier journeys as a merchant. Now, travelling for Harley, investigating local problems and passing on local opinion, he gained a deeper knowledge. It was Harley who sent him to Scotland in 1706 to prepare the way for the Union. It was not his first time there. He had travelled through the Highlands in the reign of King William, but it was his first investigative visit, and he soon became more knowledgeable about Scottish affairs than any other Englishman.

His games with Harley ended in 1715 when Harley was impeached. Middle-aged, bankrupt, ill, and convinced that he had outlived his usefulness, Defoe now felt like some marooned man on a desert island. Equally galling was the publication in 1714 of John Mackay's *Journey through England in Familiar Letters*. It was the very book that Defoe – with all his experience of the country – should have written. Furthermore, it was badly written, ill-organized and inaccurate, little more than a padded-out road book. He remained in that state of depression for four years until the publication of *Robinson Crusoe*.

His success with *Robinson Crusoe*, and with his other novels, did not distract him from the major task he now set himself, to outshine Mackay and write his own *Tour through the Whole Island of Great Britain*. The timing, a decade after Mackay's book, could not have been better. Readers were growing tired of travelling with explorers to the far ends of the earth. Britain itself, unconsciously lumbering towards the Industrial Revolution, was more interesting. A new edition of Stow's *Survey of London* came out in 1720, and a new translation of Camden's *Britannia* in 1722. The travel book, like Robinson Crusoe, had come home. Curiously, Defoe's *Tour*, mile for mile, never took place. Like Crusoe's journey, it was a fiction, a structure to make it readable.

> To describe a country by other men's accounts of it, would soon expose the writer to a discovery of the fraud; and to describe it by survey, requires a preparation too great for anything but the public purse, and persons appointed by authority. But to describe a country by way of a journey, in a private capacity, is giving an account by way of essay, or, as the moderns call it, by memoirs of the present state of things, in a familiar manner.

What made the book so radically different from its nearest rivals, Mackay and the re-printed Camden, was Defoe's sense of the movement of a country. There was an awareness of Past, Present and Future. 'No cloth can be made to fit a growing child; no picture carry the likeness of a living face'.

*   *   *

The first circuit *did* take place. Defoe set out from London for East Anglia, where he had business, on 3 April 1722. He passed through Aldgate, crossed Bow Bridge and rode east. Stratford had doubled in size in a quarter of a century. The same had happened to all the villages around: Leytonstone, Walthamstow, Woodford, Wanstead, West Ham and Plaistow. Many of the new houses were second homes for London merchants. 'The present wealth in the city of London spreads itself into the country, and plants families and fortunes, who in another age would equal the families of the ancient gentry, who perhaps were bought out.'

The road led through Hainault Forest, and at a crossroads, marked by an upright whalebone, he turned off for Barking, 'chiefly inhabited by fishermen, whose smacks ride in the Thames, from whence their fish is sent up to London to the market at Billingsgate, by small boat'. The land was flat and marshy, but the soil rich, held by

London grazing butchers, fattening sheep and cattle brought down from Lincolnshire and Leicestershire for the London market. He continued east, past the pentagon-shaped defence works at Tilbury towards Colchester, which produced 'the best and nicest, though not the largest, oysters in England'.

> All along the mouth of Colchester Water, the shore is full of shoals and sands, with some deep channels between them; all of which are so full of fish, that it is not only the Barking fishing smacks come hither to fish, but the whole shore is full of small fisher-boats in very great numbers, belonging to the villages and towns on the coast, who come in every tide with what they take; and selling the smaller fish in the country, send the best and largest away upon horses, which go night and day to London market.

Colchester was large, very populous, the streets fair and beautiful, and 'though it may not be said to be finely built, yet there are abundance of very good and well-built houses'. The town was still recovering from the siege it suffered during the civil war. 'The lines of contravallation, with the forts built by the besiegers, and which surround the whole town, remained very visible in many places; but the chief of them are demolished.'

Harwich, sixteen miles further on, a ferry port to Holland, was altogether too grasping. 'The inhabitants are far from famed for good usage to strangers, but on the contrary, are blamed for being extravagant in their reckonings, in the public houses.' It was understandable. There was less money in Harwich than previously. The town was losing the Continental ferry trade, the traffic going directly from London to Holland.

He crossed the Stour over a timber bridge and took a boat up the Orwell to Ipswich, once 'the greatest town in England for large colliers or coal-ships, employed between Newcastle and London'. Now Ipswich, like Harwich, was in decay. 'The great ships go to sea no more, but lie by, the ships are unrigged, the sails carried ashore, the top masts struck'. The town was 'thinly inhabited' and had an air of genteel poverty, making it 'one of the most agreeable places in England for families who have lived well, but may have suffered in our late calamities of stocks and bubbles, to retreat to, where they may live within their own compass'.

The next stop on his itinerary was Bury St Edmunds. It had changed much since William Worcestre passed through in 1479. 'The abbey is demolished, its ruins are all that is to be seen of its glory.' His rival Mackay, whose book had provoked such jealousy in Daniel Defoe, had implied that the young women of East Anglia were brought to Bury as if to an auction.

> I shall believe nothing so scandalous of the ladies of this town and the county around it, as a late writer insinuates. That the ladies round the country appear mighty gay and agreeable at the time of the fair in this town, I acknowledge; one hardly sees such a show in any part of the world; but to suggest they come hither as to market. This is a terrible character for the ladies of Bury, and intimates in short, that most of them are whores, which is a horrid abuse upon the whole county.

There was an 'abundance of the finest ladies', but:

> the scandalous liberty some take at those assemblies, will in time bring them out of credit with the virtuous part of the sex here, as it has done already in Kent and other places; and that those ladies who most value their reputation, will be seen less there than they have been and the scandalous behaviour of some of them, will in time arm virtue against them.

All the world travelling: a detail from Hogarth's painting 'The Polling'.

From Bury he rode east through Woodbridge to Dunwich on the coast. The town was in danger of being swallowed up by the sea, 'a testimony of the decay of public things'. He continued along the coast to Southwold, where the Dutch had defeated the British fleet in 1672.

> I was surprised to see an extraordinary large church, capable of receiving five or six hundred people, and but twenty-seven in it besides the parson and clerk; but at the same time the meeting house of the dissenters was full to the very doors, having, as I guessed, from six to eight hundred people in it.

Perhaps that too was a testimony of decay. It was here at Southwold, Defoe discovered, that the swallows embarked on their cross-sea migration to warmer climes.

> About the beginning of October, and lodging in a house that looked into the churchyard, I observed in the evening an unusual multitude of birds sitting on the leads of the church; curiosity led me to go nearer to see what they were, and I found they were all swallows; and that such an infinite number that they covered the whole roof of the church, and of several houses near, and perhaps might, of more houses which I did not see.

He asked a nearby gentleman what was the meaning of it. The old man smiled, observing that Defoe must be a stranger to ask, and told him that the swallows were 'waiting for a gale, for they are all wind-bound'. Next morning, after a strong wind from the north-west, the swallows had vanished.

It was good farming country, the first district in England where cattle were fed on turnips; and in September and October, after the harvest but before the frost, 'when the roads begin to be too stiff and deep for their broad feet and short legs to march in', the roads from East Anglia were crowded with geese and turkeys on their way to London.

Norfolk was rich from weaving, 'a face of diligence spread over the whole county', yarn coming to the market towns and villages such as Thetford, Diss, East Dereham and Harling from as far afield as Yorkshire and Westmorland. There was work for all, the manufacturers assured Defoe, 'the very children after four or five years of age could every one earn their own bread'.

Norwich was the centre of the trade.

If a stranger was only to ride through or view the city of Norwich for a day, he would have much more reason to think there was a town without inhabitants, than there is really to say so of Ipswich; but on the contrary, if he was to view the city, either on a Sabbath-day, or on a public occasion, he would wonder where all the people could dwell.

In spite of the industry there was no ugliness. The cathedral was fine and its steeple beautiful, and there were still open fields within the three miles of city walls.

East of Norwich lay the Broads – which fed the fattest cattle in England – stretching to Yarmouth, which was older than, and almost as large as, Norwich. The town was built on a peninsula between the River Yare and the sea. Unable to expand its girth, it was hopelessly overcrowded.

He rode the semicircle of the north Norfolk coast, passing through Cromer (which had nothing to recommend it but good lobsters), Cley (where there were salt works), and Wells-next-the-Sea, before turning inland to King's Lynn, well-built and well-situated on the Wash, 'the sink of more than thirteen counties'. The ruins of the fortifications looked eerily beautiful, and around the town on three sides lay the Fens.

Defoe followed the Great Ouse through the Fens south to Downham Market, crossed the river on 'an ugly wooden bridge' and turned north-west, his horse splashing through the shallow fenny waters to Wisbech. There was nothing here but 'deep roads, innumerable drains and dykes of water'. The only beautiful sight was the Isle of Ely through the fog, 'wrapped up in blankets, and nothing to be seen, but now and then, the lanthorn or cupola'.

He re-crossed the Nene and made for Newmarket, where he went to the races. Here there was:

a great concourse of the nobility and gentry, as well from London as from all parts of England; but they were all so intent, so eager, so busy upon the sharpening part of the sport, their wagers and bets, that to me they seemed just as so many horse-coursers in Smithfield, descending (the greatest of them) from their high dignity and quality, to picking one another's pockets, and biting one another as much as possible.

He went on to Cambridge, arriving during Stourbridge Fair. It was the biggest horse, corn and hop market in the country, taking up a half square mile alongside the River Cam: a city of tents, with booths and stalls in rows, like streets.

Scarce any trades are omitted, goldsmiths, toyshops, braziers, turners, milliners, haberdashers, hatters, mercers, drapers, pewterers, china-wharehouses, and in a word all trades that can be named in London; with coffee houses, taverns, brandy shops and eating houses innumerable.

The Fairlop Oak (the thickest oak in Epping Forest) and picnickers.

Understandably for a man educated at a college for Dissenters and without knowledge of Greek and Latin, the university paled beside 'the greatest fair in the world'. King's College and its chapel are not even mentioned. The sight of the colleges – and all the lost opportunities that they implied – must have hurt.

He rode south towards London, 'and at Saffron Walden I saw the ruins of the once largest and most magnificent pile in this part of England, Audley End; built by, and decaying with, the noble Dukes and Earls of Suffolk'. Soon he was in Epping Forest, 'spangled with fine villages, and these villages filled with fine seats, most of them built by citizens of London'. The villages merged into suburbs, and by evening he was in London. He had completed his first circuit.

*   *   *

Defoe's second itinerary – this time a fictitious one, but based on previous journeys – was a circuit of south-east England. With Kent, as with Essex and Suffolk, he followed the Thames estuary shoreline. It was a progress from one naval town to the next. Greenwich, his first stop, which he came to by boat, was peopled by down-at-heel gentry, the honest, modest class and retired army officers, and graced by the lines of Wren, Hawkesmore and Vanbrugh. It was:

> the most delightful spot of ground in Great Britain; pleasant by situation, those pleasures increased by art, and all made completely agreeable by the accident of fine buildings, the continual passing of fleets of ships up and down the most beautiful river in Europe, the best air, best prospect, and the best conversation in England.

Three miles down the estuary was Charlton, site of an annual horn fair. The Dissenter in him disapproved of it. 'The mob indeed at that time take all kinds of liberties, and the women are especially impudent for that day; as if it was a day that justified the giving themselves aloose to all manner of indecency and immodesty, without any reproach.'

Woolwich lay a mile along the shore, its waterfront taken up by shipyards, docks, naval warehouses and arsenals. On the other side of Woolwich the land was marshy as far as Gravesend and Shooters Hill, where the soil became chalky and the landscape overgrown by woodland.

Soon Defoe was crossing the Medway over Rochester Bridge, 'the largest, highest and the strongest built of all the bridges in England except London Bridge'. The castle was in ruins and the cathedral was dismissed as 'ancient but not extraordinary'. The docks, however, were alive.

> The building yards, docks, timber yard, deal yard, mast yard, gun yard, rope walks and all the other yards and places, set apart from the works belonging to the navy, are like a well ordered city; and though you see the whole place as though it were in the utmost hurry, yet you see no confusion, every man knows his own business.

He explored the coast around the Isle of Sheppey, and meandered through the hop fields of Kent to Canterbury. It was old, very old, and long past its best. 'The city will scarce bear being called populous, were it not for the two or three thousand French Protestants, which, including men, women and children, they say there are in it, and yet they tell me the number of these decreases daily.' They were employed in silk-weaving, but the silk industry had decayed since Celia Fiennes's visit, the number of broad looms being reduced from 300 to twenty.

A 40-mile semicircle through Ramsgate, Sandwich and Deal took him to Dover.

Paul Sandby's lime kilns in Charlton: 'a pleasant place', according to Daniel Defoe.

Neither Dover nor its castle has anything of note to be said of them, but what is in common with their neighbours; the castle is old, useless, decayed, and serves for little; but to give the title and honour of government to men of quality, with a salary.

He rode west through Folkestone and Romney Marshes to Winchelsea, 'rather the skeleton of an ancient city than a real town, where the ancient gates stand near three miles from each other over the fields, and where the ruins are so buried, that they have made good corn fields of the streets'.

At Pevensey he turned inland, through Sussex and Kent, 'traversing the deep, dirty, but rich part of these two counties', mostly passing through forest, clouded with the smoke of iron foundries. He carried on through Tunbridge Wells, where 'those people who have nothing to do anywhere else, seem to be the only people who have something to do', and continued west, 'through the deepest, dirtiest, but many ways the richest, and most profitable county in all that part of England'. On the way to Lewes the road was so muddy that he saw a lady being driven to church in a coach pulled by six oxen.

He came down to Bright Helmston, or Brighton, on the other side of the Downs, 'a poor fishing town, old built, and on the very edge of the sea', its front slowly crumbling under the force of the waves. From there he struck north-west for Petworth, 'one of the finest piles of building, and the best modelled houses then in Britain, with its elbows to the town'.

He descended the Downs into Chichester. 'The cathedral here is not the finest in England, but is far from being most ordinary.' A few years earlier the spire had been hit by lightning. 'The breach it made in the spire, though within about forty-five feet of the top, was so large, that as the workmen said to me, a coach and six horses might have driven through it.'

Ten miles to the west lay Portsmouth, 'the largest fortification, beyond comparison, that we have in England'. West of Portsmouth the land was low and flat, and after an extremely uncomfortable crossing of Southampton Water he disembarked in the New Forest. It stretched for miles.

As I rode through New Forest, I could see the ancient oaks of many hundred years standing, perishing with their withered tops advanced up in the air, and grown white with age, and that could never yet get the favour to be cut down and made servicable to their country.

He came into Southampton, a town 'dying with age'. It had lost almost all its trade to London, and the only ships that came into port were either traders from the Channel Islands or the occasional smuggler.

This was the furthest west his imaginary circuit took him, so he rode north-east towards London, stopping at Petersfield, 'a town eminent for little, but its being full of good inns', Farnham, 'the greatest cornmarket in England', and Alton, 'a small market town of no note'. His route now took him over Bagshot Heath.

Those that despise Scotland, and the north part of England, for being full of waste and barren land, may take a view of this part of Surrey, quite sterile, given up to barrenness, horrid and frightful to look on, not only good for little, but good for nothing. Much of it is a sandy desert, and one may frequently be put to mind here of Arabia Deserta, where the winds raise the sands, so as to overwhelm whole caravans of travellers.

Beyond the desert was the Great West Road, but instead of returning to London immediately, he took a diversion, through Woking, Guildford and Dorking to Epsom

Wells, 'where you drink the waters, or walk about as if you did'. Epsom was as middle-class as Tunbridge was upper-middle-class, and Bath upper-class; and to Daniel Defoe, with his bourgeois background, it was infinitely more respectable.

> 'Tis all rural, the houses are built at large, not many together, with gardens and ground about them; that the people who come out of their confined dwellings in London, may have air and liberty.

Already it was part of the commuter belt.

> The greatest part of the men, I mean of this grave sort, may be supposed to be men of business, who are at London on business all the day, and thronging to their lodgings at night, make the families, generally speaking, rather provide suppers than dinners; for 'tis very frequent for the trading part of the company to place their families here, and take their horses every morning to London, to the Exchange, to the Alley, or to the warehouse, and be at Epsom again at night.

In the winter the town was deserted, 'good houses shut up, and windows fastened; the furniture taken down, the families removed, the walks out of repair, the leaves off the trees'.

He came into London through Richmond, ultra-fashionable since the Prince of Wales (the future George II) had taken to spending the season there. Defoe remembered it from its more genteel days as 'a most agreeable retreat for the first and second rate gentry'. He liked bourgeois England, and the road along the riverside represented the best of bourgeois England.

> Nothing can be more beautiful; here is a plain and pleasant country, a rich fertile soil, cultivated and enclosed to the utmost perfection of husbandry, then bespangled with villages; those villages filled with these houses, and the houses surrounded with gardens, walks, vistas, avenues, representing all the beauties of building.

*   *   *

Pope's house at Twickenham. 'The banks of the Seine are not thus adorned.'

Defoe's third circuit took him west, out of London and along the banks of the Thames again. He stopped at Hampton Court, where the formal Dutch garden came down to the river banks.

> The river is high enough to be navigable, and low enough to be a little pleasantly rapid; so that the stream looks always cheerful, not slow and sleeping, like a pond. This keeps the water always clear and clean, the bottom in view, the fish playing, and in sight; and, in a word, it has everything that can make an inland river pleasant and agreeable.

He had known the old palace and watched it being rebuilt by King William, when 'Hampton Court put on new clothes, and being dressed gay and glorious, made the figure we now see it in'. It gave him an affection for the place.

He left the river, crossed the 'Black Desert' of Bagshot Heath again and took the Great West Road through 'woods and pastures, rich and fertile' to Basingstoke, before turning left at North Waltham for Winchester.

Winchester looked old – 'venerable', he called it. The outside of the cathedral was completely devoid of decoration, 'as if the founders had abhorred ornaments, or that William of Wyckam had been a Quaker'. In the northern suburbs was Hyde Abbey, dissolved in Leland's time. It had been bought by a Catholic family and now, 200 years later, it was 'still preserved to the religion, being the residence of some Roman Catholic gentlemen, where they have an oratory, and, as they say, live still according to the rules of St Benedict'. The writer of *The Shortest Way with Dissenters*, who had stood three times in the pillory, was a tolerant man.

A short day's ride to the west lay Old Sarum. Save for a single farmhouse it was a ghost town. Yet it returned two Members of Parliament. 'Who those members can justly say they represent, would be hard for them to answer.'

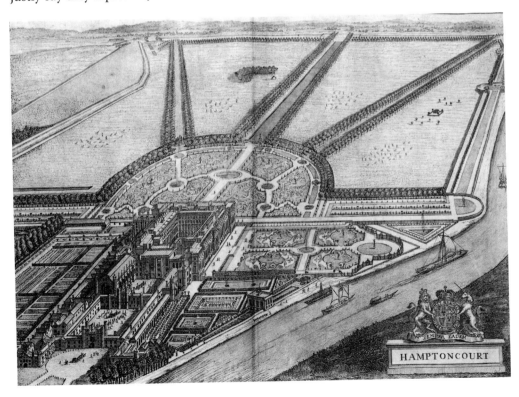

He left Old Sarum and rode 'over the most charming plains that can anywhere be seen (far in my opinion), excelling the plains of Mecca', to Salisbury, a boom town where even the poor were rich from the cloth trade with Turkey. Above the city rose the cathedral spire, 'without exception the highest and handsomest in England'.

Four rivers met at Salisbury, and the waters of three of them – polluted by dyers and clothiers – ran through the streets.

> I do not think it at all the pleasanter for that which they boast so much of; namely, the water running through the middle of every street, or that it adds anything to the beauty of the place, but just the contrary; it keeps the streets always dirty, full of wet and filth, and weeds, even in the middle of summer.

One of the rivers, the Wylye, led to Wilton House, a Benedictine convent when Leland passed through and now a 'noble princely palace' by Inigo Jones. Its owner, the Earl of Pembroke, had collected so many paintings, sculptures and antiquities that it had become a living museum, 'a chamber of rarities'.

> When you entered the apartment, such variety seizes you every way, that you scarce know to which hand to turn yourself. First, on one side you see several rooms filled with paintings all so curious, and the variety such, that 'tis with reluctance, that you can turn from them; while looking another way, you are called off by a vast collection of busts and pieces of the greatest antiquity of the kind, both Greek and Roman; among these there is one of the Roman emperor, Marcus Aurelius, in *basso relievo*.
>
> Passing these, you come into several large rooms, as if contrived for the reception of the beautiful guests that take them up. Those together might be called the Great Gallery of Wilton, and might vie for paintings with the gallery of Luxemburg in the Faubourg of Paris.
>
> After we have seen this fine range of beauties, for such indeed they are; far from being at the end of your surprise, you have three or four rooms still upon the same floor, filled with wonders, as before. Nothing can be finer than the pictures themselves, nothing more surprising than the number of them.

Next day Defoe was at Stonehenge. 'How they came hither, or from whence, no stones of that kind being now to be found in any part of England near it, is still a mystery.' He rode on, turning sharply to the south and riding through the New Forest to Lymington, a seaport facing the Isle of Wight, with no commerce but smuggling. Twelve miles west lay Christchurch, hardly worth noting, it had so declined since Taylor's escapade. Six miles on, 'over a sandy wild and barren country', was Poole, whose oysters were the biggest in southern England.

He rode inland to Dorchester. Here the population was less divided by religious and political factions than anywhere else in England, and wild flowers grew right up to the edge of the town. He returned to the coast at Portland, where white stone was being quarried for the rebuilding of St Paul's Cathedral.

> This island, though seemingly miserable, and thinly inhabited, yet the inhabitants being almost all stone-cutters, we found there was no very poor people among them; and when they collected money for the rebuilding of St Paul's, they got more in this island than in the great town of Dorchester, as we were told.

Bridport – a fishing town without a harbour, where the mackerel were so plentiful and cheap that farmers used them to manure their fields – led to Lyme Regis, 'a town of good figure' with a splendid seafront.

It is a massy pile of building, consisting of high and thick walls of stone. The walls are raised in the main sea, at a good distance from the shore; it consists of one main and solid wall of stone, large enough for carts and carriages to pass on the top, and to admit houses and warehouses to be built on it. This work is called the Cobb.

Defoe liked Lyme; it was bourgeois, but not pretentious.

The ladies here do not want the help of assemblies to assist in match-making; or half-pay officers to run away with their daughters, which the meetings, called assemblies in some other parts of England, are recommended for. Here's no Bury Fair, where the women are scandalously said to carry themselves to market, and where every night they meet at the play, or at the assembly for intrigue. The ladies are not nuns, they do not go veiled about the streets, or hide themselves when visited; but a general freedom of conversation, agreeable, mannerly, kind, and good, runs through the whole body of the gentry of both sexes, mixed with the best of behaviour, and yet governed by prudence and modesty.

North-west of Lyme Regis, about ten miles inland, through one of the most beautiful landscapes in England, was Honiton, with little streams running along either side of the streets. The lovely landscape continued to Exeter.

The city was 'large, rich, beautiful, populous', with a lucrative shipping trade with Holland, Portugal, Spain and Italy. Its cathedral was 'beautiful for its antiquity' and 'the serge market held here every week is well worth a stranger's seeing, and next to the Brigg Market at Leeds in Yorkshire, is the greatest in England'.

He meandered south and west on his imaginary journey, crossing the River Dart by the stone bridge at Totnes, then following the west bank of the river to Dartmouth. He had once been in the town when a school of pilchards had got trapped in the harbour and 40,000 had been caught in three fishing nets.

Twenty miles west was Plymouth, which he came into through Plympton, 'a poor and thinly inhabited town, though blessed with the privilege of sending members to Parliament, of which I have little more to say'. Plymouth was a considerable town, turned into a naval arsenal and dock by William III during the wars with France. Far out to sea stood the new Eddystone Lighthouse. The old one had been blown down in the Great Storm of 1703, its designer, Henry Winstanley, killed inside it.

On the other side of the Tamar was Cornwall. The ferry journey was awful. Defoe continued along the coast to Fowey, a 'fair town' with a pirate past, now earning its living from the pilchard industry, and rode inland through Truro to Falmouth, the richest trading town in the county. The further west he went, the more the moorland was dotted with tin and copper mines. Soon he was in Penzance, the last major town before the ocean. He passed through bleak and barren hills and came to Land's End. There, just as at Selsey Bill (his furthest point south) and Lowestoft in Suffolk (his furthest point east), he took off his boots and dangled his feet in the water.

He put his boots on again, turned round and headed for St Ives. From there it was thirty miles to Padstow, the next town of any size. The countryside was 'fruitful and pleasant'. Defoe liked it. Padstow, on the mouth of the River Camel, was the centre of the local herring-catching industry and Cornwall's main port trading with Ireland. He watched the local game of hurling but found it 'brutish and furious', suitable only for country boors. He preferred the wrestling, 'a much more manly and generous exercise, and that closure, which they called the Cornish Hug, has made them eminent in the wrestling rings all over England'.

He crossed Bodmin Moor and came into Devon through Launceston, where the Catholics still paid reverence to the statue of Mary Magdalen on the church tower. The town looked old. 'It was a frontier town, walled about, and well-fortified, and had, also, a strong castle to defend it; but these are seen now only in their old clothes, and lie all in ruins.'

He was now in the most desolate part of Devon. Even the tin mines were abandoned. After some miles the 'wild, barren, poor country' faded away and became more populous, the people more industrious. Soon he was in Tiverton on the River Exe, a hive of activity. 'We found people here all fully employed, and very few, if any, out of work, except such as need not be unemployed but were so from mere sloth and idleness.'

Wellington, across the border in Somerset and on the road to Taunton, was just the opposite. Defoe was immediately surrounded by beggars, scurrying under his horse's heels.

The third Eddystone Lighthouse.

It was our misfortune at first, that we threw some farthings and halfpence, such as we had, among them; for thinking by this to be rid of them, the whole town came out into the street, and they ran in this manner after us through the whole street, and a great way after we were quite out of the town.

Taunton was only six miles on, and it was as industrious as Tiverton. One merchant told him 'there was not a child in the town, or in the villages round it, of above five years old, but if it was not neglected by its parents and untaught, could earn its own bread'.

From Taunton he made an excursion north over Exmoor, 'a vast tract of barren and desolate lands', to Minehead, rich from trade with Ireland. He rode east along the shore to the Parrett estuary, then up the river to Bridgwater and Glastonbury, where the 'venerable marks of antiquity' shown him by the local people struck him with awe.

They went over the ruins of the place with me, telling me which part every particular piece of building had been; and as for the white thorn, they carried me to a gentleman's garden in the town where it was preserved, and I brought a piece of it away in my hat.

Four miles on came Wells, 'one of the neatest and in some respects the most beautiful cathedrals in England', its west front 'one complete draught of imagery'. Beyond Wells lay Cheddar Gorge, 'a deep and frightful chasm'. Defoe was glad to be out of it. The lowlands on the other side of it were cheese country, and the farm pigs which fed on the whey made the best bacon in England. The highlands, on the other hand, were cloth country, and there were impoverished outworkers in every hamlet, spinning yarn for the master clothiers who lived in the towns. All along the way were reminders of the Great Storm of 1703, the signs reading, 'This high the waters came in the great storm' and 'Thus far the great tide flowed up in the last violent tempest'.

Keeping to the north of Salisbury Plain, he continued on through Newbury to Reading, lying on the River Kennet and within easy reach of the Thames. The main trade was water haulage, and the riverside was lined with barges loaded with malt and meal for the journey to London. He had been there during the tumultuous days preceding the Glorious Revolution, when the town had almost been burnt by Irish troops supporting King James II. But the lasting memory of Reading that he retained was not of fire and revolution, but of riverside warehouses and overloaded barges.

He rode to Great Marlow on the River Thames, another water haulage town. All along the river were corn mills, paper mills, thimble-making mills, oil-pressing mills and copper foundry mills. The line of water mills led to Windsor, 'the most beautiful and most pleasantly situated castle and royal palace in the whole isle of Britain'.

He admired the terrace walk with its fine gravel, and lawns as smooth as carpets; and, like Celia Fiennes, he toured the state rooms, stopping at a piece of needlework by Mary, Queen of Scots on one of the chimneypieces. In St George's hall he was completely taken in by the *trompe-l'oeil* of King William sitting on horseback.

I was going forward towards the end of the hall, intending to go up the steps, as I had done formerly. I was confounded, when I came near to see the ascent was taken down, the marble steps gone, the chair of state or throne quite away, and all that I saw, was only painted upon the wall.

From there he descended down to the lower court and its spectacular Chapel of St George.

The chapel is not only fine within, but the workmanship without is extraordinary; nothing so ancient is to be seen so very beautiful. The Chapel of St Stephen's in Westminster Abbey, called Henry VII's Chapel, and King's College Chapel in Cambridge, built by Henry VI, are fine buildings; but they are modern compared to this.

Next day, after a brief visit to Eton College, 'the finest school for what we call grammar learning in Britain', he came into London.

*   *   *

His fourth journey took Defoe to Wales and the Midlands. He started from London and rode west through Harrow, 'a little town on a very high hill', and on through Uxbridge and Aylesbury to Oxford:

> the greatest (if not the most ancient) university in this island of Great Britain; and perhaps the most flourishing at this time, in men of polite learning, and in the most accomplished masters of science, and in all the parts of acquired knowledge in the world.
>
> It is a noble flourishing city, so possessed of all that can contribute to make the residence of the scholars easy and comfortable, that no spot of ground in England goes beyond it. The situation is in a delightful plain, on the bank of a fine navigable river, in a plentiful country, and at an easy distance from the capital city.

Wren's Sheldonian Theatre was 'in its grandeur and opulence, infinitely superior to anything in the world of its kind; it is a finished piece, as to its building, the front is exquisitely fine, the columns and pilasters regular, and very beautiful'.

From Oxford he rode north to Woodstock, once a royal palace, and given to the Duke of Marlborough by a grateful nation.

> Nothing else can justify the vast design, a bridge or *ryalto* rather, of one arch costing £20,000, and this, like the bridge at the Escurial in Spain, without a river. Gardens of near 100 acres of ground. Offices fit for 300 in family. Outhouses fit for the lodgings of a regiment of guards rather than livery servant.

Now it was empty, the duke dead and the duchess – who hated the place – abroad.

He continued on through Chipping Norton, and in the village of Bloxham witnessed a 'mop' or labour fair, where the country people stood in the market place, each carrying a tool – the carter a whip, the shepherd a crook, the labourer a shovel, the domestic servant a brush. Defoe was overheard calling it a 'jade fair' and was almost lynched. He did not stay and soon he was in the Cotswolds, 'so eminent for the best of sheep and finest wool in England'.

> Upon these downs we had a clear view of the famous old Roman highway called the Fosse, which evidently crosses all the middle part of England, and is to be seen and known (though in no place plainer than here) quite from the Bath to Warwick, and thence to Leicester, to Newark, to Lincoln, and on to Barton upon the banks of the Humber. Here it is still the common road, and we followed it over the downs to Cirencester.

From Cirencester, 'a very good town, populous and rich, full of clothiers and driving a great trade in wool', he travelled on through Malmesbury, 'famous for a monastery and a great church built out of the ruins of it', to Bath.

In former times this was a resort hither for cripples; and we see the crutches hang up in several baths, as the thank-offerings of those who have come hither lame, and gone away cured. But now we may say it is the resort of the sound rather than the sick; the bathing is made more a sport and diversion than a physical prescription for health; and the town is taken up in raffling, gaming, visiting and, in a word, all sorts of gallantry and levity.

The whole time indeed is a round of the utmost diversion. In the morning you (supposing you to be a young lady) are fetched in a close chair, dressed in your bathing clothes, that is, stripped to the smock, to the Cross Bath. There the music plays you into the bath, and the women that tend you, present you with a little floating wooden dish, like a basin; in which the lady puts a handkerchief, and a nosegay, of late the snuff-box is added, and some patches; though the bath occasioning a little perspiration, the patches do not stick so kindly as they should.

Here the ladies and gentlemen pretend to keep some distance, and each to their proper side, but frequently mingle here too, as in the King and Queen Bath, though not so often; and the place being but narrow, they converse freely, and talk, rally, make vows, and sometimes love; and having thus amused themselves an hour or two, they call their chairs and return to their lodgings.

In the afternoon there is generally a play, though the decorations are mean, and the performances accordingly; but it answers, for the company here (not the actors) make the play.

He followed the River Avon to Bristol, the second city of the kingdom, rich in Saxon times from the Irish slave trade, rich from wool between slave trades, and rich again from the North Atlantic slave trade. He did not think much of it, except for its wealth. It was overcrowded, lying in low ground, and hemmed in by a hill. But no one could be unimpressed by its size. It had its own cathedral (though 'very mean') and twenty-one parish churches.

'All ship-shape and Bristol fashion': the city's docks and quay, c. 1730.

Ludlow Castle: the seat of the Prince of Wales and 'the very perfection of decay'.

Here Defoe resolved to follow the course of the River Severn, cross it by ferry from Aust to Chepstow, as William Worcestre had done, and ride on into Wales. But the weather was terrible, and the fame of the Severn Bore more terrible still. So instead he followed the river along its eastern bank, riding past Berkeley Castle, 'a noble though ancient building' where Edward II had been so horribly murdered, and on through rich and fertile country, via Gloucester, to Tewkesbury. It lay at the confluence of the Avon and Severn, and the junction was crowded with barges carrying sugar, oil, wine, tobacco, iron, lead, corn and cheese.

Twelve miles upstream was Worcester, another great cloth centre, but 'not a very well-built city because the town is close and old, the houses standing too thick'. The cathedral was decaying, its outside absent of ornamentation and with a low tower and no steeple. Inside was the grave of King John, between those of two bishops, St Oswald and St Woolstan. 'Whether he ordered his interment in that manner, believing that they should help him *up* at the last call, and be serviceable to him for his salvation I do not know.'

He crossed the Severn by Worcester's bridge and rode into the Welsh Marches, following the River Teme, a tributary of the Severn, to Ludlow, its castle 'the very perfection of decay'. There he turned south to Leominster.

One would hardly expect so pleasant and fruitful a country as this, so near the barren mountains of Wales; but 'tis certain, that not any of our southern counties, the neighbourhood of London excepted, comes up to the fertility of this county.

From Leominster it was thirteen miles to Hereford, 'the chief city, not of this county only, but of all the counties west of the Severn'.

It is truly an old mean built and very dirty city, lying low, and on the banks of the Wye, which sometimes incommodes them very much by the violent freshes that come down from the mountains of Wales. The church is a magnificent building, however ancient, the spire is not high, but handsome, and there is a fine tower at the west end, over the great doorway or entrance. The choir is very fine, though plain, and there is a very good organ. The revenues of this bishopric are very considerable, but lie under some abatement at present, on account of necessary repairs.

He followed the Wye, shortcutting its more impossible meanders to Monmouth, 'a place of great antiquity', Chepstow, where he crossed the Wye into Wales, and the Brecon Beacons, which reminded him of the Alps.

Defoe liked Wales. Provisions were plentiful and the inns were good.

The Welsh gentlemen are very civil, hospitable and kind; the people very obliging and conversable, and especially to strangers. They believe their country to be the pleasantest and most agreeable in the world, so that you cannot oblige them more than to make them think you believe so too.

He followed the River Taff downstream to Cardiff.

The south part of this country is a pleasant and agreeable place, and is very populous; 'tis also a very good, fertile and rich soil, and the low grounds are so well covered with grass and stocked with cattle, that they supply the city of Bristol with butter in very large quantities salted and barrelled up, just as Suffolk does the City of London.

At the coast he turned west and, passing through Swansea, came to Carmarthen, where Merlin had been born and the Ancient Britons held their parliaments. The town was old and well-built, and surrounded by some of the richest corn fields and meadows in Wales.

We found the people in this county more civilized and more courteous than in the more mountainous parts, where the disposition of the inhabitants seems to be rough, like the country. But here as they seem to converse with the rest of the world by their commerce, so they are more conversable than their neighbours.

He came into Pembrokeshire, passing through Tenby on the coast, 'the most agreeable town'. Pembroke he found 'the largest and richest, and at this time, the most flourishing town in all south Wales'. West of Pembroke, on the way to St David's, 'the country begins to look like Wales again, dry, barren and mountainous'. The cathedral there was venerable and beautiful but much decayed, its roof still open to the sky, as it had been when John Taylor lamented its fate.

He next turned north and rode along the shore of Cardigan Bay. The further north he went, the more mountainous the land became: 'innumerable summits and rising peaks of nameless hills, and still every hill we saw, we thought was higher than all that ever we saw before'. Soon he was in Snowdonia. Mount Snowdon, topped with snow in the middle of June, was 'a monstrous height'. He pressed on through the mountains to Caernarfon, where 'the people are very courteous and obliging to strangers'.

After a disappointing excursion to Holyhead on the Isle of Anglesey, he came to Bangor and took the north coast road to Conwy, 'the poorest but pleasantest town in all the county'. There he turned south-east to Denbigh, and came into 'a most pleasant, fruitful, populous and delicious vale, full of villages and towns, the fields shining with corn, just ready for the reapers, the meadows green and flowery, and a fine river, with a mild and gentle stream running through it'.

He continued to Holywell and the healing well of St Winifred, where, like Celia Fiennes, he saw the Catholics pray before the saint's shrine.

Conwy High Street: 'the poorest but pleasantest town in all the country'.

The priests that attend here are very numerous, and appear in disguise. Sometimes they are physicians, sometimes surgeons, sometimes gentlemen, and sometimes patients, or any thing as occasion presents. No body takes notice of them, as to their profession, though they know them well enough, no not the Roman Catholics themselves; but in private, they have their proper oratories in certain places, whither the oratories resort; and good manners has prevailed so far, that however the Protestants know who and who's together; nobody takes any notice of it.

He crossed the River Dee and arrived in Chester. Neither the Rows in the town centre nor the sandstone cathedral, crumbling due to the weather, appealed to him, but he liked the cheese.

The soil is extraordinary good, and the grass, they say, has a peculiar richness in it, which disposes the creatures to give a vast quantity of milk, and that very sweet and good; and this cheese manufacture, for such it is, increases every day, and greatly enriches all the country; raises the value of the lands, and encourages the farmers to the keeping vast stocks of cows; the very number of cattle improving and enriching the land.

He meandered south to Shrewsbury, arriving at nightfall. After resting a few days in this 'beautiful, large, pleasant, populous and rich town', he set off along the old Roman road, Watling Street, 1,400 years old and still going strong, to Lichfield, 'a place of good conversation and good company'. Its cathedral, he announced with his journalist's flair for superlatives, was the most beautiful in England.

It is not easy to describe the beauty of the West End; you enter by three large doors in the porch, or portico, which is as broad as the whole front; the space between the doors are full of carved work and imagery, no place being void, where by the rules of architecture any ornament could be placed.

Paul Sandby's painting, depicting 'The Old Welsh Bridge' at Shrewsbury.

Defoe's next stop was Coventry. There had been an election there when he was first in the town in 1705 and the whole populace seemed to be rioting. 'Nor were these the scum and the rabble of the town but in short the burgesses and chief inhabitants, nay even the magistrates, aldermen and the like.'

In between elections the town made cheesecloth and ribbons. Coventry was old and much decayed, and reminded him of Cheapside before the Great Fire, 'the timber-built houses projecting forwards and towards one another, till in the narrow streets they were ready to touch one another at the top'.

Defoe, like Celia Fiennes, knew the story of Lady Godiva, but he was not taken in by the statue of the man turned blind by looking at her. 'Mr Camden says positively nobody looked at her at all.'

Six miles further on, by 'a very pleasant way on the banks of the River Avon, was Warwick. The castle stood solid, overlooking a beautiful landscape, but a fire in 1692 had destroyed the town. 'It is now rebuilt in so noble and so beautiful a manner that few towns in England make so fine an appearance.'

He rode east, crossed the Foss Way, passed through Daventry and came into Northampton. Northampton too had been the victim of a fire, ''tis now finely rebuilt with brick and stone, and the streets made spacious and wide. The great new church, the town hall, the gaol and all their public buildings, are the finest in any county town in England, being all new built.'

Turning north, through Market Harborough, along 'deep dismal roads, the dirtiest and worst in all that part of the country', he came to Leicestershire.

> The whole county seems to be taken up in country business, particularly in breeding and feeding cattle; the largest sheep and horses in England are found here, and hence it comes to pass too, that they are in consequence a vast magazine of wool for the rest of the nation; even most of the gentlemen are graziers, and in some places the graziers are so rich that they grow gentlemen.

He took the Foss Way north-east to Newark and across the Trent to Lincoln, 'an ancient, ragged, decayed and still decaying city; so full of the ruins of monasteries and religious houses the very barns, stables, outhouses and, as they showed me, some of the hog-sties were built church fashion'. He did not even think the cathedral was worth writing about, apart from its spectacular position, a landmark for five counties.

Putting Lincoln behind him, he rode north-east to Grimsby, then south through the Fens to Boston. 'This part is indeed very properly called Holland, for 'tis a flat, level and often drowned country, like Holland itself; here the very ditches are navigable, and the people pass from town to town in boats, as in Holland.' As he rode along he heard 'the uncouth music of the bittern', the long-legged wading bird of the Fens, whose call sounded to Defoe like a great groan.

Boston was 'a handsome well built seaport', and the church tower, the 'Boston Stump', seemed the highest in the country.

He continued through the Fens to Spalding and Crowland, where he saw the remains of the once mighty monastery. The water there was 'the colour of brewed ale' and the air close and fetid. The draining of the Fens was nearly complete. Giant windmill-like wind pumps, 'wonderful engines for throwing up water', stood out on the horizon. On the newly reclaimed fields grew acres of hemp.

He 'set foot on dry land' again at Peterborough. ''Tis remarkable that this church when a monastery was famous for its great revenues, so now, as reduced, 'tis one of the poorest bishoprics in England, if not the meanest.'

Here he turned sharply to the north up the Great North Road and made a short excursion to Grantham, 'famous for its very fine church and spire steeple, so finely built, and so very high, that I do not know many higher or finer built in Britain.'

> This is a neat, pleasant, well-built and populous town, has a good market, and the inhabitants are said to have a very good trade, and are generally rich. There is also a very good free school here. The town, lying on the great northern road, is famous, as

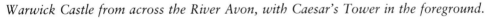

Warwick Castle from across the River Avon, with Caesar's Tower in the foreground.

well as Stamford, for abundance of very good inns, some of them fit to entertain persons of the greatest quality and their retinues, and that is a great advantage to the place.

He doubled-back down the Great North Road and came to Stamford, already old by the time the Romans left, with two markets and six parish churches. In the grounds adjoining the town was Burghley House, with so much on its roofline that it looked more like a country town than a country house. Verrio's 12-year repainting job was over. The state rooms were never to look so magnificent again. The maestro of commercial baroque had left the town, leaving behind discarded lovers and unpaid bills. After inspecting the great work, Defoe returned to the Great North Road and came down into Huntingdon.

> Here are the most beautiful meadows on the banks of the River Ouse, that I think are to be seen in any part of England; and to see them in the summer season, covered with such innumerable stocks of cattle and sheep, is one of the most agreeable sights of its kind in the world.

Turning right off the Great North Road, he came into Bedford, 'large, populous and thriving', with five parish churches, a bridge across the Ouse and a first-rate corn market. Fifteen miles away was Woburn, 'spacious and convenient rather than fine but exceedingly pleasant for its situation' and set amid oak trees 'as rich and valuable, as they are great and magnificent'. He rode on to St Albans, trotting past country people sitting by the roadside making bone-lace and straw hats. From there London was only a day away.

*   *   *

Britain south of the Trent had now been surveyed. What was left was rougher, less developed, and far less pretentious.

> The wildest part of the country is full of variety, the most mountainous places have their rarities to oblige the curious, and give constant employ to the enquiries of a diligent observer, making the passing over them more pleasant than the traveller could expect, or than the reader perhaps at first sight will think possible.

It was not entirely a wilderness, however, and the southern cities of Bristol, Exeter and Norwich were 'matched, if not outdone, by the growing towns of Liverpool, Hull, Leeds, Newcastle and Manchester'.

Defoe divided his survey of the north of England and Scotland into six letters, grouped around three journeys: the first through the North Midlands and Yorkshire; the second through the north-east of England to Edinburgh; and the third through the north-west of England and into the Scottish Highlands.

For his first two journeys he used Nottingham as his base. It was 'one of the most pleasant and beautiful towns in England', set on sandstone rock overlooking fine meadows.

> The Trent is navigable here for vessels or barges of great burden, by which all their heavy and bulky goods are brought from the Humber, and even from Hull; such as iron, block-tin, salt, hops, grocery, dyers' wares, wine, oil, tar, hemp, flax, etc, and the same vessels carry down lead, coal, wood, corn; as also cheese in great quantities, from Warwickshire and Staffordshire.

He left Nottingham and rode north into Sherwood Forest.

This forest does not add to the fruitfulness of the country, for 'tis now, as it were, given up to waste; even the woods which formerly made it so famous for thieves, are wasted; and if there was such a man as Robin Hood, a famous outlaw and deer-stealer, that so many years harboured here, we would hardly find shelter for one week, if he was now to have been there. Nor is there any store for deer, compared to the quantity which in former times they tell us was usually here.

He turned west, out of the forest, and came to Derby, where he followed the River Derwent – 'a frightful creature when the hills load her current with water' – into the Peak District. The hillsides he passed were punctured by lead mines. Once he came upon three children playing by a cave. Inside was a woman and two more children. It was her home. Her husband had been born in it, so had her children. 'The habitation was poor, 'tis true, but things within did not look so misery as I expected. Everything was clean and neat, though mean and ordinary. There were shelves with earthenware, and some pewter and brass.' Further on he encountered some of the miners. They were lean and pale, their complexions taking on the colour of the lead itself, and their accents were so thick that Defoe needed an interpreter.

If we blessed ourselves before, when we saw how the poor woman and her five children lived in the hole or cave in the mountain; we had much more room to reflect how much we had to acknowledge to our Maker, that we were not appointed to get our bread thus, one hundred and fifty yards underground, or in a hole as deep in the earth as the cross upon St Paul's cupola is high out of it. Nor was it possible to see these miserable people without such reflections, unless you will suppose a man is stupid and senseless as the horse he rides on.

He came to Chatsworth, stately amid the Peaks, its gardens, waterworks, statues, and interiors making 'a palace for a prince'. Beyond Chatsworth the Peaks rose up around him. 'This perhaps is the most desolate, wild and abandoned country in all of England.'

Chatsworth in Derbyshire, 'a most glorious and magnificent house', and its fountains.

He next turned east and came out of the Peak District into Sheffield. It was large, populous and very smoky; and had been making cutlery since before Chaucer's time. Since then it had broadened its base, manufacturing nails, swords, razors and axes. He left Sheffield, crossed the Don and rode through 'Black Barnsley' – black on account of the black hue of the moors, and blacker still from the smoke of the iron works. Ten miles on lay Wakefield, a 'clean, large, well-built town, very populous and very rich', with a cloth market every Friday. Though more populous than York, it was not legally even a town, and its highest official was a constable. Defoe's next stop was Rochdale, but the way was not easy – though easy to exaggerate.

> Here, though we were but at the middle of August, and in some places the harvest was hardly got in, we saw the mountains covered with snow, and felt the cold very acute and piercing; but even here we found, as in all those northern countries, the people had an extraordinary way of mixing the warm and the cold very happily together; for the store of good ale which flows plentifully in the most mountainous part of this country, seems abundantly to make up for all the inclemencies of the season.

Coming out of Rochdale the sun was shining, but once on the moors the rain poured down, and as Defoe and the little party he was travelling with ascended into the foothills of the Pennines, so came the snow.

> It is not easy to express the consternation we were in when we came up near the top of the mountain; the wind blew exceedingly hard, and blew the snow directly in our faces, and that so thick, that it was impossible to keep our eyes open to see our way. The ground also was covered with snow, that we could see no track, except when we were showed it by a frightful precipice on one hand, and uneven ground on the other; even our horses discovered their uneasiness at it; and a poor spaniel dog that was my fellow traveller, and usually diverted us with giving us a mark for our gun, turned tail of it and cried.

At last the wind and snow abated and they found themselves in a hollow at the foot of Blackstone Edge. They continued descending, and saw the faint outlines of a village in front of them. 'We thought now we had come into a Christian country again, and that our difficulties were over; but we soon found ourselves mistaken in the matter.' There were eight more snow-covered hills before Halifax. Defoe's exhausted party finally descended the eighth hill. The hillside was dotted with houses, each house a mill, and each mill utilizing a Pennine stream for the manufacture of cloth.

> The day clearing up, and the sun shining, we could see that almost at every house there was a tenter. I thought it was the most agreeable sight that I ever saw, the hills rising and falling so thick, and the valleys opening sometimes one way, sometimes another.

Halifax, in spite of its population which Defoe estimated as over 100,000, was only a parish, although it had sixteen Nonconformist meeting houses. The town's guillotine, of which Taylor had so approved and Fiennes so disapproved, had long gone, but the scaffold and base were still in place. There Defoe heard of the tradition whereby if a man could get his head out of the block, between the executioner releasing the cord and the blade coming down, and run down the hill without being caught by the executioner, he could keep his life. Defoe thought it impossible; but according to Halifax legend, one man not only succeeded but stopped halfway down the hill and called back to the crowd to throw him his hat.

He set off north-west. A vast conurbation stretched all the way to Leeds, one of the biggest cloth centres in the country, with a market that attracted buyers from as far away as Russia and America. Beyond Leeds Defoe's party found themselves travelling 'over a continued waste of black ill-looking desolate moors, over which travellers are guided, like race horses, by posts set up for fear of bogs and holes'. He stopped at Knaresborough, where, like Celia Fiennes, he tried the water. There were still four separate springs, each producing a different taste. Two he recommended: the Sweet Spa, whose medicinal properties had been popular since 1630, and the Stinking Spa, where Celia Fiennes had to hold her nose in order to down the purging water. Defoe thought it marvellous, and enthusiastically recommended it for 'hypochondriac distempers'.

Ripon, less than a day's ride away, he liked – it was 'a very neat, pleasant, well-built town, and has not only an agreeable situation on a rising ground between two rivers, but the market place is the finest and most beautiful square that is to be seen of its kind in England.'

Continuing north, across Wensleydale and Swaledale, he passed through Richmond, its castle slighted since the civil war, and across the River Tees ('a terrible river') to Barnard Castle, 'well-built but not large'. There, amid the Yorkshire Dales, where Bernard Baliol had built a castle in 1112, his descendant John Baliol had had it confiscated in 1295, Richard III had administered the North, Leland had admired the 'meetly pretty town' and John Taylor had rested his sore feet, Daniel Defoe brought his journey through the Peaks and the Pennines to an end.

*   *   *

Defoe returned to Nottingham and from there he set out on his journey through the north-east of England and south-east Scotland to Edinburgh and the Firth of Forth. He followed the River Trent to the Humber estuary, and the River Ouse to the city of York, where there was an abundance of unpretentious middle-class gentry, and the girls were more modest than in the south. It was a beautiful city, and the demolished fortifications had 'a reserved secret pleasantness in them for the contemplation of the public tranquility'. The bridge over the River Ouse contained an arch seventy feet wide, the widest in England. As for the minster, it was 'the beautifullest church of the old (i.e. Gothic) building in Britain'.

He left the city, riding along Walmgate, and headed south-east over moorland and sheepland to Beverley, whose 'great collegiate church is the main thing which ever did, and still does, make the town known in the world'. There were two beautiful churches, an almshouse and a free school, and 'pleasant springs running quite through its streets'. The main trades were malt-making, tanning and oatmeal, the poor scraping a living by working bone-lace. It had been a large cloth centre in the Middle Ages, but by the sixteenth century, when Leland passed through, it was already in decline.

Six miles on was Hull. It was one of the biggest ports in Europe, its ships carrying cloth from Leeds, lead from Derbyshire, butter from Yorkshire, cheese from Cheshire and corn from all the countries touched by the Trent, Ouse and Don. They sailed as far as Danzig, Riga and St Petersburg, returning with iron, copper, hemp, flax, canvas, linen, yarn and timber. Like Fiennes before him, Defoe saw the eskimo dummy and his sealskin kayak in the town hall. 'He was taken up at sea in a leather boat, which he sat in and was covered with skins, which drew together about his waist, so that the boat could never fill, and he could not sink; the creature would never feed nor speak, and so died.'

He made his way along the North Sea coast to Scarborough. Its main attraction was its spa. Daniel Defoe was an expert on spas. 'It is hard to describe the taste of the waters; they are apparently tinged with a collection of mineral salts, as of vitriol, alum, iron, and perhaps sulphur, and taste evidently of the alum.'

His destination was Durham. On the way he passed through Northallerton, which he liked. There was not a Tory in the town. He arrived in Durham:

> a little compact neatly contrived city, surrounded almost with the River Wear, which with the castle standing on an eminence, encloses the city in the middle of it; as the castle does also the cathedral, the bishop's palace, and the fine houses of the clergy, where they live in all the magnificence and splendour imaginable.

Many of the population were Catholics, 'who live peaceably and disturb nobody, and nobody them.'

Chester-le-Street, seven miles up the road, was dirty, 'empty of all remains of the greatness which antiquaries say it once had, when it was a Roman colony'.

> From hence the road to Newcastle gives a view of the inexhausted store of coals and coal pits, from whence not London only, but all the south part of England, is continually supplied; and whereas when we are at London, and see the prodigious fleets of ships which come constantly in with coals for this increasing city, we are apt to wonder whence they come, and that they do not bring the whole country away; so, on the contrary, when in this country we see the prodigious heaps, I might say mountains, of coal, which are dug up at every pit, and how many of those pits there are; we are filled with equal wonder to consider where the people should live that can consume them.

Newcastle was confined, overcrowded and covered with coal smoke, 'not the pleasantest place in the world to live in. It lay on both sides of the Tyne, the river crowded with coal ships, its banks lined with shipyards.

He was tempted to follow the route of Hadrian's Wall, but instead struck north into Northumberland, with the Cheviot Hills on his left, the North Sea on his right. His destination was Berwick-upon-Tweed – 'old, decayed, and neither populous nor rich' – and the Scottish border.

The border lay three miles beyond Berwick. The Great North Road climbed the brow of a hill, 'and I can truly say I never was sensible of so fierce a wind, so exceeding keen and cold, for it pierced our very eyes, that we could scarce bear to hold them open'. At the bottom of the hill the first town they came to was 'as perfectly Scots, as if it were 100 miles north of Edinburgh.'

Daniel Defoe knew Scotland. He had been paid to know it. He had been there in the reign of King William, and was sent there by Harley in 1706 as secret agent and propagandist to promote the union between the two countries. He ended up writing a book about it, returning to Scotland again and again. Defoe's view of Scotland was colonialist. He saw no hope for the country until it had been woken 'from thy long lethargic dream' by England; but he was an enlightened colonialist, convinced that union would only work on terms acceptable to the Scots. The Tory government's policy against the Jacobean Highlanders, a policy epitomized by the massacre at Glencoe, disgusted him.

Defoe and his little party found themselves on open moorland. 'For about eight miles you see hardly a hedge or a tree.' On the far side of the moor was Coldingham, where there had been an enormous monastery before the Reformation. They rode on.

Everywhere they passed through they were generously made welcome. The gentry of Scotland, Defoe decided, was the most civilized in Europe.

They kept to the coast road and came up to Dunbar. It was a handsome town beside a natural harbour, its cobbled quays built by Cromwell in 1650 after his army had defeated a Scottish force twice its size. The main industry was fishing and the main export smoked herrings. It was a pleasant place, but hardly somewhere to stay long. They left the town and continued through a 'fruitful and rich' country of rolling hillsides to Haddington. Defoe's only complaint was the lack of enclosures, preventing the sheep and cattle from renewing the soil with their manure and 'fattening the land'. Then he discovered that the locals used seaweed, which seemed just as effective. He followed the main road seven miles east to Haddington, 'an old half ruined, yet remaining town, which shows the marks of decayed beauty'. The main manufacturing was cloth, but by Defoe's last visit to Scotland the weavers were all English. The Scots cloth industry had been undercut and put out of business since the Union.

He rode along the shore of the Firth of Forth to Leith, the port of Edinburgh. All along the coast were villages and the homes of the gentry; the villagers employed in fishing, oyster collecting, coal mining and salt working. In Leith there was a factory for making bottles.

A 'spacious, rich and pleasant plain' lay between Leith and Edinburgh. They crossed the plain and came into the city past Holyroodhouse, casting their eyes over the policemen, 'clothed and armed as grenadiers', as they rode in. Though only just completed, Defoe found Holyroodhouse's early Palladian style distinctly old-fashioned: which is ironic, considering that the style was just coming back into vogue. In the palace grounds was an apothecaries' garden where a rhubarb bush grew.

From the palace the street went in an almost straight line for one and a half miles to the castle on the other side of the city: 'perhaps the largest, longest, and finest street for buildings and numbers of inhabitants, not only in Britain, but in all the world'. Here were the old St Giles' cathedral, built in the late fourteenth century. It was now the High Kirk of Scottish Presbyterianism, and its bells fascinated him.

> In the great tower of this church they have a set of bells, which are not rung out as in England, for that way of ringing is not known here but are played upon with keys, and by a man's hand, like a harpsichord; the person playing has great strong wooden cases

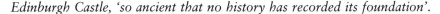

Edinburgh Castle, 'so ancient that no history has recorded its foundation'.

to his fingers, by which he is able to strike with the more force, and he plays several tunes very musically, though they are heard much better at a distance than near at hand.

South of the cathedral stood Parliament Close, the stateliest square in the city, its buildings including the parliament, law courts, council chamber, public library and treasury. At the far end of the street was the castle, 'of little use, unless for salutes and firing guns upon festivals'.

Edinburgh was not all to Defoe's liking – its sanitation was still medieval, the city was horribly overcrowded and at night the streets stank of excrement, left there to be cleared away in the morning. Yet he defended it from its English critics, who pronounced it barbarous.

> Were any other people to live under the same unhappiness, I mean as well as a rocky and mountainous situation, thronged with buildings from seven to ten or twelve storeys high, a scarcity of water, and that little they have difficult to be had, and to the utmost lodgings far to fetch, we should have a London or Bristol as dirty as Edinburgh; for though many cities have more people in them, yet I believe that in no city in the world so many people live in so little room.

*   *   *

Defoe's last journey was from Liverpool, through the north-east of England and the Scottish Highlands. Liverpool was the fastest-growing port in the kingdom. Its streets were clean, its houses well-built, its people industrious.

> The town was, at my first visiting it, about the year 1680, a large handsome well-built and increasing thriving town, at my second visit, anno 1690, it was much bigger than at my first seeing it, and, by the report of the inhabitants, more than twice as big as it were twenty years before that; but, I think, I may safely say at this my third seeing it, for I was surprised at the view, it was more than double what it was at the second; and, I am told that it still visibly increases both in wealth, people, business and buildings. What it may grow to in time, I do not know.

He left Liverpool and followed the Mersey to Warrington, where 'a stately stone bridge' crossed the river. Warrington was big, populous and had its own weekly linen market. He continued east to Manchester, rich from cotton, and 'one of the greatest, if not the greatest, mere village in England'. It was growing as quickly as Liverpool, there were new churches, new squares, new streets, as well as a college, a hospital, a free school and a library. Already the village was bigger than most cathedral cities. Here were 50,000 people, and not a single representative in Parliament.

Striking north-west through Bolton and Preston, he came to Lancaster, a town in ruins, with few people and less trade. North were the mountains of the Lake District, 'the wildest, most barren and frightful of any that I have passed over'. He came to Penrith, 'a handsome market town; and then, 'through a country full of castles, for almost every gentleman's house is a castle, we came to Carlisle, a small but well-furnished city, the frontier post'.

He crossed the River Esk and entered Scotland at Gretna Green, keeping to the coast road and passing through Annan, where there were good salmon in the River Annan and a steadily declining trade with Ireland and the Isle of Man. 'It was but a dull welcome into Scotland', and it was not until he got to Dumfries, a major port, that he saw any evidence of prosperity resulting from the Union. It shows Defoe's remarkable honesty that although he had worked actively for the Union, he never ignored the evidence against it.

Twelve miles upriver was Drumlanrig Castle, 'a fine picture in a dirty grotto'. It had been built between 1679 and 1691 by William Douglas, Duke of Queensberry, whose son negotiated the Union during Defoe's 1706 visit.

> He best understood his own design; for the house once laid out, all that unequal descent is so beautifully levelled and laid out in slopes and terraces, that nothing can be better designed, or indeed, better performed than the gardens are, which take up the whole south and west sides of the house; and, when the whole design will be done, the rest will be more easy, the ground being a plain the other way, and the park and avenues completely planted with trees.

He rode on, south-west to Kirkcudbright, once a busy port on the banks of the Dee. Now it was 'a harbour without ships, a port without trade, a fishery without nets, a people without business'. Further along the coast was the Rhinns of Galloway, the hammer-shaped peninsula poised to strike Ireland. Soon sick of Galloway and its rough and wild landscape, Defoe continued up the coast, north now to Ayr. The further he went, the more fruitful and cultivated the country became. It was 'the pleasantest county in Scotland', the capital Ayr 'showing the ruins of a good face'. Irvine, further up the coast, was more prosperous, thanks to the coal trade with Ireland. The streets were handsome and there was a good quay crowded with ships.

He passed through Renfrewshire, 'pleasant, rich and populous', and came to Greenock on the Clyde. It was the centre of the herring industry, 'and where the ships ride that come into and go out of Glasgow, just as the ships for London do in the Downs'.

> The country between Paisley and Glasgow, in the bank of the Clyde, I take to be one of the most agreeable places in Scotland. Take its situation, its fertility, healthiness, and nearness of Glasgow, the neighbourhood of the sea, and altogether, at least, I may say, I saw none like it.

Continuing up the south bank of the Clyde, he crossed the river on horseback at low tide and came into Glasgow.

> Glasgow is, indeed, a very fine city; the four principal streets are the fairest for breadth, and the finest built that I have ever seen in one city together. The houses are all of stone, and generally equal and uniform in height, as well as in front; the lower storey generally stands on vast square Doric columns, not round pillars, and arches between give passage into the shops, adding to the strength as well as beauty of the building; in a word, 'tis the cleanest and beautifullest, and best built city in Britain, London excepted.

It stood on a hill, sloping down to the river. There was a market place where the four main streets met. On the north-east corner of the crossing was the Tolbooth and Guildhall, marked by a seven-storey tower. North of the market was the university, 'a very spacious building' containing two courts. Beyond the university rose St Mungo's, the cathedral. It had two west towers and the highest spire in Scotland.

It was a city of business, and it was doing well out of the Union, 'though the rabble in Glasgow made the most formidable attempts to prevent it'. The city's main business came from trade across the Atlantic, and Glasgow sent fifty ships a year to the New World, bringing back cotton, sugar and tobacco. In return the city exported servants:

> and these they have in greater plenty, and upon better terms than the English; without the scandalous art of kidnapping, making drunk, wheedling, betraying, and the like; the poor people offering themselves fast enough, and thinking it their advantage to go; as indeed it is, to those who go with sober resolutions to serve out their time, and become diligent planters for themselves.

He made his way over Campsie Fells to Stirling, crossing the River Carron on the way.

> Great stones, square and formed, as if cut out by hand, of a prodigious size, some of them at least a ton, or ton and a half in weight, lay scattered, and confusedly, as it were, jumbled together in the very course of the river, which the fury of the water, at other times, I doubt not, had hurried down from the mountains, and tumbled them thus over one another.

Daniel Defoe came down into the valley of the Forth, passing the village of Bannockburn, and saw Stirling, a castle on a crag, on his right. The view from the castle's battlements of the Forth Valley, and the wide river meandering through it, had nothing to compare to it in all Europe.

He rode along the south bank of the Forth to Linlithgow. The palace was far less decayed than most of the other great buildings in Scotland. He liked the town.

> The people look here as if they were busy, and had something to do, whereas in many towns we passed through they seemed as if they looked disconsolate for want of employment. The whole green, fronting the lough or lake, was covered with linen-cloth, it being the bleaching season, and, I believe, a thousand women and children, and not less, tending and managing the bleaching business.

From Linlithgow he rode twenty-five miles to Lanark, and made his way east along the valley of the Tweed. The hills on either side were thickly dotted with sheep, the wool sent to England, 'to the irrepairable damage of the poor; who, were they employed to manufacture their own wool, would live much better than they do'.

He passed the ruins of Melrose Abbey, 'the greatness of which may be a little judged of by its vastly extended remains'.

> The building is not so entirely demolished but that we may distinguish many parts of it: the great church or chapel of the monastery, which is as large as some cathedrals, the court, the cloister. But the Reformation has triumphed over these things, and the pomp of Popery is sunk now into the primitive simplicity of the true Christian profession. So I leave Melrose with a singular satisfaction at seeing what it now is, much more than that of remembering what it once was.

He returned north to Edinburgh, where he enjoyed the last comforts of civilization before venturing into the Highlands – still tribal, still unpacified, still unmapped, 'the true and real Caledonia'.

He left Edinburgh by boat across the Forth at Queensferry, and rode five miles to Dunfermline, once the capital of Scotland, now 'a perfect picture of decay'. He set off the following morning east along the coast to the Marquis of Tweedsdale's pile at Aberdour Castle. It was 'old and magnificent', facing the Firth of Forth, its terraces dropping down to the estuary.

From Aberdour he turned north to Kinross, where he looked out over Loch Leven at the island castle and fourteenth-century tower house where Mary, Queen of Scots had been held captive before her escape in 1568. By the western shores, close to Kinross itself, was Kinross House, the town 'a little distance from it, so as not to annoy the house'. It had been built by the architect Sir William Bruce, 'the Kit Wren of North Britain'. 'The house is a picture, 'tis all beauty; the stone is white and fine, the order regular, the contrivance elegant, the workmanship exquisite.'

His excursion to Kinross over, he returned to the Firth of Forth, at Burntisland. There was a good harbour. 'But want of trade renders all this useless; for what is the best harbour in the world without ships? And whence should ships be expected without commerce to employ them? The place is unhappy, and must decay yet further.'

The next village on the coast was Kinghorn, where, among other activities, the town earned a living by shooting porpoises. Only Kirkcaldy, a few miles to the north, showed any benefits from the Union. It was 'a larger, more populous and better built town than any other, and indeed than any on this coast'. Corn and linen were shipped to England and Holland, and there were small but efficient coal and salt industries. The coal mines multiplied the further Defoe went along the coast.

> The people who work in the coal mines in this country, what with the dejected countenances of the man, occasioned by their poverty and hard labour, and what with the colour or discolouring, which comes from the coal, both to their clothes and complexions, are indeed frightful fellows at first sight.

He followed the coastline to the North Sea before turning north himself for St Andrews, a university and cathedral city, in spite of its tiny size. The old cathedral here was a noble structure, longer than St Paul's in London by twenty-five feet. 'The building is now sunk into a simple parish church.'

St Andrews's steadily dilapidating cathedral, 'ancient pieces mourning their own decay'.

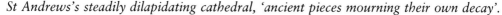

'The colleges are handsome buildings, and well supplied with men of learning in all sciences, who govern the youth they instruct with reputation.' It was a very ancient university. There were three colleges: St Salvadore, the oldest, opened in 1456, St Leonard's, a Benedictine abbey until the Reformation, and St Mary's, a postgraduate college, where King Charles I once held a parliament.

Soon he was following the Firth of Tay to Perth.

> The chief business of this town is the linen manufacture; and it is so considerable here, all the neighbouring country being employed in it, that it is a wealth for the whole place. This town was unhappily, for some time, the seat of the late rebellion; but I cannot say it was unhappy for the town, for the townswomen got so much money from both parties.

He explored the country inland, then rode about a mile north from Perth to Scone Palace, where the Kings of Scotland had once been crowned and the Old Pretender held court during his fruitless rebellion of 1715.

From Scone he mounted his horse and rode east along the Firth of Tay's north coast to Dundee, 'a pleasant, large and populous city, that well deserves the title Bonny Dundee'. The market place in the middle was the largest and fairest in Scotland after Aberdeen, and the merchants, who shipped corn and linen to Scandinavia and Holland, and herrings to the Baltic, were all gentlemen.

A half-day in the saddle took him to Montrose. The way was pleasant, the country fruitful and the people civilized. They were English settlers who had taken over lands forfeited from rebels. Forty miles further along the coast came Aberdeen. There were two parts to it, Old Aberdeen and New Aberdeen, each on the mouth of a river, the Dee and the Don, about a mile from one another. There were two colleges, one in the old town and one in the new, a beautiful and spacious market place and a cathedral. Defoe liked Aberdeen, both Old and New, and he approved of the predominantly Presbyterian people's religious tolerance towards those who, in England, would be worshipping in the Church of England: a tolerance that would never have been matched by the Anglican authorities in England at the time.

He continued along the coast past Peterhead and around Kinnairds Head, and turned with the coastline sharp west to Elgin and the Moray Firth. It was 'a pleasant country, the soil fruitful, watered with fine rivers and full of good towns'. Across the River Spey he noticed the land becoming flatter and the climate milder. 'Nor is the forwardness of the season the only testimony of the goodness of the soil here; but the crops are large, the straw strong and tall, and the ear full'.

He rode through Elgin, where 'the cathedral shows, by its ruins, that it was a place of great magnificence', to Inverness, a garrison town at the north-east end of Loch Ness, controlling the only bridge across the loch and the River Ness for miles.

> Oliver Cromwell thought it a place of such importance that he built a strong citadel here and kept a stated garrison always in it, and sometimes more than a garrison, finding it needful to have a large body of his own veteran troops posted here to preserve the peace of the country and keep the Highlands in awe.

Many of the soldiers had settled in the vicinity, which accounted for the English accents of the population.

> When you are over this bridge you enter that which we truly call the north of Scotland, and others the north Highlands; in which are several different shires, but cannot call

for a distinct description, because it is all one undistinguished range of mountains and woods, overspread with vast and almost uninhabited rocks and steeps filled with deer innumerable.

He was now in the wildest, most remote and most desolate part of Britain – barren range upon barren range, as far as the eye could see. The life of the people who lived there matched the landscapes. You could not avoid the poverty. The houses were hovels, with walls of turf or dry stone, the children went barefoot, and the men, as if to compensate for their humiliations, carried swords all the time. There was no law but tribal law, while the tribal chiefs ruled like petty monarchs, keeping their tribesmen in abject poverty to pay for their retinues and petty wars. It was a 'frightful country'.

Our geographers seem to be almost as much at a loss in the description of this north part of Scotland, as the Romans were to conquer it; and they are obliged to fill it up with hills and mountains, as they do the inner parts of Africa, with lions and elephants, for want of knowing what else to place there.

The western Highlands and the Western Isles were even wilder, the people more primitive, and the English more unpopular. The accent of the natives was quite impossible to fathom.

We could understand nothing on this side of what the people said, any more than if we had been in Morocco; and all the remedy we had was, that we found most of the gentlemen spoke French, and some spoke broad Scots; we found it also much to our convenience to make the common people believe we were French.

The people, 'poor abandoned creatures', were hardly Christians. Missionaries were as urgently needed in Scotland as they were in Africa. What religion there was, was due to 'the diligence of the Popish clergy, who to do them justice, have shown more charity, and taken more pains that way, than some whose work it has been, and who it might much more have been expected from'.

After a visit to the coast opposite the Isle of Skye he came down with his guides to Fort William, at the bottom of the Great Glen, which, with Fort Augustus and Inverness, completely sealed the north of Scotland from the rest of Britain. The garrison commander, Lieutenant-General James Maitland, was an enlightened soldier. 'This wise commander did more to gain the Highlanders and keep them in peace, and in a due subjection to the British government, by his winning and obliging behaviour, and yet by strict observance of his orders, and the duty of a governor, than any other before him had been able to do by force and the sword.'

He turned south-east and came down through the Grampians.

The Grampian mountains, which are here said to cut through Scotland, as the Muscovites say of their Riphaean hills, that they are the girdle of the world. As is their country, we are the inhabitants, a fierce fighting and furious kind of men; so I must add that they are much changed and civilized from what they were formerly. And though the country is the same, and the mountains as wild and desolate as ever, yet the people, by the good conduct of their chiefs and heads of clans, are much more civilized than they were in former times.

It was the last great mountain range Defoe had to encounter. Ahead lay Edinburgh and, beyond Edinburgh, London. He was coming back into civilization. His *Tour through the Whole Island of Great Britain* was complete.

6
RURAL REVOLUTIONARY

He came from farming stock, born in 1741, the youngest of four children and always a little spoilt. His father, a modest though trifle obsessive clergyman, he had little affection for. About his mother he felt differently. 'Her kindness and affection for me never failed the course of her life.' The family farm was at Bradfield Combust, a few miles south-east of Bury St Edmunds. The father, somewhat eccentrically, spent his only inheritance pulling the house down and rebuilding it according to exactly the same plan, so there was 'not a single room free from every fault that could be found, whether as to chimneys, doors, windows and connecting passages'. At the age of nine, in danger of becoming a mother's boy, he was sent to boarding school in Lavenham. Arthur Young hated it.

The boy proved unsatisfactory. He was sent to be apprenticed to a wine merchant in King's Lynn. Arthur Young hated that too. His only consolation was a pamphlet he had written on the French wars in America. It had been well received. He wrote another one on America in general. It was a disaster. 'The reflections of a youth aged 15,' wrote the *Gentleman's Magazine*. Young was stung. He was already eighteen and a half. He came to London, 'without education, profession or employment, and started a magazine, *The Universal Museum*. It was another disaster. So he took over the family farm at Bradfield Combust. 'I had no more idea of farming than of physics or divinity.'

He began reading books on farming. It was the high point of the agricultural revolution. He believed everything. 'There is fifty times more lustre in the waving ears of corn, which cover a formerly waste acre, than in the most glittering star that shines.' Later he was to recant, like so many others in middle age, calling his revolutionary fervour 'nothing but folly, presumption and rascality'; but at the time things looked different – they always do.

The enclosing of England was on the way to completion. The population had risen from 5 million in Defoe's day to 7.5 million in Young's. As the population increased, so did the poor, though at a higher rate, driven from the land so rapidly being enclosed. For Arthur Young the poor had to be sacrificed for the agricultural revolution. They were perfectly happy with their diet of black bread, cheese, potatoes, soup and beer; and if they spent their money on tea – 'which impairs the vigour of the constitution and debilitates the human mind' – they had nobody but themselves to blame.

He began writing on the revolution. His first success was *A Farmer's Letters*. 'Too much praise cannot be said in recommendation of these letters,' wrote the *Gentleman's Magazine* in 1667.

Young had already been married for two years. 'The colour of my life was decided in 1765,' he wrote ambiguously. His wife was Martha Allen, whom he had met in King's Lynn. It was not a happy marriage at first, and the lack of money made it unhappier. They moved to a new farm at Stampford Hall in Essex, 'a noble farm of 300 acres'. It was far too large, and now he had two daughters to support. 'Young, eager and totally ignorant, it is not surprising that I squandered much money under golden dreams of improvements: especially as I connected a thirst for experiment without the knowledge of what an experiment demands.'

Short of money as usual, and able to pay bills only by producing a steady stream of agricultural publications, he determined to find another farm. He took out advertisements in the newspapers for land in the southern half of England. His replies were so numerous that it took six weeks in June and July 1767 to view them all. With bills piling up, and never a writer to miss an opportunity, he turned the experience into a book: *A Six Weeks Tour through the Southern Counties of England and Wales*.

*   *   *

His aim was clear:

> to display to one part of the kingdom the practice of the other, to remark wherein such practice is hurtful, and wherein commendable, to draw forth such spirited examples of good husbandry from obscurity, and display them the proper objects of imitation.

It was not all agriculture, however. Arthur Young may have been an unprofessional farmer, but he was a professional writer, always willing to give the public what it wanted; and what it wanted was obvious. Doing stately homes had been fashionable for over a decade. Thousands of the respectable upper-middle-class passed from one stately home to the next, pronouncing vulgar anything they could not afford themselves. Some houses were so popular that the owners had to limit the opening times: Chatsworth two days a week, Woburn on Mondays, and Keddleston from twelve to two on weekdays. Some, like Holkham, Houghton and Wilton, published their own guide books. Holkham was so popular that visitors had to stand in a queue in the vestibule. Lady Beauchamp Proctor was disgusted.

> Nothing could have been more disagreeable than this situation: we all stared at each other, and not a creature opened their mouths. Some of the Masters amused themselves with trying to throw their hats upon the heads of the busts, whilst the Misses scrutinized one another's dresses.

Stately gardens were just as popular, though fashions in gardens changed even more quickly than those in houses. The formal Dutch gardens so beloved by Defoe were already out before he had written his *Tour*, Joseph Addison announcing in 1712 that he preferred artificial rudeness to 'neatness and elegance'. Pope concurred. 'All gardening is landscape painting.' The new style's finest exponent was William Kent. 'Mr Kent always used to stake out his grovettes before they planted and to view the stakes every way, to see that no three of them stand in line,' a professor of poetry at Oxford recalled. Inevitably the trend towards Nature reached its most unnatural conclusion: a perfect imitation of Nature. Capability Chic. Soon serpentine lakes were replacing straight canals and man-made hillocks, burying geometrical lawns in a carefully arranged wilderness tamed by classical temples, Greek goddesses and naked obelisks. Classical gardens were the most common, but they were not *de rigueur*. There were Chinese gardens with pagodas, dragons and latticework bridges, growing out of the *chinoiserie* fad in the middle of the century; and Turkish gardens for the admirers of Lady Mary Wortley Montagu. Sir William Chambers wrote a book on the Oriental garden.

Holkham in Norfolk was Arthur Young's first stop after his departure from the family home at Bradfield Combust. He deposited his bags at the Leicester Arms in the village of Holkham, which looked out on a landscape of sea, sand and pine trees, and rode down the main street, which got more main as the line of cottages disappeared and it became the main drive into Holkham Hall. Just in case any of the visitors were to mistake the spot where the village ended and the grounds began, there was a triumphal arch. The drive was long, very long. A mile and a half on was an obelisk. From there he could see the south front of the house, the spire of Holkham church rising about the trees on the summit of a hill, the triumphal arch, acres of plantations, and Wells-next-the-Sea, 'a parcel of scattered houses appearing in the wood'.

Holkham Hall was a Palladian palace, built of extraordinarily ugly, dull pink bricks and only just complete. It was magnificent, and beautiful from a distance, though – 'Will you excuse these criticisms from one who knows nothing of architecture, but the power of pleasing the taste of individuals?' – spoilt only by the rather tatty line of top windows.

It had been started by Thomas Coke, Earl of Leicester, in 1734 (his great-grandson and heir, the future Coke of Norfolk, who picked up the banner of the agricultural revolution from Arthur Young, was only fifteen years old during his mentor's visit). He had been on the Grand Tour. It showed. The hall was a 48-foot cube, lined with Greek statuary, carrying a gallery of Ionic columns and clad in polished pink alabaster. The saloon was a mere half the size, but still enormous, with 'a proportion much condemned but by no means displeasing to me'. There was furniture by William Kent, crimson wall-hangings and a profusion of ceiling carvings. The other rooms were equally overdressed, their marble walls extravagantly wasted behind Brussels tapestries and Renaissance paintings. In paintings, as in houses, Young had fashionable tastes. He liked Cignani's 'Joseph and Potiphar's Wife', Van Dyke's 'Duke of Aremberg', Salvator Rosa's 'Rock', Claude Lorrain's landscapes and Parmegiano's 'Woman in the Cave'. Titian's 'Venus' was 'hard and disagreeable', and the Mary in Rubens's 'Flight into Egypt' 'a female mountain'. The statue gallery, its Venetian windows looking out on Capability Brown's grounds, was 'without exception the most beautiful room I ever beheld'. Arthur Young may not have known much about art, but he knew what he liked. 'The *Venus* in wet drapery is exquisite, nothing can exceed the manner in which the form of the limbs is seen through the clothing.'

Houghton, which rivalled Holkham in 'taste, expense, state and parade', was only a few miles away.

> All the country from Holkham to Houghton was a wild sheep-walk before the spirit of improvement seized the inhabitants; and this glorious spirit has wrought amazing effects; for instead of boundless wilds and uncultivated wastes, inhabited by scarce anything but sheep; the country is all cut into enclosures, cultivated in a most husband-like manner, richly manured, well-peopled, and yielding a hundred times the product that it did in its former state.

Houghton Hall, classical enough for a statesman and vulgar enough for a politician.

It had been built for Sir Robert Walpole in 1722, the work of Colen Campbell, James Gibbs and Thomas Ripley. Walpole, who had paid for it, hardly lived there, except for three weeks each autumn. Now, owned by the former Prime Minister's unstable grandson, the Third Earl of Offord, it was fading, its finest works sold, its rooms dilapidated and open to the weather, and the beautiful lawns trampled over by horses.

The approach was magnificent, though, and lined by plantations, 'with openings left judiciously in many places to let in the view of more distant woods, which changes the shade, and gives them that solemn brownness'.

The house, a central block, crowned on its corners by domes and cupolas, and faced entirely in stone, was as magnificent, but the inside was a disappointment. The hall was another cube, graced with the kinds of statues you would expect from a class that regarded Greek deities as honorary Englishmen. A balcony 'pushed out in defiance of all the ideas of grace, elegance or proportion' surrounded three sides of it. The cherubs frolicking on the ceiling were quite unnecessarily vulgar.

The saloon cheered him up. It was softer and warmer, with a fireplace relief of 'The Sacrifice of Bacchus' by Rysbrack; 'one of the finest rooms in the world'. Off it was a drawing room, the walls adorned with the paintings of Carlo Maratta. The house-keeper took Young from room to room. It was difficult walking, looking, listening, consulting the guide book and making notes all at the same time. The doors, doorcases, windows, ceilings, sculptures and mantlepieces followed each other so quickly that it was impossible to remember one from the other. Rembrandts, Rubens, Titians, Marattas, Poussins, Van Dycks, Guidos and Salvator Rosas vied for attention.

He spent the night at King's Lynn, where he stayed at the Duke's Head. It was 'civil and reasonable'. Next morning he rode south through Thetford, where he slept at the

Bell. The third day from Houghton took him to Bury St Edmunds, where he stayed at the Angel. It was 'very civil and reasonable'.

> The road to that town lies for some miles over a wild heath, overrun with bushes, the wild luxuriance of whose growth displays evidently enough how greatly it would answer to break it up and convert it into arable farms.

He had dual feelings about Bury, for it had been his local town.

> Bury is a tolerable well built town, in a dry and healthy situation; many of the streets cutting each other at right angles; but a parcel of dirty thatched houses are found in different streets not far from the centre of the town, which has a very bad effect.

He rode south in his chaise across country, first to his old home at Bradfield Combust and then to Lavenham, where he stayed at the Swan. He had dual feelings about Lavenham too. He had spent eight hateful years at school there. He meandered on through East Anglia, inspecting progressive farms on the way. The Reverend Tanner's lucerne crop at Hadleigh, which he passed through on 19 June 1767, was particularly praiseworthy. West of Hadleigh was Sudbury, rich from wool, 'an exceedingly dirty but a great manufacturing town'.

Suffolk ended and Essex began. There were hop and barley fields on either side of the road. At Lord Clare's farm near Braintree he was pleased to see oxen pulling ploughs. It was the only place in the south-east that he saw them. Elsewhere farmers were still using teams of horses, an inefficient, extravagant and barbarous custom. He went on to Billericay, 'the country very rich, woody and pleasant, with abundance of exceeding fine landscapes over extensive valleys'. The road, needless to say, was appalling.

> Of all the cursed roads that ever did disgrace this kingdom in the very ages of barbarianism, none ever equalled that from Billericay to the King's Head at Tilbury. It is for near 12 miles so narrow, that a mouse cannot pass by any carriage; I saw a fellow creep under his waggon to assist me to lift my chaise over a hedge. The trees everywhere overgrow the road, so that it is totally impervious to the sun; and to add to all the infamous circumstances which concur to plague a traveller, I must not forget the

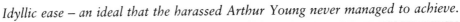

Idyllic ease – an ideal that the harassed Arthur Young never managed to achieve.

eternal meeting with chalk waggons, themselves frequently stuck fast, till a collection of them are in the same situation, and 20 or 30 horses may be tacked to each, to draw them out, one by one.

Tilbury bored him, and after a short excursion across the estuary to Gravesend ('Wapping in miniature'), he was driving through London, coming out on the other side of the Oxford road. All the way through west London there were market gardens, and in Acton he saw tidy fields of peas and beans. He came to High Wycombe, passing the night at the 'exceedingly good, civil and not unreasonable' Antelope. The farms were large, their fields abundant in turnips, barley, clover and wheat, all the crops rotated in the theoretically correct manner.

He went on to Oxford, resting for the night at the Angel. The country was 'extremely disagreeable, barren, wild and almost uninhabited'. He spent a day in Oxford. Most of it he dismissed as 'second-rate Gothic', but he marvelled at the new front quad for Queen's and at Gibbs's Radcliffe Camera, before continuing to Blenheim, where he stayed at the Bear.

From the Bear he went to the Elephant, the white baroque elephant of Blenheim Palace: 'a pile raised at the expense of the public, and meant to be great and magnificent, and would have been effected, had not the execution fell to such a miserable architect as Vanbrugh; whose buildings are monuments to bad taste'.

Inside Blenheim, the saloon was altogether too magnificent; the ceiling, painted by Laguerre, showing the four continents and the duke himself in the middle, was held up by a colonnade of classical columns. He admired the drawing room leading off it through a marble doorway. Its walls were lined with paintings by Rubens: 'Holy Family', 'Roman Charity', 'Virgin and Child', 'Flight into Egypt', 'The Three Wise Men', 'Lot Driven Out of Sodom', 'Christ Blessing the Children' and 'Pope Gregory the Great'. In the breakfast room were more paintings by Rubens, and three by Rembrandt; while in the rooms leading off from the other side of the saloon were paintings by Giordano, Holbein and Brueghel. It was not all bad, though. The library, where there was a statue of Queen Anne by Rysbrack, was 'the noblest room applied to this use I ever saw'.

He liked the grounds by Capability Brown – 200 acres of temples, grottoes, pyramids and obelisks – but found the Rialto 'a most miserably heavy, ungracious piece of architecture'. Finally, to ensure that Arthur Young did not merely dislike Blenheim, but hated it, the servants showing him round complained at the meagreness of his tip.

He drove his chaise west through fields of wheat, beans and barley to Witney on the edge of the Cotswolds, a prosperous wool town doing booming business with the North American colonies. His horses dragged the chaise through some of the worst roads he had encountered. One even had the gall to call itself a turnpike.

He found the Cotswolds 'dull and disagreeable'. Beyond Stow, the land improved, tightly constricted by checkerboard patterns of dry stone walling. Here the horses pulling the plough gave way to oxen, an infinitely more efficient beast of burden. Soon he reached the Vale of Gloucester. There was a spectacular view from Crickley Hill, 'a complete piece of sublime nature, well worthy of attention from those whose nerves will suffer them to relish those sorts of objects'. He continued to Gloucester, where he was told that the manufacture of pins employed 'near 400 hands, of whom a great number are women and children'.

'The same stony, hard, rough and cursed roads, miscalled turnpikes' went all the way from the River Severn to the Forest of Dean, jolting the chaise and cutting the horses' hoofs. He liked the country, 'very hilly and picturesque', and Chepstow was 'one of the sweetest valleys I ever beheld'.

He crossed the border into Wales and followed the coast to Cardiff on roads as bad as those in the Cotswolds and the Forest of Dean. 'Whatever business brings you into this country, avoid it, at least until they have good roads.' He felt the same about the Welsh, a nation of peasants, too conservative to learn.

He drove his chaise across the Brecon Beacons to Monmouth. Some of the way took him through 'a landscape too beautiful for such a daubing pencil as mine to attempt to paint', which 'might make amends for the want of a Claude Lorrain'. From Monmouth he came down the River Wye. Mountains, valley and river were:

> wonderfully romantic, and what makes the whole picture perfect, is being entirely surrounded by vast rocks and precipices, covered thick with wood, down to the very water's edge. The whole is an amphitheatre, which seems dropped from the clouds, complete in all its beauty.

Young returned to Chepstow, crossed the Severn and took the road to Bristol. Three miles from Bristol he stopped at Mr Champion's copper-works. The liquid ore reminded him of the eruptions of Mount Vesuvius. 'All the machines and wheels are set in motion by waters; for raising which there is a prodigious fire engine, which raises, it is said, thirty hogsheads every minute.'

Beyond Bristol the land declined in quality, he noted. He stayed little in Bath, for it was insufficiently agricultural to justify more than a passing glance. The city was one vast Georgian building site. Still, it 'greatly exceeds London in regularity of building, and in being proportionately a much finer city; the Circus is truly beautiful, and ornamented in just such an elegance which, if I may be allowed the expression, lies between profusion and simplicity'.

He followed the River Kennet to Devizes and drove south across Salisbury Plain, 'a dreary tract of country', to Salisbury. 'The flocks of sheep they keep on the plain, I believe, are the greatest in England.' A few miles before Salisbury he stopped at Wilton House.

Coming up to it he understood why the Inigo Jones façade was reckoned so fine, though the famous Palladian bridge disappointed him. He climbed out of the chaise and looked around him, selecting what he saw with a weary traveller's eye. 'In one of the niches of a pedestal in the inner court is a statue of Venus picking a thorn out of her foot; the turn of the body is inimitable and the expression of the pain in her countenance, fine.'

He arrived in Salisbury, exhausted, and stayed at the Three Lions.

> Salisbury is one of the prettiest towns in England, the market place is well-built, the whole exceedingly clean, and with one circumstance I never observed in any other place, a small transparent stream runs through every street, in many of them two, one on each side instead of gutters. The effect of this in cleanliness and beauty is very great.

He liked Salisbury, and could have stayed there longer; but the roads to Winchester were surprisingly good, and when he came to Farnham he found himself surrounded by hop fields.

> The country is a very pleasant one, a due mean between a hilly and a flat one; the small risings give a variety, and open to agreeable landscapes; and the number of scattered houses and villages render it lively, particularly as they are so neat.

The convenience of being male: a study by the eighteenth-century artist, Paul Sandby.

From Farnham the soil was weak and sandy all the way to London. On the other side of the city, on the Epping road, he went into raptures over the potatoes, 'which afforded me a pleasure superior to that which any palace could confer'. Appalling roads led him to Chelmsford, and took him on to Bradfield Combust. He arrived there on 23 July 1767. His chaise had covered 600 miles.

*   *   *

The farm Young finally chose, after his six-week tour, was Bradmore Farm in North Mimms, near Hatfield. Even here he was not satisfied. 'A nabob's fortune would sink in an attempt to raise good arable crops,' he exclaimed, in between churning out pamphlets to pay for his agricultural experiments. Worse than that, he discovered he no longer loved his wife. He started going to London, where he developed an obsession for Hetty Burney, sister of Fanny Burney, who was living off Poland Street in Soho. The Burneys were related to the Youngs by marriage. He had failed in farming and now he was failing in marriage. So to escape the one, he packed up his bags and left North Mimms; and to save the other he took his wife with him. This time, however, it was not a six-week tour, it was a six-month one: and Martha Young was pregnant.

On his six-week tour he stayed at inns. For a six-month tour, with a pregnant wife, he preferred something more comfortable, and less expensive. So he inserted advertisements in the London newspapers.

> The author of the *Six Weeks Tour through the Southern Counties of England and Wales*, proposing to undertake this summer a TOUR through the North of England, begs leave to request such of the nobility, gentry, landlords, farmers and others, as possess, or are acquainted with, any particular improvements, experiments, customs, implements etc in the agriculture of the following counties, *viz.* Hertfordshire, Bedfordshire, Huntingdonshire, Northamptonshire, Rutlandshire, Leicestershire, Nottinghamshire, Lincolnshire, Derbyshire, Yorkshire, Durham, Northumberland, Cumberland, Westmoreland, Lancashire, Cheshire, Shropshire, Staffordshire, Worcestershire, Warwickshire and Buckinghamshire.

There were few replies, but then there is no such thing as a free lunch. He set out all the same from North Mimms in June 1768, driving along 'wretched roads' to Luton, where they turned off the road to look over Luton Hoo.

The approach was exquisite. The house was the home of the Earl of Bute, and was being rebuilt by Robert Adam. The grounds – 1,500 acres of 'hill, dale, wood and water' – were a delight. In the lower of the two lakes were a couple of pleasure boats and a full-sized sloop with flying colours.

Rough roads over a gravelly loam soil took them to Dunstable, where the local industries were basket-weaving, hat-making and box-manufacturing, and on to Woburn, where the modernization by Flintcroft had just been completed.

> The house forms a large quadrangle, with a handsome court in the centre. Behind are two quadrangles of offices, distinct from the house, which are very beautiful buildings; plain and simple, but extremely proper for their destination. They are built like the house of white stone. In the centre of the principal fronts is a small dome rising over a porticoed centre supported by Tuscan pillars, which have a very good effect.

Young marched through the house, with his long-suffering wife waddling along behind him. The Rysbrack mantlepieces, the paintings, the tapestries and the rococo ceilings came and went as the Tavistocks' servant took them from room to room. The grotto, a pre-Flintcroft survival of the 1630 Woburn, was pretty for what it was, he thought, but its bas-reliefs in shell seemed strangely incongruous.

The silent couple explored the grounds. There was a great glade cut through the park for several miles, at the end of which was a Chinese temple, large enough for thirty people to dine in.

They took the road to Bedford, 'if I may venture to call such a cursed string of hills and holes by the name of road'. All along the way they passed fields of beans. Bedford was thriving, thanks to the Ouse being made navigable, but Arthur Young found it merely uninteresting, 'noted for nothing but its lace manufactory, which employs five hundred women and girls'.

He was surprised how good the road was on the way to St Neots. The sandy soil had a rich black texture, and there were lots of carrots, always a good sign. He turned north for Stamford. The land was open and unenclosed. On a hill near Kimbolton he counted twelve steeples.

Stamford was pretty, a 'well-built town, all of stone, a quarry lying under the whole country'. They wandered the streets between lines of weather-beaten grey stone houses, and crossed the bridge to inspect Burghley House. There were lots of paintings. He liked the Poussins.

They took the road north to Grimsthorpe, 'the country mostly open and the roads extremely bad'. He looked over the Duke of Ancester's park and pile at Grimsthorpe Castle and pronounced it magnificent. Possibly he did not realize it was by Vanbrugh.

They now continued to Grantham. The way was 'picturesque and beautiful', and they made a short diversion to Belvoir Castle, 'which is seen, almost in the clouds on the top of a vast hill, for many miles around'.

Their next stop was Newark. The needle-sharp spire of St Mary Magdalen stood out on the horizon. They liked the town, but they left the next morning, crossing the Trent and coming into Sherwood Forest, 'the first large and continued tract of wasteland that I have met with since I left Hertfordshire'.

North of Sherwood Forest lay Doncaster, where they turned sharp left for Rotherham. 'There cannot be a more pleasant ride than from Doncaster to Rotherham; from every part the road varies and agreeable prospects are seen, which vastly enliven the country.' The view of Conisbrough Castle, in a break between two hills, was particularly fine. 'A broad river winds in a charming style through the irregular valley that it is impossible not to be struck by rapture at the view.'

Rotherham, on the River Don, was very different: one vast soot-covered iron foundry.

> Near the town are two collieries, out of which the iron ore is dug, as well as the coals to work it with; these collieries and works employ near five hundred hands. The ore is here worked into metal and then into bar iron, the bars sent to Sheffield to be worked. This is one branch of their business. The other is the foundry, to which they run the ore into metal pigs, and then cast them into all sorts of boilers, pans, plough-shares etc.
>
> But what gave me much more satisfaction than the iron works of Rotherham was the cabbage culture of Samuel Tucker Esq, who lives just outside the town. This excellent spirited and accurate cultivator has, I apprehend, carried that branch of farming to its *ne plus ultra*.

Sheffield was less than an hour away. It had 30,000 inhabitants, 100 hands employed in the plate works, and many more in the steel mills and silk-weaving factory. The grinders, sharpening knives, razors, scissors and lancets, made the most money.

> The mechanism of these grinding wheels is very curious. Many grindstones are turned by a set of wheels which all receive their motion from one water-wheel, increasing velocity from the first movement to the last, which is astonishing. In the finishing wheel it is so great that the eye cannot perceive the least motion.

The silk mill, weaving silk from India, China, Turkey, Piedmont and America, employed 152 people, the majority women and children. Once again the entire machinery – thousands of revolving wheels – was powered by water.

Sheffield impressed Young even more than Mr Tucker's cabbage culture.

> I would advise you, in case you take this place in your way to the more northerly parts, to view all the mills in the town; among others, do not forget the tilting-mill, which is a blacksmith's immense hammer in constant motion on an anvil, worked by water-wheels, and by the same power the bellows of a forge adjoining kept regularly blown. The force of this mechanism is prodigious, so great that you cannot lay your hand on a gate at three perches distance [sixteen yards], without feeling a strong trembling motion, which is communicated to all the earth around.

They continued to Barnsley. The road passed through beautiful countryside, and they stopped on the way at the Earl of Strafford's Wentworth Castle.

'The new lawn to the front is one of the most beautiful in the world,' he pronounced, calling the classical façade of Corinthian columns 'surprisingly light and elegant'. Over the chimney in the hall were some carvings by Grinling Gibbons. Opposite the chimney was the drawing room, its walls lined with paintings by Carlo Maratta, Salvador Rosa and Guido Reni. Upstairs the 180-foot-long gallery was 'one of the most beautiful rooms in England', graced with paintings by Borgognone, Van Dyck, Bassan, Marratt, Titian and Michelangelo. Her Ladyship's reading closet, in complete contrast, was hung in painted satin, with a mosaic ceiling festooned in honeysuckle. Young thought it 'a sweet little room'.

They wandered through the woods and passed the ornamental lake, encountering on their way a Chinese temple, a statue of Ceres, a menagerie and the figure in stone of the late earl who had built the place.

The next day they were driving into Leeds. 'The business of this town flourished greatly during the war, but sunk much at the peace, and continued very languid till within these two years, when it began to rise again.'

They crossed the River Wharfe at Tadcaster and arrived in York. From the window of the chaise Young saw acre upon acre of potatoes. Their first stop was at the minster. 'The entrance strikes the mind with that awe which is the result of the magnificence arising from the vastness,' he later recalled. Once used to the dark light, however, he found the proportions displeasing. He preferred the delicate Decorated chapter house, 'the most peculiar Gothic building in the world'.

The assembly rooms, built by Lord Burlington in the style of Ancient Egypt, were as dull as the minster.

> An assembly room which is always dedicated to liveliness and gaiety, should undoubtedly be adorned in a gay and elegant manner, with carving, gilding and glasses. If a profusion of ornamentation was anywhere excusable, it would certainly be in the temple of pleasure; but this room is totally devoid of decoration, the plainness of it must strike everyone.

He enjoyed walking along the banks of the River Ouse, and he thought York's prison, the converted castle, 'the most airy, healthy and pleasant prison in Europe'.

They left York and took the road to Beverley. It was pretty and well-built, though the west end of the minster *did* look like the front of a cake shop.

They reached Castle Howard, which had been started by Vanbrugh in 1700 and had taken thirty-seven years to complete. Up until then Vanbrugh had built nothing, was thirty-five years old, and an ex-captain of Marines who wrote plays. It was the

York Minster from the north-west, showing the north transept and chapter house.

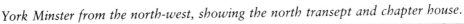

grandest of grand baroque: a central block surmounted by dome and cupola, its two wings forming a magnificent 300-foot façade on the garden side. Pity it was by Vanbrugh. 'The house loses the grandeur as well as the beauty that ought to attend so large and expensive a building, in the want of a unity of its parts.'

The proportions in the hall were all wrong. It was immense, made up of two storeys rising to the cupola, so the stone Greek and Roman gods and goddesses appeared diminutive beneath the gorgeous painted ceiling of the Trojan Wars.

In the park were the requisite mausoleum by Hawkesmore, temple by Vanbrugh and fountain by the appropriately named John Thomas.

> Besides these, there are several other ornamental buildings about the park, but all are so heavy and clumsy in style as to be perfectly disgusting. Even the mausoleum is far enough from being free from these objections. It is not very light in itself, but the steps up to the chapel, and the walls that surround it in the fortification style, are detestable. The Ionic temple is a cluster of porticoes; the bridge is heavy, and even ugly.

They came to Kirkby, where the soil was gravelly sand. The men were employed as shepherds, the women and children spinning flax. The Youngs' chaise crossed the Yorkshire Moors and Cleveland Hills. Progressive farms were few and far between. They arrived at the Great North Road, and continued north through dales and moorland to Middleton-in-Teesdale, before turning north-east for Durham.

> Advancing towards Middleton from the hill before you descend in to the village, the most glorious prospect opens to the view that imagination can picture; you look down upon the left over a noble extensive valley intersected with hedges and a few walls into sweet enclosures, which being quite below the point of view are seen distinct, though often numberless; the scattered trees, the houses, villages, ornament the scene, in a manner too elegant to admit to description. Beneath your feet at the bottom of a vast precipice rolls the Tees, which breaks into noble sheets of water, and throws a magnificence over the scene.

Beyond Durham, where they marvelled at castle and cathedral rising out of the rock, they temporarily abandoned their chaise for horses and hired a good guide to take them into the Pennines. They found themselves on wild moorland. Arthur loved it. His poor wife, getting bigger every day, is never mentioned.

> Here you ride through rapid streams, struggle along the sides of rocks, cross bleak mountains, and ride up the channel of torrents as the only sure road over bogs; listening to the roar of the waterfall, which you begin to think tremendous. Upon arriving at the banks of the Tees, where it pours down the rock, steeps of wood prevent you seeing it, but the roar is prodigious. Making use of our hands and our feet, and descending almost like a parrot, we crawled from rock to rock, and reached from bough to bough, till we got to the bottom under this noble fall. Noble indeed! The whole river (no trifling one) divided by one rock, into two vast torrents, pours down a perpendicular precipice of near fourscore feet. The deluging force of the water throws up such a foam and misty rain, that the sun never shines without a large and brilliant rainbow.

He dismissed his guide in a fit of enthusiasm and promptly got lost. After a few miles they found themselves in an enchanted landscape, 'as if dropped from heaven'. They dismounted, Young leading, Martha trying to keep her balance as she followed him down.

Durham, 'half church of God, half castle 'gainst the Scots', by William Daniell.

Encircled by a round of black mountains, we beheld a valley which from its peculiar beauty, one would have taken for the favourite spot of nature, a sample of terrestrial paradise. Half way up the hills in front many rugged and bold projecting rocks discovered their bare points among thick woods which hung almost perpendicularly over the precipice. In the dark bosom of these rocky shades a cascade glittering in the sun pours as if from a hollow in the rock, and at its front forms an irregular basin prettily tufted with wood, from whence it flows in a calm tranquil stream around this small but beautiful vale, losing itself among rocks in a most romantic manner.

They reached the Wear and followed it back to Durham, where they were reunited with their chaise. All the fields were covered in mustard flowers. They continued to Newcastle. It had a population of 40,000, a fleet of 400 colliers, and boasted the world's first railway.

The coal waggon roads, from the pits to the water, are great works, carried over all sorts of inequalities of ground, so far as the distance of nine or ten miles. The track of the wheels are marked with pieces of timber let into the road, for the wheels of the waggon to run on, by which means one horse is enabled to draw, and that with ease, fifty or sixty bushels of coal.

Five miles away, through delightful countryside overlooking the River Tyne, was Crawley's iron works, 'supposed to be the greatest manufactory of the kind in Europe', making anchors, chains, hooks and cannons. It had done well out of the recent wars, but now only orders for anchors and chains kept the works busy. Here again, everything – copper rollers, iron bar cutters, cranes and hammers – was moved by water.

The Young couple pressed on north into Northumberland, to Alnwick, where they looked over the house of the Duke of Northumberland. It had been the home of the Percys in the Middle Ages. Now the insides were being completely rebuilt in fashionable

'Gothick' by Robert Adams. Young liked it, though others found it as vulgar as the owners, who had changed their names from Smithson to Percy and taken over the title of Duke of Northumberland. Further on, at the village of Hetton, he encountered a farmer who grew carrots the size of a man's fist.

They reached Berwick-upon-Tweed, their furthest point north, and drove south-west towards Carlisle, getting out of the chaise and walking about half a mile along Hadrian's Wall. Twenty-five miles south of Carlisle was Penrith, and, west of Penrith, the Lakes.

They rode through the mountains and came to Derwentwater, 'a most elegant sheet of water, of the finest colour imaginable, spotted with islands'. The shoreline lost itself amid the surrounding woodland, and the top of Skiddaw seemed to rear up above the clouds. The water itself had such 'limpid transparency' that you could see the bottom, while the shore was girdled by 'stupendous rocks, broken and irregularly pointed, in the most abrupt and wild manner imaginable, with monstrous fragments as large as a house'. Young rowed around the lake and explored the shoreline. Borrow-dale, on the far side, was 'a whole sweep of rocks, crags, mountains and dreadful chasms'.

Hardly had he returned to dry land than he was climbing Skiddaw. From the top he could see Scotland, the Isle of Man and even the coast of Ireland, while the lake below appeared no more than a little basin. The beauty was spectacular, 'the rich luxuriance of nature's paintings', but the site was inconvenient, requiring much strenuous effort. Young recommended winding paths cut through the rock, and benches for the weary traveller to rest on.

Windermere was equally spectacular. Again he rented a rowing boat. The turns in the lake gave the impression of several different sheets of water. The shoreline varied from meadows to cornfields, to woods, to hanging rocks, 'an edging as elegant as ever fancied by Claude himself'.

Francis Wheatley's rendering of Arcadian bliss on the shores of Lake Windermere.

They left the Lakes and came down to Lancaster. The countryside was becoming tighter, disciplined by hedgerows. Lancaster was a flourishing port, with over 100 ships of sail trading with Africa and the Americas. There were lots of new Georgian houses, a sign of prosperity. They continued down through Lancashire, stopping at Warrington, where canvas sails were made and there was a pin factory employing between 200 and 300 children.

They arrived in Liverpool and established themselves at an inn. Martha, with her arched back and mandarin walk, must have been a total wreck. He dragged her through the town, inspecting the sights. Their first impression was disappointment. The assembly rooms were so small that the musicians' gallery was 'a mere overgrown shelf', and the new church of St Paul's, which should have been so delightful, was spoilt by clumsy columns. Liverpool's pride was its docks, though many were still empty from the post-war depression, in spite of the wealth that accrued from the North Atlantic slave trade.

They turned east for Manchester. Young wanted to see the new factories, and the canal that Lord Bridgwater had built. Manchester was the biggest cotton town in the country, three-quarters of its finished articles going to America. 'Large families in this place are no incumbrance, all are set to work,' Young enthused. Like its port, Liverpool, Manchester's wealth was tied to the vicious circle of the slave trade. Finished cotton was sent to West Africa where it was exchanged for slaves, the slaves were sent to America where they were exchanged for raw cotton, and the raw cotton was sent to Manchester and turned into finished cotton.

Cotton was not its only boast. Manchester was the terminus of the most modern waterway in the world: the Duke of Bridgwater's canal from his coal mines at Worsley right into the streets of Manchester, with an extension being built to Liverpool. It was one of the first of the country's great canals, its opening heralding a new age of transport in Britain.

Everyone recognized it as a stupendous undertaking, 'the most extraordinary thing in the kindgom', according to the *Annual Register* of 1760. 'The boats in some places are to go underground, in another place over a navigable river, without communicating with its waters.'

In Manchester they searched for a boat to take them to the duke's coal mines at Worsley, and were quite put out to discover that there were no pleasure boats available for the right sort of members of the public. Sightseers, Young warned, might have to spend two days in Manchester looking for a suitable boat.

The canal started in a subterranean quay, with yards and warehouses above, where the coal was unloaded by water-powered cranes. Coming into daylight, Young found the canal running along the sides of natural banks, stream and rivulets diverted beneath it. Just before Langford Bridge the canal divided in two, the right-hand branch continuing to Worsley, the left-hand one leading towards Liverpool. He took the right-hand one. Soon his narrowboat, drawn by a single horse, came to Barton aqueduct, 200 yards long, over the River Irwell.

> The effect of coming at once on to Barton Bridge, and looking *down* upon a large river, with barges of great burden sailing on it; and *up* to another river, hung in the air, with barges towing along it, form altogether a scenery somewhat like enchantment.

On the far side of the valley was the final stretch to Worsley. It was marked by a brick kiln, producing the thousands of bricks required for the great undertaking. Young could see the duke's house and grounds in the distance between two hills in front of him. It was a fine prospect.

Soon the canal entered a tunnel. Mr and Mrs Young disappeared into it, like Charon and a spirit that had died in pregnancy. It extended right to the heart of the coal mine, where it divided again into two branches. The whole hill was rich with coal seams, and from the surface shafts dropped down to both the canal tunnel and the coal tunnels. Where the seams were above the level of the canal, shafts dropped directly 'into the boat beneath, either promiscuously, or directed through a tube to fill a box at a time'. Where the seams were below the level of the canal, the coal was hoisted up to the surface through one set of shafts, and dropped down into the narrowboats through another.

Having completed a tour of the Manchester–Worsley branch, Young decided next morning to explore the Manchester–Liverpool branch, which had reached the village of Altrincham, about twenty miles outside Manchester. They sailed across valleys and through hills until they came to Altrincham, where the waterway abruptly stopped. The canal head was crowded with hundreds of navvies, carpenters, smiths, masons and boatmen. Two houseboats floated on the water. One was a carpenter's workshop, the other a blacksmith's forge.

He came on to dry land and rode down through the West Midlands, stopping in every farmyard he passed. When he got to Cheshire he wanted to know why the cheese was so good.

> Their cows are of an ordinary breed, loose boned; some farmers have aimed at improvement by Lancashire bulls, but it does not answer except in beauty. The average quantity of milk is about five gallons; but some of Mr Vernon's near this place have given ten.

Within a couple of days they were in the Potteries, visiting Burslem, where another canal to Liverpool was being excavated. There were over 300 kilns employing 10,000 people.

> In general we owe the possession of this most flourishing manufacture to the inventive genius of Mr Wedgwood; who not only originally introduced the present cream coloured ware, but has since been the inventor of every improvement, the other manufacture being little better than mere imitators.

Staffordshire was beautiful after the Potteries, even though farmers' lives were made difficult by the extortionary poor rate of one and sixpence in the pound, which only encouraged laziness and tea-drinking. The Youngs arrived in Birmingham. 'I was nowhere more disappointed than at Birmingham.' The new industrialists were so secretive, after some French industrial spies had stolen patents, that they told them nothing. Nor did the manufacturers have much to tell. The town, with its population of 28,000, had done well out of the war but had still not recovered from the slump of peace.

They came down into Worcester. In Leland's time 'no town in England made so many clothes yearly as this town', but by the 1760s it had diversified and was glove-making, porcelain-manufacturing and market gardening. The porcelain, in particular, was very fashionable. The guildhall, by a pupil of Wren's, epitomized the new Worcester, as did the Georgian houses. There was a cathedral too, but that was Gothic and did not interest Young. On the other side of the Severn he could see the

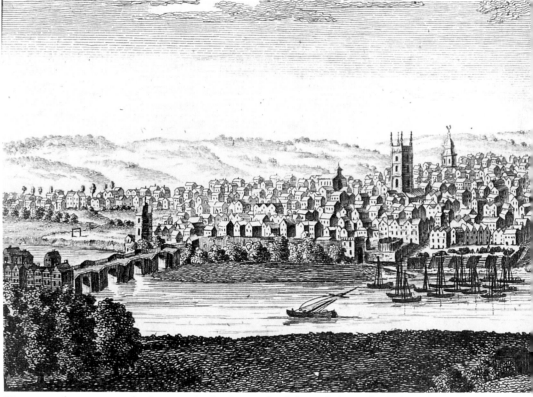

Worcester from across the Severn: the bridge to the left, and the cathedral to the right.

Malvern Hills. There were no industries, but there were no beggars either. The women and children were all employed in the market gardens.

Their next goal was Oxford, and they drove through the Vale of Evesham and passed the row of gabled almshouses in Chipping Norton, before stopping, resting and sightseeing at Ditchley Park, three miles from Blenheim.

Ditchley Park was the seat of the Earl of Litchfield. Gibbs had designed it; Kent and Flintcroft had worked with him on it; and in its early days it was one of the most fashionable houses in England. It was typically Palladian, a main block with wings and a projecting centre, where the figures of Loyalty and Fame hovered above the doorway.

Inside, the stucco work was by Vassali, Artari and Serena. Young found the hall, with Kent's kitsch mural 'The Assembly of the Gods' beneath a two-storey high stuccoed ceiling, and lined by busts of Milton, Livy, Homer, Virgil, Cicero, Sappho, Shakespeare and Dryden, 'a handsome room'. He went into the music room, where there were paintings by Rubens and Wotton, and passed through a doorway. The stony figures of Arts and Science lounged above them. There was a Holbein in the dining room; and he loved the almost rococo fantasy of the saloon – Diana and Minerva in the doorway and Flora on the ceiling.

In the grounds a lake was being excavated beside a domed temple. Capability Chic.

> The gardens are disposed with taste; the sloping banks scattered with wood, and hanging to the serpentine lake, with the rotunda, finely placed on a rising ground among the trees, is a very beautiful landscape.

Their next stop was Oxford, where he gazed in wonder once again at the Radcliffe Camera. It was 'a beautiful building'; but this time he was more critical. The dome, with its ribbing, was altogether too busy, and the Ionic pillars seemed rather ineffectual.

They took the road to London via Henley and Maidenhead. Poor Mrs Young must have been in agony at every jolt. Hammersmith was crowded with market gardens, varying in size between five and fifty acres. There were more market gardens in Kensington, producing peas, turnips, wheat, horse-beans, barley, potatoes and clover. Young turned north through Enfield for North Mimms. Enfield saddened him. It was all waste. He was depressed. A farm too large and expensive awaited him. A reminder of failure. A family too large and expensive awaited him. Another failure.

*　　*　　*

Soon after their return Martha gave birth to a son. They now had three children, and not enough money to bring even the daughters up adequately. That same year Arthur won the Society of Art's Gold Medal for his *Essay on Hogs*. He had the choice of a medal or cash. Being a gentleman he chose the medal. His wife was in despair. Fanny Burney (a prejudiced source) gives a picture of the unhappy couple on a visit to London.

> Mrs Young has been on a visit to us for some days. She and her *caro sposo* are a very strange couple, she has grown so immoderately fat, I wonder he could ever marry her. They have however given over those violent disputes and quarrels with which they used to entertain their friends. Not that Mrs Young has any reason to congratulate

herself upon it, quite the contrary, for the extreme violence of her overbearing temper has at length so entirely wearied Mr Young that he disdains any controversy with her, scarce ever contradicting her, and lives a life of calm easy contempt.

Back in North Mimms he had to try to earn a living. The more unsuccessful he was as a farmer, the more he had to write, and the more he wrote, the more he was regarded as a successful farmer and standard-bearer of the agricultural revolution. The following year, 1770, he wrote even more: on hops, hiring and stocking, *rural oeconomy*, and four volumes on agricultural experiments.

What a year of incessant activity, anxiety and wretchedness was this! No cart horse ever laboured as I did, spending like an idiot, always in debt, in spite of what I earned with the sweat of my brow and almost my heart's blood, such was my anxiety, yet all was clearly vexation of spirit.

He still managed to make time, though, for a third tour, this time without his long-suffering wife.

In his new book, *A Farmer's Tour Through the East of England*, he wrote copiously, as usual, about the progressive farms at which he stayed on the way and, like his *Six Month Tour*, *A Farmer's Tour* can be seen as a 2,000-page circular bread-and-butter letter. Not that he gave that as his public reason for writing the book; his public reason shows him more vulnerable. 'My design was to be some service to British agriculture, an object I cannot possibly succeed in except by publishing.'

He left North Mimms in the summer of 1770 and rode through St Albans on the road to Berkhamstead. It was rich land, and the rich land continued to Tring. All along the way he saw the thick-wheeled Hertfordshire plough. At Tring he came into a range of chalk hills, and on the other side of the hills in a vale was Aylesbury. The town had been doing well out of the agricultural revolution. There was a new, red-bricked town hall, and in Aylesbury's tiny squares, triangles and open spaces, which you always came upon when you least expected them, were newly built houses.

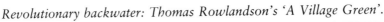

Revolutionary backwater: Thomas Rowlandson's 'A Village Green'.

Next morning he left for Buckingham, and the thick-wheeled Hertfordshire plough gave way to a light, swing one. 'The soil ranks among the richest I ever saw.' There in Buckingham, a market town modestly flaunting its new Georgian gentility after a major fire in 1725, he crossed the Ouse and rode up the resolutely straight and stately approach to Stowe. It was probably the grandest approach any stately house in Britain could boast of, as rational, confident and arrogant as the century itself.

The house he saw before him, 'more beautiful than any in the surrounding country', had been given a classical garb by Lord Cobham since Celia Fiennes visited it and wrote of its 'cupelow'. The bricks had been stuccoed, a portico of Ionic columns built on the front, and the side wings given square Palladian towers. Now a balustrade was being built on the top.

He passed under the gigantic portico. In the drawing room were works by Poussin, Holbein, Guerchino, Rubens, Rembrandt, Claude Lorrain, Van Dyck and Dürer. The gallery was lined with Brussels tapestries. He looked up at the ceiling, stuccoed in compartments. Further on, in the dressing room, he saw a buxom Venus blinding Cupid. It was by Titian.

He walked the grounds, ornamented with statues at strategic points. From the Temple of Bacchus there was a charming view of the Temple of Venus on the water's edge. Passing the inevitable hermit's cave (designed by Kent) he came to the pavilions at the park's gate, 'from which the water is seen differently winding, in a very natural taste, at the bottom of several pastures; as just an imitation of a real stream as can anywhere be seen'. He stomped up to Queen Caroline's pillar and on through a perfect man-made landscape to the rotunda. Further on was Gibbs's Temple of Friendship, and a stone bridge, built to designs by Palladio. Ahead of him was the Temple of Concord. He passed a statue of Venus rising from the bath, 'the attitude naturally taken', and a grotto patterned with shells. There the woodland opened up into the Elysian Fields and he could see on the hill the Temple of Ancient Virtue.

Young left Stowe and took his chaise north to Northampton.

> The view of Northampton from the hill at the Towcester entrance is very fine. It is built on an easy slope, and shows itself to great advantage. It is in general well-built, contains many good houses and several streets that are straight and broad. The market is a fine one, but by no means the best in England.

He did not approve of the farming practices, however. The hedges were a mess, there was nothing that deserved the name of ditch, and there was absolutely no appreciation of the finer points of manuring.

> All this country, and I believe through all Northamptonshire (and I observe much of it through Buckinghamshire) they have a most execrable custom of collecting all the cow dung from the fields, and kneading it up with short straw to burn instead of coals. They daub it in lumps on all the walls of their houses, barns and stables to dry, and from hence take it to their chimney; any traveller would suppose the country a colony from the wild Irish.

Market Harborough and Leicester took him to Nottingham. It was good farming country all the way. North of Nottingham, Sherwood Forest ('waste land but highly improvable') led to Newstead Abbey, seat of Lord Byron.

In front of the house was a large lake. On the far bank were two Gothic castles, built by 'Mad Jack' Byron in 1749. Their cannons were levelled directly at the parlour window. 'A twenty-gun ship, with several yachts and boats lying at anchor, throw an air of most pleasing cheerfulness over the whole scene.'

Derby, his next stop, was large; made up of five parishes. It turned out stockings, silk and porcelain. The porcelain was 'something in the style of Worcester but inferior'. A few miles to the west of the town's centre lay Kedlestone Hall, home of Viscount Scarsdale, and 'one of the finest houses in the kingdom'.

The 360 feet of Palladian façade – only ten years old – were unforgettable, a centre and two wings. The formal front by James Paine was so monumental and palatial that Dr Johnson though it would make a first-rate town hall.

The hall was lined with Corinthian columns. In between the columns were Greek and Roman deities. Above the mantlepiece was a relief showing the Rape of the Sabine Women. The arabesque stucco ceiling was by Adam's own plasterer, Joseph Rose. In the north music room, finished in stucco and with an Ionic entablature, were paintings by Guido, Giordano, Rembrandt and Bassan. The drawing room was huge, hung with blue damask and with coved ceiling edges and a relief, in marble, of Virtue rewarded with riches and honour. Hanging on the blue damask were paintings by Veronese, Cuyp, Raphael, Guido, Zuccarelli, Claude Lorrain and Tintoretto. The floor in the library was marble, the ceiling mosaic. Corinthian columns flanked the chimneypiece. Above it was a frieze of Cupid and Psyche. The saloon, or rotunda, was elegant and simple, crowded with statues but with only four pictures in niches in the walls. All were by Rubens: a land storm, a sea storm, a rural scene and a hunting scene. Further on, the ceiling of the dining room astonished him. Painted on it were circles representing Europe, Asia, Africa and America. A fifth circle in the centre depicted Love embracing Fortune. The great staircase was filled with paintings. Upstairs the state dressing room and state bedchamber were both hung in blue damask. The Scarsdales' own private rooms were hung in blue paper.

> The stables are very spacious and well-built; and peculiar in one circumstance, which is having a range of vaults underground across a paved yard in their front, with a door into each opposite those of the stables; these are receptacles for the dung, which is moved here in barrows as fast as made, quite out of the way, and the yard kept perfectly clean. The dung is also most valuable as manure, from not being exposed to the rains: but gutters should have been made into them from the stables for the conveyance of the urine: or if it was found to fill them too much, then into a reservoir with a pump; and his Lordship would find the watering his lawns would improve them to a high degree.

He passed through Ashbourne and came to Dove Dale, a two-mile gorge of crags and cliffs and caves worn through soft limestone.

> It is bounded in a very romantic manner by hills, rocks and hanging woods; which are extremely various; and the hills in particular of a very bold and striking character. They are spread on all sides in vast sweeps, inexpressably magnificent, and are much more striking than anything else in Dove Dale. The rocks are in some places very romantic, rising in various shapes from banks of hills and woods, and forming a wide assemblage of really romantic objects; but are much exceeded in magnitude by others in different parts of the kingdom. The course of the river is various, from a gentle current to great rapidity over broken rocks; and in some places falls, but not in a bold manner. The fragments of rock in it, with branches of wood growing from them, are truly romantic and picturesque.

'He who has seen Dove Dale has no need to visit the Highlands' (Dr Johnson).

He made his way up the River Derwent. 'In some places the breadth is considerable, the stream smooth; in others it breaks upon the rocks and falls over the fragments; besides forming slight cascades.' At Hag Rock near Matlock he looked down a 'perpendicular' precipice at the river, 'a fine sheet of water fringed with wood on the opposite side'.

The river led to Chatsworth. It did not take him long to hate it. An earlier age might have been impressed by 'Nile's leaky body, dolphins, sea-nymphs and dragons vomiting water, trees spiriting it from their branches, and temples pouring down showers from their roofs', but he just sneered. The house was an improvement, but even that did not change his mood. The inn he had stayed at the previous night, only a quarter of a mile from Chatsworth, had been abominable, and he had found 'nothing but dirt and impertinence'.

He left the Peaks at Chesterfield. He was still in a furious temper.

The town of Chesterfield has nothing to entertain the traveller, unless he chooses to admire the ingenuity of a crooked steeple. Their architect, full of Hogarth's idea of the line of beauty, thought no form so proper as a crooked billet: in which he has very happily succeeded, to the great improvement of taste in that neighbourhood.

He did not stay, but took the road to Doncaster to visit a particularly progressive farmer, a Mr Crowle. 'Mr Crowle's cabbages weighed on an average nineteen pounds seven ounzes each,' he noted approvingly, before turning south through Sherwood Forest again. The land could not have been more different from Mr Crowle's. The soil was light and sandy, and hardly cultivated. It looked wild and desolate, useful for nothing but grazing a few sheep on. It disgusted him. Treated with good marl or clay, like in Norfolk, it would be perfectly capable of raising turnips, barley and wheat.

He crossed the Trent and drove his chaise to Lincoln. There was nothing worth a stranger's glance, save the cathedral. It had 'a most pleasing edifice'. Beyond Lincoln, heathland stretched south and east all the way to Sleaford. It would yield fine sainfoin, he thought. The land was getting flatter, and soon it would be horizontal, broken by nothing but the spires of Fen churches. He crossed the Welland and came into Long Sutton. Here were 3,500 acres of salt marsh, exposed since the Fen draining of the last hundred years. It was a common, and on it grazed 30,000 sheep and 1,000 horses. The Fens, once drained, possessed some of the richest grazing land in the country. He continued east to King's Lynn. He knew it well. It reminded him of his wife.

He had reached Norfolk, the kernel of the agricultural revolution. It was like coming home. In north Norfolk, in particular, he noted, they were taking a very uncompromising line on carrots. It was a serious matter. One of the leading Norfolk exponents of carrots, a Mr Billing of Weasenham, had renounced them, though he was still committed to the turnip culture. Young was shocked. He did not think he was the only one. 'The reader will naturally ask, how can this be with a man who wrote so clearly an account of carrots.' Young dismissed him.

> I take the real case to be this. He was advised to try carrots, but against his own opinion; and finding them better than he expected at first, repeated the trials for some time. When he came to enlarge the culture to whole fields, the attention they required in hoing and the expense being much superior to turnips, gave him a disgust. The largeness of his business made more compendious crops agreeable. His men went regularly to work with turnips almost without directions; nor would he spare a sufficiency of hands from the other crops to do justice to the carrots; and these circumstances, I have little doubt, were his reason for leaving off the practice.

Every revolution has its Billings. Every revolution has its Youngs.

He passed through Burnham Market to Wells-next-the-Sea, where marshland was still being reclaimed. The crops were improving every mile into the revolutionary heartland. Most of the cattle were of 'the little mongrel Norfolk sort', he jotted down, but they gave five gallons of milk a day, and some even seven. Blakeney Point, Cley and Holt passed by. The land on either side of the Norwich road was 'rich and well cultivated, but improves as you advance'.

Norwich was still one of the biggest cities in England with 38,000 houses. As well as wool cloth it produced satin and damask. Men and women were paid the same, seldom more than five shillings a week, and boys and girls got ninepence. They could all earn more if they worked harder, but those who did only spent it in the ale house, which was hardly a good example of industriousness. Besides, the insurrection in America led by George Washington was having a bad effect on trade, and had deprived Norwich of one of its major cloth markets.

From Norwich Young took the road to Great Yarmouth, through the Norfolk Broads. The husbandry on the way was generally good, some of it quite exceptional.

A rural scene by John Augustus Atkinson: horses and workmen at a gravel pit.

Carrots were doing well, he noted smugly. One farmer, a Mr Ramsey, had made some fascinating experiments with lucerne and Scotch cabbage. His wife, Mrs Ramsey, was equally industrious. Her copies of Roman ruins, Dutch ice-skating scenes and English landscapes, executed with a hot poker, showed 'a spirit in the strokes superior to the original prints'.

He came down through Suffolk to Woodbridge, 'a place of famous husbandry', which had seized the revolutionary initiative from Norfolk.

> Upon the whole, this corner of Suffolk is to be recommended for practising much better husbandry, all things considered, than any other tract of country with which I am acquainted. Their culture of carrots, their breed of horses, their management of the pea and bean crop, is much more masterly than anything met with in most parts of the kingdom.

On the way to Ipswich he stopped at the Nacton Poor House, a model of its kind. With 144 paupers it was quite an attraction.

> It stands in a high airy situation: a healthy spot, and the whole appearance to be kept in a very clean and wholesome manner. There are various appartments for men with their wives, for single men and lads, and also for single women and girls. There are likewise proper rooms for the different manufactures carried on, such as spinning, weaving, making twine, making sacks; also offices for baking and brewing, with proper storerooms: the whole open to the view of any person that comes to see them.

The poor were allowed tuppence in every shilling earned. They spent it on tea. 'Indulgence renders it necessary to let them do as they please with it, but it would be better expended on something else.' All in all, the destitute should feel extremely grateful for the place. 'Nothing has such good effects as workhouses,' he enthused. 'No neighbouring poor live near so well in their own cottages.'

He meandered along the Stour Valley and through Colchester to Chelmsford, made a half-circle round London and crossed the Thames at Clapham. The soil was poor and sandy, but he was delighted to meet a Mr Duckett, 'whose mechanical abilities are so well-known by the invention of two most excellent ploughs'. Strolling round the Clapham farm, whose meadows went down to the Thames, he noted how neat Mr Duckett's hedges were. 'All the tillage of his land is performed with ploughs of his own invention.' At Kew he inspected the exotic plants. Then he drove south to Morden and east to Kent. The road took him through Rochester, Chatham (there was a small field of lucerne in the dockyard), Feversham, Canterbury and Maidstone. It was chalky and hilly.

He came to Dover, one of the prettiest seaports he had ever seen. 'The situation is very romantic, at the foot of several bold hills, and the harbour in the centre of the town, quite built round, is surrounded by quays, that are more agreeable to the view than any I know.' He climbed up to the castle, from where he had a clear view of France, and remounted his chaise for the 'six or seven very romantic miles' to Folkestone. 'The road runs along the edge of vast precipices, the shore very high and bold, and nobly varied.' It was a perfect day under an azure sky. The view of Folkestone, with its church on a point of land close to the sea, was 'as beautiful outline as can be imagined: the union of sea and land complete'.

West of Folkestone was Romney Marsh, 'the richest tract of grazing land in this part of the kingdom'. Most of the sheep were the local Romney breed, without horns. Further on, driving inland, the world seemed idyllic.

> The country is all hill and dale, the prospects extensive over a rich varied woodland; the road is good and leads through many scattered villages, with numerous single cottages, remarkably neat, well built, clean and snug; little gardens well kept, the hedges regular and all clipped; many of the walls whitewashed, the paling whole and in order, and even the pigsties tiles quite neat and strong; the whole uniting to raise the

A dockside butcher's shop in the mid-eighteenth century: a study by Paul Sandby.

Rowlandson's watercolour of the Old Church, at Newtown on the Isle of Wight.

most pleasing idea of warm comfortable inhabitants. One's humanity is touched with pleasure to see cottages the residence of cheerfulness and content. A country so decorated is beautiful indeed, and more entertaining to travel through, than if splendid temples and proud turrets arose on every hill.

It all changed in West Sussex, where the air was thick with smoke from iron furnaces, but once in the Downs the views of the Weald, 'walled in by the sweeps of bare hill, projecting in the boldest manner', were glorious.

He stopped at Portsmouth and visited the dockyards. They depressed him. So he took a ferry to Ryde on the Isle of Wight, and rode to Newport, in the middle of the island. He liked the Isle of Wight, where they mixed seaweed with cow dung before laying it on the bean fields, and where there were no foxes ('Consequently they are without a species of vermin by no means so innocent, the hunters of them'). 'No place is happier in the beauties of a varied country: here are hills, dales, mountains, rocks, wood and water, all in perfection.'

> The farmers on this island are much the neatest people for stacking that ever I saw: all their hay and corn stacks are round, drawn up as regularly as possible to a point which is ornamented with a little knob of straw. It is surprising with what exactness they build, and with what neatness they thatch them: they are really beautiful, nor can you easily imagine how much these stacks ornament the country.

Young returned to the mainland at Southampton and arrived in the New Forest. The uselessness of its 80,000 acres drove him to distraction.

> I enquired particularly into the utility of this great tract of land, in furnishing timber for the Royal Navy, and I found the benefit of it very inconsiderable. Fells of ship timber are not often made.
>
> An open forest, stocked with deer and quite scattered over with villages and single houses, could not possibly yield a product of timber nearly proportional to its extent.

The cattle that are kept wild on it, and the deer, destroy nine young trees out of ten. There is not a shadow of a reason for leaving it in its present melancholy state.

Nor were the farmers mixing seaweed in their manure, as on the Isle of Wight. It lay unemployed, washed up against the shore all along the coast to Christchurch and the Dorset border. He turned inland and rode through Dorchester to Bridport. The farms were inefficient and the sheep were not kept in folds; but the landscape of hills and fields and distant sea was spectacular. 'A more varied or beautiful country is nowhere to be seen in England', and it continued all the way to Axminster, where the men were employed in the cloth trade, and the women and girls in the carpet factories.

He was now in the Vale of Taunton. It was thickly enclosed. He had planned to go on into the West Country, but autumn had come and the weather was changing, so he turned north instead, and started back to North Mimms.

He rode through Bridgwater and came to King's Sedgemoor, a black peat bog, undrained and unused, though possessing some of the richest soil in England. He saw it all from the top of Glastonbury Tor.

His next stop was Bath. The scaffolding had come down from the Circus. Now the Crescent was being built; 'amazing edifices for a town supported by pleasure and disease'. He skirted the north of Salisbury Plain, riding through Devizes, Marlborough and Hungerford. Reading, Uxbridge and Barnet passed by and he was back in his farm at North Mimms before the frost set in.

Arthur Young wrote no more topographical descriptions of England. He continued travelling the country, both as a writer and later as secretary to the Board of Agriculture, but his pen gives us no more pictures of England on the eve of the Industrial Revolution. Instead he travelled abroad, giving us topographical descriptions of Ireland and Italy, and France during the French Revolution. The Board of Agriculture gave him a proper job so that he could abandon farming; his marriage improved, in spite of (or possibly because of) numerous family tragedies; and when he died he was remembered, not as an agricultural revolutionary or spendthrift farmer, nor even as an English traveller, but as a respected public servant.

Milsom Street, Bath: some of the 'amazing edifices supported by pleasure and disease'.

7

THE DISCOVERY OF SCOTLAND

I mentioned our designs to Voltaire. He looked at me, as if I had talked of going to the North Pole, and said, 'You do not insist on my accompanying you?' 'No, sir.' 'Then I am very willing you should go.'

James Boswell, *Journal of a Tour to the Hebrides*

'I SMELL YOU in the dark,' the old man muttered, as the young one carefully manoeuvred him through the dollops of human excreta thrown out into the Edinburgh street for the nightwatchmen to sweep up in the morning.

He was sixty-three-years old, and 'unwieldy from corpulency'. He wore a brown greatcoat, so large it almost touched the ground, and with pockets so deep it seemed they could hold both volumes of his dictionary. His eyes were bad and he was getting deaf; and his physical features were so peculiar that Sir Joshua Reynolds's sister, Frances, refused to give a detailed description of him on the grounds that 'I might have the mortification of seeing it hung up at a print shop as the greatest curiosity ever exhibited.'

He sniffed the air; not that he was the cleanest person himself. He rarely had a bath, last night's menu was imprinted on his shirt front and he seldom changed his clothes. He had had a bad day. You could tell by the sniff. The journey by post-chaise from London had been exhilarating; he always liked coaches. Then came Scotland. The inn at Edinburgh, Boyd's, was appalling. When he had asked for more sugar in his lemonade, the waiter had taken a lump with his fingers and dropped it into the glass. Dr Johnson, enraged, flung it out of the window.

Why Samuel Johnson had come to Scotland in the first place was a mystery. The kindest thing he had said about the Scots was that there were too many of them in England, and that their success was unmerited.

'The truth is,' James Boswell later tried to justify, 'like the ancient Greeks and Romans, he allowed himself to look on all nations but his own as barbarians.' The truth was, Boswell also admitted, Johnson was like a child sometimes.

Samuel Johnson was born in Lichfield, the son of an impoverished bookseller, 'a poor diseased infant almost blind'. He grew up ugly and ungainly, enjoying idleness as

much as study. Right up until the age of thirty he made no effort to impress anyone, 'considering the matter hopeless'. He failed at childhood, failed at Oxford, failed at marriage and failed at schoolmastering. The depressions he had first suffered in childhood got steadily worse, until 'all his labours, all his enjoyments, were but temporary interruptions from its baleful influence'. He went to London, where he mixed with scholars and scrubbers, classicists and criminals; and was compromised by none of them. Sometimes he was so poor that men took him for a vagrant. He made a living of sorts on Grub Street, where in his writings he took the side of the American Indian and negro slave. He was a mass of contradictions: a Tory on the side of the underdog; a virtual teetotaller whose first hero had been a drunken poet; a man who believed in the truth yet deferred unquestioningly to George Pslamanazar, a famous confidence trickster. Somehow, amid all this, and while his wife died slowly of gin and opium, he found time to edit the works of Shakespeare and compile an English dictionary. 'I dreamt of being a poet and woke up a lexicographer.'

He had wanted to come to Scotland since he was a child, when his father gave him a copy of Martin Martin's *Description of the Western Islands of Scotland*. He always talked of going to Scotland. Then Thomas Gray went to Scotland. Next Thomas Pennant went to Scotland. His *Tour in Scotland* had come out only a couple of years before. Pennant was a good writer. Dr Johnson admired him. He reminded the old man of his childhood ambition, and of that copy of Martin. Johnson kept saying he wanted to go, Boswell kept pressurizing him to go, now Mrs Thrale wanted him to go. He had to go. The Scotland that he had wanted to see was the Scotland of Martin: the Scotland of clans and tribes and ancient loyalties, which had died at Culloden. He knew before he left that he had come too late.

They were walking up Cannongate. Samuel Johnson heaved his bulk clumsily. His health had never been good, and he was rarely free from pain. Cannongate was Edinburgh's main street, from the castle to the palace. The young man pointed out the height of the buildings, towering so that the alleys appeared like miniature canyons. The old man acknowledged that they were noble. They also reeked. Already the smell was becoming too much for civilized people. Some, like James Boswell's former neighbour, the saintly atheist David Hume, had moved to New Town in the north-east suburbs. Boswell was relieved Hume was no longer a neighbour. Hume was not really Samuel Johnson's type. There would have been trouble.

Johnson was not an easy companion, 'hard to please and easy to offend, impetuous and irritable in his temper, but of a most humane and benevolent heart'. Boswell loved him.

James Boswell first met Samuel Johnson in the back parlour of Tom Davies's bookshop ten years earlier. It was a chance meeting that Boswell had been planning for months. He was typical of a type – on the make. He had left Scotland, whored and drunk in London, written an amusing book about Corsica and was looking for fame. He was also looking for a father figure. Johnson recognized that. He was in deep need of love, and he was looking for a son.

They reached the top of the Royal Mile, and turned under an archway into a filthy alley. It led to James's Court, where Boswell had lodgings. It was a smart address for Edinburgh, as you would expect from a reasonably successful lawyer. Inside Margaret Boswell waited nervously. The man, she had ascertained from her husband's stories, could be a saint. He could also be a monster, and when he was most monstrous, he was most pathetic. She had given up her bedroom for Johnson: and she, with a four-month child. She watched him as he sat in the best chair talking. He was almost human. Perhaps he would have been, had it not been for some of his personal habits.

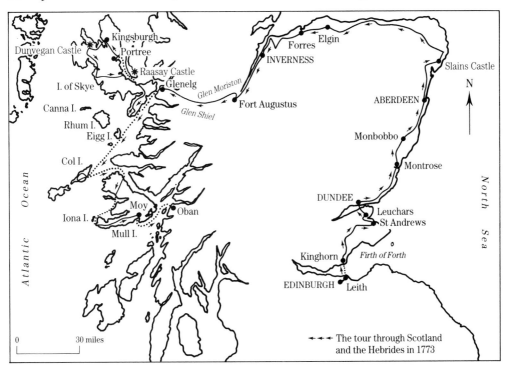

The tour through Scotland and the Hebrides in 1773

'I smell you in the dark': from Samuel Collins's 'Picturesque Beauties of Boswell'.

The next day was Sunday, 15 August 1773. The streets were deserted. Edinburgh was a Presbyterian city. Johnson wanted to be off to the Highlands quickly. He was hungry for wilderness. Boswell delayed. He wanted to show off his friend, the Man of Letters, in Edinburgh. The Man of Letters was irritated. He had come to Scotland to see things he would not see in the normal course of London life, and here he was surrounded by a provincial imitation of London. At least Hume was not in the vicinity. Hume may have been the 'mildest man that ever scuttled a creed' but he was also a Scotsman, and the mildness disappeared when he spoke of England and the Union. 'Nothing but rebellion and bloodshed will open the eyes of that denuded people,' he had written. Johnson, a High Church Tory, hated all that Hume stood for.

> A man who has so much conceit as to tell all mankind that they have been bubbled for ages, and he is the wise man who sees better than they − a man who has so little scrupulosity as to venture to oppose those principles which have been thought necessary for human happiness − is he to be surprised if another man comes and laughs at him?

He was irritated by Boswell's friends, with their romantic nationalism and dour provincialism.

'Sir, never talk of your independency, who could let your Queen remain twenty years in captivity, and then be put to death, without even a pretence of justice, without your ever attempting to rescue her; and such a Queen!' he burst out after an insufferable tour of the Houses of Parliament, sessions house, and advocate's library.

'Half our nation was bribed with English money,' James Kerr, the Edinburgh Keeper of Records, replied in a huff.

'That is no defence, that makes it worse.'

There was another bad moment in the evening. They had been talking about Lord Monboddo's assertion that the orang-utan could be taught English. Samuel Johnson pronounced the idea ridiculous. Someone said that Lord Monboddo, an extremely learned prehistorian, was merely asserting that all things were possible, and thus it was possible that the orang-utan could speak.

'But, sir, it is just as possible that the orang-utan does not speak, as that he speaks. However, I shall not contest the point. I should have thought it not possible to find a Monboddo; yet *he* exists.'

Johnson was tired, and sad, and suffering from overcrowding and constipation; he had left the only servant he could tolerate, the former black slave, Francis Barber, in London, and there was no Mrs Thrale.

He loved Mrs Thrale in his own clumsy egotistical way; but his Christian principles forbade even the thought of that love being consummated. He had met her eight years ago. He had been suffering one of his terrible depressions. She recognized him for what he was – 'ever sighing for the tea and bread-and-butter of life, when satiated with the turtle and the burgundy of it' – and took him into her house at Streatham. She was rich. Her husband, a brewer, had a succession of mistresses. She was extraordinarily well educated, speaking and reading Latin, French and Italian, and she was bored. Hester Thrale was diminutive, vivacious and one of the beauties of the age. She was also extremely unhappy. Samuel Johnson was big, difficult and one of the ugliest men in England. His demands were unlimited. He told her everything, forced her to share his burdens. Now her mother was dying and her husband losing money. She could not cope with Samuel Johnson on top of all that. So she sent him off to the Highlands with that fool Boswell; and he knew she had.

Johnson was a sad man, and the only time he seemed happy in Edinburgh was when he was with Boswell's four-month-old daughter. She had the appearance of listening to him, her father thought. So Johnson was glad to leave Edinburgh on Wednesday, 18 August. Boswell's wife was tearful, but he would have none of that.

'Madame, we do not go there as to paradise. We go to see something different from what we are accustomed to.'

*   *   *

They left the city in a chaise and rode north to Leith, where they took a ferry across the Firth of Forth. Boswell said the view was as fine as from Constantinople or Naples. Johnson concurred.

'Water is the same everywhere.'

As they crossed the Forth, Johnson spotted an island. It was Inchkeith, and he was determined to land there. They came ashore. The island was rocky, and there was a fort with the inscription: 'MARIA 1564'. Johnson 'stalked like a giant among the luxuriant thistles and nettles'.

'I'll have this island. I'd build a house, make a good landing place, have a garden, and vines, and all sorts of trees.' As they got back in the boat he called out to his sycophant, 'Come, now, pay a classical compliment to the island on quitting it.'

Boswell thought.

'Unhappy Queen!
Unwilling I forsook your friendly state'

he declaimed in Greek.

They dined at Kinghorn and took a post-chaise to St Andrews, on the eastern coast, passing through Kirkcaldy and Cupar, where they stopped for tea – 'places not unlike the small and straggling market towns of those parts of England where commerce and manufactures have not yet produced opulence,' Johnson thought.

They arrived at St Andrews late at night. It was a dreary drive. Supper at the Glass revived the old man. Then, led by the landlord with a candle, and followed by a waiter with a lantern, they were taken to what was left of St Leonard's College, where they were to stay. One of St Andrews University's academics, Dr Watson, had bought the ground and turned the remains into his house.

They spent the morning with Dr Watson. Johnson liked him. Boswell was making a nuisance of himself folding and unfolding a map of Scotland. The old man ignored him, happy with Watson, and reminisced of days gone by.

'I remember when all the *decent* people in Lichfield got drunk every night, and were not the worse thought of. Ale was cheap, so you pressed strongly. When a man must bring a bottle of wine, he is not in such haste. Smoking has gone out. To be sure, it is a shocking thing, blowing smoke out of our mouths into other people's mouths, eyes and noses, and having the same thing done to us. Yet I cannot account, why a thing which requires so little exertion, and yet preserves the mind from total vacuity, should have gone out.'

Watson took them on a tour of the town. It had once been the metropolitan see of Scotland. The monastery had been founded in the eleventh century, the cathedral in the twelfth, the castle in the thirteenth and the university in the fourteenth. Now town and university were slowly dying. There was a silence about the place.

Johnson surveyed the ruins of the cathedral, ostentatiously keeping his hat off.

'It is surely not without just reproach that a nation, of which the commerce is hourly extending, and the wealth increases, denies any participation of its prosperity to its literary societes; and while its merchants or its nobles are raising palaces, suffers its universities to moulder into dust.'

Someone mentioned dinner.

'Ay, ay, amidst all these sorrowful scenes, I have no objection to dinner.'

They left next morning, at noon. It was a Friday. Johnson was bored.

The roads of Scotland afford little diversion to the traveller, who seldom sees himself either encountered or overtaken, and who has nothing to contemplate but grounds that have no visible boundaries, or are separated by walls of loose stone. From the banks of the Tweed to St Andrews I had never seen a single tree, which I do not believe to have grown up far within the present century.

They crossed the Firth of Tay by ferry. It cost four shillings. Necessities were cheap in Scotland, but luxuries such as ferries were the same price as in the rest of Britain, so they seemed dearer.

The inn at Montrose, where they arrived at 11 p.m., was as bad as the one in Edinburgh. Once again a waiter picked up a lump of sugar in his dirty fingers and put it in Dr Johnson's lemonade. Johnson called him a rascal and started ranting about Scotland. Boswell told him that the landlord was an Englishman. Johnson sulked.

He became angry again later in the evening when Boswell suggested that he take a store of lemons with him into the Highlands. He felt old and lonely and superfluous and humiliated.

'I do not wish to be thought that feeble man who cannot do anything. Sir, it is very bad manners to carry provisions to any man's house, as if he could not entertain you. To an inferior it is oppressive; to a superior it is insolence.'

The only memorable thing about Montrose was the beggars. Johnson found them fascinating.

> It must, however, be allowed that they are not importunate, nor clamorous. They solicit silently, or very modestly, and therefore though their behaviour may strike with more force the heart of the stranger, they are certainly in danger of missing the attention of their countrymen. Novelty has always some power, an unaccustomed mode of begging excites an unaccustomed degree of pity. But the force of novelty is by its own nature soon at an end.

They left the coast and rode inland. It rained most of the day and all next morning. They found themselves on a dreary moor. It was Macbeth country.

'So foul and fair a day I have not seen,' the editor of Shakespeare declaimed to the wind. He was in a better mood.

At Monboddo they were entertained by Lord Monboddo, the man who believed the orang-utan could be taught English. Boswell thought it 'a wretched place, wild and naked, the baron's house marked by two turrets'.

The noble lord solemnly took them over the house. He was dressed in a rustic suit, and said he saw himself as Farmer Burnett. He had become an agricultural revolutionary.

'In such houses our ancestors lived, who were better men than we,' he said.

'No, no, my lord. We are as strong as they and a great deal wiser,' Johnson contended.

There was an awful silence. This was an assault on one of Lord Monboddo's capital dogmas. Boswell changed the subject. The evening improved. The two old men began pontificating to each other.

'Learning has decreased in England, because learning will not do so much for a man as formerly.'

'You, sir, have lived to see its decrease in England, I its extinction in Scotland.'

Monboddo asked them to stay the night, but Boswell nervously interjected something about them having to be in Aberdeen by evening. Monboddo accepted it.

'Well, I am like the Romans: I shall say to you, "Happy to come – happy to depart!"'

Gory, Monboddo's black servant, led them to the highway. When they got there the doctor called out from his chaise.

'Mr Gory, give me leave to ask you a question! Are you baptized?'

Gory said he was, and that he had been confirmed by the Bishop of Durham.

Johnson gave him a shilling.

The old man's spirits had improved from the previous day, and he talked of abandoning the chaise in the Highlands and riding.

'Why, sir,' Boswell mocked him, 'you seemed to me to despond yesterday. You were a delicate Londoner; you are a macaroni; you can't ride.'

'Sir, I shall ride better than you. I was only afraid I should not find a horse able to carry me.'

They arrived at Aberdeen at 11.30. The New Inn was full, but a waiter, who remembered Boswell's father, the formidable judge, let them in, and found a single room, which the two men had to share.

They awoke in the morning and walked down to the harbour in the new part of the town. Johnson laughed to hear that Cromwell's soldiers had taught the people of Aberdeen to plant cabbages and make shoes and stockings.

It was a Sunday. Quiet. At dinner Johnson stuffed himself with Scotch broth. He picked up a book, Massilon's *Discourses on the Psalms*, then threw it down. He picked up Ogden's sermons, then threw that down too. It should have been a bad sign, but the doctor was in a good mood. He talked all night about transubstantiation. He had a captivated audience.

On the Monday the two men went to the town hall, where Johnson received the freedom of the city. He walked through the street with the diploma stuck in his hat, as was the custom. Aberdeen seemed a different place from on the deserted Sunday. The New Town was bustling and prosperous. All the houses were built of granite. They moved on through the streets to the Old Town, and King's College, and the honorary freeman was pleased to walk where Boethius, the fifteenth-century historian of Scotland, had walked.

They set out from Aberdeen about 8 a.m. on the morrow and breakfasted at Ellon. The landlady thought Dr Johnson was a doctor, and wanted to bring her sick child to him.

'But he is not a doctor of physic,' Boswell told her.

'Is he an occulist?' asked the landlord.

'No, he is only a very learned man.'

At 3 p.m. they arrived at Slains Castle. It was all pink granite. They reached the castle just as the dinner bell was ringing. Boswell had a tendency that way.

They stayed that night, entertained by the Earl of Errol's brother, Charles Boyd, who had been out in '45 with Bonnie Prince Charlie. He escaped the Duke of Cumberland's troops and hid on the Isle of Arran for a year before reaching France. There he married a French lady and brought her to Scotland.

Boswell liked him, but Johnson found him too pompous. When Boyd praised his sister-in-law, Lady Errol, for never beating her children, Johnson interjected.

'Sir, she is wrong; I would rather have the rod to be the general terror to all, to make them learn, than tell a child, if you do this or thus, you will be more esteemed than your brothers or sisters. The rod produces an effect which terminates itself. A child is afraid of being whipped, and gets his task, and there's an end on't; whereas, by exciting emulation, and comparisons of superiority, you lay the foundation of lasting mischief; you make brothers and sisters hate each other.'

While on Arran, Boyd had found a chest full of medical books left by a surgeon. He learnt medicine and administered to the poor there. He kept up the practice every afternoon and left the two visitors to walk in the grounds while he conducted his surgery. The house was built on what Johnson called 'the margins of the sea, so that the walls of one of the towers seem only a continuation of a perpendicular rock, the foot of which is beaten by the waves'. The nearest neighbour to the east was the King of Denmark. Johnson loved it.

'I would not for my amusement wish for a storm; but as storms, whether wished or not, will sometimes happen, I may say, without violation of humanity, that I should willingly look upon them from Slains Castle.'

That evening Johnson sat by a bow-window, repeating an ode by Horace, *Jam satis terris*. There was a full-length portrait of Lord Errol by Sir Joshua Reynolds on the wall.

'Sir Joshua Reynolds, sir, is the most invulnerable man I know; the man with whom if you should quarrel, you would find the most difficult how to abuse.'

The Earl came in about 9 p.m. Boswell was obsequious. Johnson was not. There was a moment when Boswell feared that Errol would start a drinking session, but it never happened. He stuck to alternate glasses of port and water.

That night, in his room, Boswell listened to the blazing fire and the beat of the wind against the windows as he wrote up his journal.

> I observed that Dr Johnson, though he shewed that respect to his lordship, which, from principle, he always does to high rank, yet, when they came to argument, maintained that manliness which becomes the force and vigour of his understanding. To shew external deferences to our superiors, is proper: to seem to yield to them in opinion, is meanness.

He lay down to sleep. The window panes rattled. Beyond the glass the sea roared. The pillow was made of the down of sea-birds. It smelt disgusting.

He was up at breakfast, enthusing about the feudal system, and how mankind was happier then, when Johnson came down. Boswell's subservience was excruciating.

'To be sure, the *chief* was: but we must think of the number of individuals. That *they* were less happy seems plain; for that state from which all escape as soon as they can, and to which none return after they have left it, must be less happy; and this is the case with the state of dependence on a chief or great man.'

They left the following morning. 'I had now travelled two hundred miles in Scotland and seen only one tree not younger than myself,' the doctor wrote.

That night they reached Banff. They hoped to stay with the Earl of Fife at Duff House. It was baroque and built by William Adam, but the earl was not there, so they stayed at an indifferent inn instead. The old man wrote a long letter to Mrs Thrale, then cursed at Scottish windows, so impossible to open. 'The necessity of ventilating human habitations has yet to be found in our northern neighbours.'

Next day they came to Elgin, and walked round the ruins of the cathedral in the rain. It had been stripped of lead in the Reformation, left naked by Knox.

They returned to their inn, walking under the piazzas in the middle of the town. The old man did not like them, they made the street too dark. No, he would eat no dinner.

They reached Forres the next evening, after crossing the heath where Macbeth had seen the witches.

> 'How far is't called to Forres? What are these,
> So wither'd, and so wild in their attire?
> That look not like the inhabitants o' the earth,
> And yet are on't?'

Johnson declaimed to the winds. Then he turned to Boswell, who also had the titles Dalblair and Auchinleck, and continued, 'All hail Dalblair! hail to thee, Laird of Auchinleck.' It had been a good day.

At Nairn, where they had their next breakfast, the doctor first saw peat fires and heard the Erse language. There he placed the frontier to the Highlands. Boswell thought it miserable. They rode on to Cawdor, and after dinner visited the castle. 'The tower is very ancient,' the editor of Shakespeare wrote, 'its walls are a great thickness, arched on the top with stone, and surmounted with battlements. The rest of the house is later, though far from modern.'

They stayed with the local Presbyterian minister. He was hardly Johnson's type, and the Man of Letters did not come down to prayers in the morning, on the grounds that a man may as well pray when he mounts a horse, or a woman when she milks a cow. He was particularly irritated by Boswell's and the minister's enthusiasm for maps. They cluttered the floor. Later he softened and gave the minister's 11-year-old son his copy of Sallust.

Cawdor: where Duncan was murdered by Macbeth.

They came to Fort George, where they were presented to Sir Eyre Coote, a brilliant soldier intensely disliked by the military establishment, who ended up a commander-in-chief. He invited the two travellers to dine with him. They toured the fort until 3 p.m., when the drum beat for dinner. Samuel Johnson enjoyed good food, and enjoyed listening to Sir Eyre Coote telling them of his overland journey from India to England, while the regimental band played in the background. He was one of the first of the British bedouin-lovers, and regaled his company with stories of their endurance, their fidelity and their honour.

After two courses and some excellent wine, they left, between 6 and 7 p.m., Sir Eyre Coote accompanying them down the stairs from the mess room.

An hour later they were in Inverness. On their way they passed the field of Culloden, but neither mentioned it. Boswell had been looking forward to his arrival in Inverness, and hoped to find letters waiting for him from his wife. There were none.

> I felt a momentary impatience to be at home. Transient clouds darkened my imagination, and in those clouds I saw events from which I shrunk; but a sentence or two of the *Rambler's* conversation gave me firmness, and I considered that I was upon an expedition for which I had wished for years, and the recollection of which would be a treasure to me for life.

It was a Sunday. They attended a 'mean' Episcopalian chapel, then crossed the deserted streets to Macbeth's castle, where Boswell solemnly shouted out:

> 'The raven himself is hoarse,
> That croaks the fatal entrance of Duncan
> Under my battlements.'

They dined with the local Episcopalian minister, Mr Keith, and ate roast kid. Johnson had never had it before. He pronounced it excellent. The conversation turned to the recent discovery of an odd animal in New South Wales, the kangaroo. The grave-looking moral philosopher rose from his chair, put his hands out like feelers, gathered up the tails of his coat to form a pouch and made three vigorous hops across the room. He was like that sometimes.

The following morning Johnson and Boswell abandoned their chaise and mounted horses. They were no longer riding north or north-west, but south-west. Their destination was Fort Augustus, at the far end of Loch Ness and halfway down the Great Glen that cuts the Highlands diagonally in two.

'We were now to bid farewell to the luxury of travelling, and to enter a country over which perhaps no wheel has ever rolled,' the doctor wrote.

They had four horses, one for Johnson, one for Boswell, one for Joseph Ritter, Boswell's Bohemian servant, and one for the baggage. Two Highlanders, who owned the horses, ran along beside them, acting as guides.

Boswell had never seen his hero on a horse. 'To see Doctor Johnson in any new situation is always an interesting object to me.'

It was a lovely autumn day. They rode under birch trees, looking out over Loch Ness at the mountains beyond. After a few hours they came to a meagre hut built of loose stones. Inside was an old lady, boiling a goat. Dr Johnson, ever inquisitive in the pursuit of knowledge, wanted to find out where she slept. She thought he wanted to rape her. When she realized their intentions were honourable, she offered them a dram of whiskey and a prayer in Eske.

Riding on, Boswell taunted Johnson. It was *his* face that had frightened her.

'No, sir,' the older man replied, 'she'll say, "There came a wicked young fellow, a wild dog, who I believe would have ravished me, had there not been with him a grave old gentleman, who repressed him, but when he gets out of sight of his tutor, I'll warrant you he'll spare no woman he meets, young or old."'

'No, sir, she'll say, "There was a terrible ruffian who would have forced me, had it not been for a civil decent young man who, I take it, was an angel sent from heaven to protect me."'

As evening came down they arrived at Fort Augustus, where they were entertained by Governor Trapaud, an old friend of Boswell. In the morning the officers told them stories of the American Indians.

They left the fort and after some miles came upon a party of soldiers hacking out a road. The two travellers gave them two shillings, on the reasonable grounds that as they were benefiting from the soldiers' labour they should pay something towards it.

They were riding over General Wade's military road, climbing and descending a desolation of rocks and rivulets and brush-sweeps of heather. It was the wildest landscape they had yet passed through. At the end of eleven miles they descended to the tiny hamlet of Anoch in Glen Moriston. It stood at the bottom of the glen, watered by a winding river. There were only three houses, and only one of them had a chimney. It was the inn. Like the others it was built of dry stones, but the dining and sleeping parts were lined with turf and wattle.

The landlord came as a surprise to the two travellers. His name was Lachlan McQueen. He could read French and Latin and compose Celtic verses. Johnson envied

A highland chambermaid – by Paul Sandby.

him some of the books in his library. They included Prideaux's *Connections*, Cyrus's *Travels*, a treatise against drunkenness and a volume of *The Spectator*. The daughter charmed him, and he presented her with a book, Cocker's *Arithmetic*.

McQueen joined them and the subject turned to emigration, as it so often did. Seventy men had just left the Glen for America, he told them. He himself was going out there next year.

Johnson asked him if he would have stayed if he had been better treated.

'No man leaves his native country willingly,' McQueen snapped back.

As they drank their tea they could hear the soldiers, to whom they had given money on the road, spending it in McQueen's bar. 'Come, let's go and give them another shilling apiece,' said Dr Johnson. He did, and the soldiers saluted him, and he said he felt quite feudal. Long after the gentlemen left they could hear the soldiers carousing and fighting; and in the morning the barn was speckled with blood.

Sleeping accommodation was rudimentary: two beds in a room, the room divided by a woman's gown hanging from a rope. Boswell had his servant put out sheets, and stripped down naked to face the vermin. Johnson, after hesitating like a man about to get into a cold bath, faced the fleas in his greatcoat.

Lying in bed the younger man announced that he would write an epic poem about the doctor's Scottish experience.

The old one laughed and asked in whose name he would sign it.

'Mrs Thrale's,' said Boswell.

The old man was furious. 'Sir, if you have any sense of decency and delicacy, you won't do that!'

It was cruel. Boswell knew how Londoners mocked the old man for his love for Mrs Thrale. Johnson knew it too.

Boswell slept with difficulty, understandably. Johnson had no difficulty, and was still fast asleep after Boswell was up, his coloured hankerchief tied around his head.

They left Anoch. McQueen walked with them for a few miles. He had been out in '45, and as he told the story of the exhilaration and the despondency, the courage and the crassness, Boswell's eyes filled with tears.

They were riding over 'the bosom of the Highlands', as Johnson called it, 'the last shelters of national distress'. When they were not climbing over cleavages, they were splashing through bogs or negotiating streams whose winter torrents gorged out the mountainside. In the far distance Johnson discerned a mountain topped in white. One of the guides told him it was snow – and it was only the first day of September.

Regions mountainous and wild, thinly inhabited, and little cultivated, make a great part of the earth, and he that has never seen them, must live unacquainted with much of the face of nature, and with one of the great scenes of human existence.

Johnson was still furious over Boswell's quip about Mrs Thrale.

'There is a mountain like a cone,' Boswell called out to him, trying to draw him out of his ill-humour.

'No, sir. It would be called so in a book; and when a man comes to look at it, he sees it is not so. It is indeed pointed at the top, but one side of it is larger than the other.'

Boswell called the next mountain immense.

'No; it is no more than a considerable protuberance.'

They descended to the shores of Loch Cluanie and stopped to rest the horses. Samuel Johnson moved apart from the rest.

I sat down on a bank, such as a writer of Romance might have delighted to feign. I had indeed no trees to whisper over my head, but a clear rivulet streamed at my feet. The day was calm, the air soft, and all was rudeness, silence and solitude. Before me, on either side, were high hills, which by hindering the eye from ranging, forced the mind to find entertainment for itself. Whether I spent the hour well I know not; for here I first conceived the thought of this narration.

They rode along the shore to a broad and shallow river. It led to Glen Shiel. There was a tiny village of some twenty hovels. It was called Auknasheals.

The inhabitants crowded round the travellers. None of them spoke English. 'There was great diversity in the faces of the circle around us,' Boswell recalled. 'Some were as black and wild in their appearance as any American savage whatever. One woman was as comely almost as the figure of Sappho.' The two travellers passed around snuff and tobacco. Boswell gave them slices of white bread (which they had never had before) and distributed a penny to each of the children. He asked for some milk. An old woman brought some. At first she wanted no money: when pressed, she asked only for a shilling. One of the bystanders told her in Eske to demand half-a-crown. She refused. Boswell looked on, proud and ashamed of the standards of his country.

By late afternoon Johnson and the horses were getting fatigued. Such was his weight that the horses had to take turns bearing him. Mount Ratiken was so steep he thought his horse would collapse under him. Boswell and the two guides took turns leading it, one of the guides trying to divert the doctor from his discomfort by making the wild goats jump at his whistles.

Little did he conceive what Doctor Johnson was. Here now was a common ignorant Highland clown imagining that he could divert, as one does a child, *Dr Samuel Johnson*! The ludicrousness, absurdity, and extraordinary contrast between what the fellow fancied, and the reality, was truly comic.

But Dr Johnson was only a child. Boswell had said so himself, many a time. And, like all children, he was capable of rages. It was getting dark. No one had spoken for some time. They descended the slopes to Glenelg, the fishing port from where they would get a boat to the Isle of Skye. Suddenly, without explanation, Boswell rode ahead to arrange accommodation. Tired, left alone like some surplus piece of baggage, humiliated by his old and cumbersome body, lonely and peevish, Samuel Johnson screamed at Boswell in fury.

'I should as soon have thought of picking your pocket. Doing such a thing makes one lose confidence in him who has done it, as one cannot tell what he may do next.'

Boswell, insensitive to anyone but himself, understood nothing. He could not even understand that the old man's fury was hiding his tears. He returned to Johnson amazed at the outburst. Later Johnson told him that if he had not turned round he would never have spoken to him again.

There was almost nothing in the inn; but a hospitable laird, hearing that there were strangers, sent them some rum and sugar. Dr Johnson fell into bed in his greatcoat. 'Mr Boswell, being more delicate, laid himself sheets with hay over and under him, and lay in linen like a gentleman.'

Breakfast was easier for Johnson than for Boswell. Johnson's anger comprised sudden storms and was soon forgotten. After breakfast they boarded a boat to take them over the sea to Skye. It was raining.

*　　　*　　　*

They landed at Armadale on the southern shore of the island a little after midday. The sky had cleared. Sir Alexander Macdonald was there to meet them. Boswell knew him and did not like him. He was pompous, priggish and mean, and the epitome of the anglicized Scot – rather like Boswell himself. Besides, Boswell used to fancy his wife.

On their first night in Sir Alexander's house Boswell, looking for pen and paper, came upon Sir Alexander in Dr Johnson's room. Boswell was bitterly abusive, rounding on his host for ill-treating his tenants and mistreating his wife. Understandably Macdonald was 'thrown into a violent passion'. One sympathizes with Macdonald. Johnson, who was no more attracted to Macdonald than Boswell, and who described Lady Macdonald's conversation as heavy enough to sink a 90-gun ship, was easily egged on the following morning.

'Were I in your place, sir, in seven years I would make this an independent island. I would roast oxen whole, and hang out a flag as a signal to the Macdonalds to come and get beef and whiskey.'

Sir Alexander, infamous for his tight-fistedness, objected. Johnson would not listen.

'Nay, sir; if you are born to object, I have done with you.' He had not done with him, however, and went on mocking. 'I would have a magazine of arms.'

'They would rust.'

'Let there be men for cleaning. Your ancestors did not use to let their arms rust.'

It poured with rain for the next two days. Macdonald's politeness was beyond reproach. The weather cleared on Sunday. It was a beautiful day. Boswell's spirits improved and, as they improved, so his hero-worship increased. 'I looked on him, as a man whose head is turning giddy at sea, looks on a rock.'

The old man played the role allotted to him. 'Sir, when a man retires to an island, he is to turn his thought entirely to another world. He has done with this.'

They left Armadale the next day and rode inland, making for Coirechatachan, the farm of Mr McKinnon, one of Macdonald's tenant farmers.

> In the islands there are no roads, nor any marks by which a stranger may find his way. The horseman has always at his side a native of the place, who, by pursuing game, or tending cattle, or being employed in messages or conduct, has learnt where the ridge of the hill has breadth sufficient to allow a horse and his rider a passage, and where the moss or bog is hard enough to bear them. The bogs are avoided as toilsome at least, if not unsafe, and therefore the journey is made generally from precipice to precipice; from which if the eye ventures to look down, it sees below a gloomy cavity.

There was something idyllic about Coirechatachan. Boswell thought McKinnon 'a big jolly man' when he met him. He took them into the parlour. It was low and covered in a thick carpet. They had tea. The whole McKinnon family was there. Supper was sumptuous and there was a large bowl of punch. More important than that was the warmth and generosity of the McKinnon family. When Boswell went to bed Mrs McKinnon kissed him on both cheeks.

> We here enjoyed the comfort of a table plentiful furnished, the satisfaction of which was heightened by a numerous and cheerful company; and we for the first time had a specimen of the joyous social manners of the inhabitants of the Highlands. They talked their own language, with fluent vivacity, and sung many Erse songs with such spirit, that, though Dr Johnson was treated with the greatest respect and attention, there were moments in which he seemed to be forgotten.

Dr Johnson left early, and went upstairs to write an ode to Mrs Thrale.

They were rainbound all next day. No one seemed to mind. McKinnon was a warm and civilized man. McKinnon's wife wanted to go to America and said how agreeable it would be if the two gentlemen would visit them there.

Samuel Johnson, supremely happy, spent his time compiling his notes on Skye. It was not easy.

> He that travels in the Highlands may easily saturate his soul with intelligence, if he will acquiesce in the first account. The highlander gives to every question an answer so prompt and peremptory, that scepticism itself is dared to silence, and the mind sinks before the bold reporter in unresisting credulity; but, if a second question be ventured, it breaks the enchantment; for it is immediately discovered, that what was told so confidently was told at hazard, and that such fearlessness of assertion was either the sport of negligence, or the refuge of ignorance.

On food, which had an important place in his scheme of things, he noted that there were fish, fowl, stags, oxen, beef, sheep and goats. Only the geese he disliked. Fed from the sea, they stank of fish. Breakfast, dinner and supper were profuse; though he found the habit of eating cheese at breakfast repulsive.

The next day, the weather clear, they said goodbye to the McKinnons and sailed to Raasay, an island off the eastern coast of Skye. Before they embarked they met Donald McQueen, the local minister, and Malcolm Macleod, a Highland laird who had been out in '45. They were sailing with them. Malcolm Macleod made a deep impression on James Boswell.

> He was now 62 years old, hale, and well proportioned, with a manly countenance, tanned by the weather, yet having a ruddiness in his cheeks, over a great part of which his rough beard extended. His eyes were quick and lively, yet his look was not fierce, but he appeared at once firm and good-humoured. He wore a pair of brogues, tartan hose which came up only near to his knees, and left them bare, a purple camblet kilt, a black waistcoat, a short green cloth bound with gold cord, and yellowish bushy wig, a large blue bonnet with a gold thread button. I never saw a figure that gave a more perfect representation of a Highland Gentleman.

The sea was calm, according to Samuel Johnson, and squally, according to James Boswell. On the way across the water Macleod told them of his experiences in 1745. He had escaped to Raasay to hide Bonnie Prince Charlie after Flora Macdonald had brought him over from the mainland dressed as a lady's maid.

Boswell, the romantic, noted it all down.

> The distressed Wanderer, whose health was now a good deal impaired by hunger, fatigue, and watching, slept a long time, but seemed to be frequently disturbed. Malcolm told me he would start from broken slumbers, and speak to himself in different languages, French, Italian, and English. One of his expressions in English was, 'O God! Poor Scotland!'

They came to Raasay. It was pure pastoral.

> We saw before us a beautiful bay, well defended by a rocky coast; a good family mansion; a fine verdure about it, with a considerable number of trees; and beyond it hills and mountains in gradation of wilderness. Our boatmen sung with great spirit. Dr Johnson observed that naval music is very ancient. As we came near the shore, the singing of our rowers was succeeded by that of reapers, who were busy at work.

Raasay House by William Daniell, and 'a beautiful bay, well-defended by a rocky coast'.

They landed and were met by the Laird of Raasay and numerous relations and retainers. The laird led them to his house, where he introduced them to his three sons and ten daughters. It was a delightful place. The carpet was rolled up, a fiddler was called, and the young in the company started to dance. The doctor did not dance, but sat to one side, 'sometimes deep in meditation, sometimes smiling complacently, sometimes looking upon Hooke's *Roman History*'. After they had eaten supper one of the ladies sung a song in Erse. Johnson asked for it to be translated. It was a farewell by an islander on going to America.

'This is truly the patriarchal life,' he told Boswell the next day. 'This is what we came to find.'

They planned to leave, but the rain kept them island-bound. The old one did not mind. 'Without is the rough ocean and the rocky land, the beating billows and the howling storm. Within is plenty, elegance, beauty and gaity, the song and the dance.' Boswell's only complaint was about the lavatorial arrangements. 'You take very good care of one end of a man, but not of the other,' Johnson told him.

They finally left on Sunday, 12 September. It was a beautiful day. Their destination was Dunvegan Castle in the north-west of Skye, where Macleod, the chief of the clan, resided; but first they had a visit to make.

They returned to the Skye mainland in an eight-oar sailing boat, Donald McQueen and Malcolm Macleod going with them. The boat landed at Portree, where an emigration ship, the *Nestor*, lay waiting to dispeople the island.

McQueen and Macleod rode with them north-west across Skye. It was raining. Their first stop was Kingsburgh House, home of Flora Macdonald – 'a name that will be mentioned in history, and if courage and fidelity be virtues, mentioned with honour,' as the doctor put it. It was not a chance meeting, though it may have been kept secret. Flora Macdonald was as much James Boswell's heroine as Samuel Johnson was his hero; and Johnson himself had always had a sympathy for the Good Old Cause.

Boswell had been planning the meeting for months. Flora Macdonald too knew of it. A fortnight earlier she had been told that Mr Boswell was coming to Skye to see her, with 'a young English buck' called Johnson.

'She is a woman of middle stature, soft features, gentle manners and elegant presence' was how the buck described her. She was married now, middle-aged and the mother of seven children. Soon she would be taking them to America.

Boswell was enthralled. 'To see Dr Samuel Johnson, the great champion of the English Tories, salute Miss Flora Macdonald in the Isle of Skye was a striking sight.'

She took the old English Tory to his room. The bed he was to sleep in was the same as that in which Prince Charlie had slept. Boswell, who came in later, drunk, and woke the doctor, asked him how he felt in it. 'I have had no ambitious thoughts,' he replied through his nose. He had a cold. There was a print by Hogarth of Wilkes with the cap of Liberty beside him, on the wall. It looked out of place.

At breakfast the old man was at his most charming. Flora Macdonald asked how he had slept. Johnson turned the conversation to the prince.

'We were told in England there was one Flora Macdonald with him.'

'They were right,' she said, then told her story.

She had brought the prince to Skye in an open boat. He was given the name Betty Bourke, a lady's maid from Ireland. All over the mainland Cumberland's troops were searching for him. The coasts were patrolled by the Royal Navy. There was a £30,000 reward for his head. A few shots were fired at them when they set off from the coast, but they reached Skye unharmed. Flora took her kinsman, Lady Margaret Macdonald, into her confidence and they decided the prince should be taken to Raasay. That night, while the Pretender hid, the two ladies entertained the officer in command of the Redcoats stationed on the island. In the morning they again dressed the prince as Betty Bourke and set off on foot to Portree – along the same route that Johnson and Boswell had taken but in the opposite direction. At the first stream they crossed, the prince lifted his skirt so that it would not get wet and reveal everything.

'He was very awkward in his female dress. His size was so large, and his strides so great.'

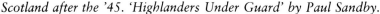

Scotland after the '45. 'Highlanders Under Guard' by Paul Sandby.

Many who passed by realized who he was. None betrayed him. Outside Portree he changed his clothes, putting on a tartan short coat and a waistcoat, with philibeg and short hose, plaid and bonnet. Most of the boats had been commandeered by the military. A rowing boat was found in an inland loch and dragged several miles over hills and bogs. He boarded it and was gone into the night.

The old man listened intently. 'All this should be written down,' he said. Boswell, still suffering from a hangover, wrote it down.

After a day at Kingsburgh, Johnson and Boswell crossed Loch Snizort Beag by boat, thus saving eight miles' riding, picked up their horses and continued to Dunvegan Castle. Johnson disliked riding in Skye.

'The way is narrow,' he complained to Boswell, 'one only at a time can travel, so it is quite unsocial; and you cannot indulge in meditation by yourself, because you must be always attending to the steps which your horse takes.'

They were riding over moorland. It was rough and barren, and almost completely devoid of trees. In some places it was so boggy that the riders had to dismount and walk. Johnson was continually sinking. Once he fell off.

They arrived at Dunvegan, a peel-tower wrapped in ivy, late in the afternoon.

'The great size of the castle,' Boswell wrote, 'which is partly old and partly new, and is built upon a rock close to the sea, while the land around it presents nothing but wild, moorish, hilly and craggy appearances, gave a rude magnificence to the scene.'

They were received by Lady Macleod, mother of the laird, who himself was expected back in a few days. She charmed them, particularly the old man. 'At Dunvegan I had tasted lotus, and was in danger of forgetting that I was ever to depart.'

'Boswell, we came in at the wrong end of the island.'

'Sir, it was best to keep this for the last.'

'I would have it both first and last.'

The days were idyllic and telescoped into each other. The laird returned. He was as kind as his mother. Johnson still had a cold, but it hardly bothered him. The Macleods worried for him. Miss Macleod knitted him a nightcap that he would not wear, and Lady Macleod tried to get him to take some brandy. He would not touch it.

'It carried me. I took the opportunity of a long illness to leave it off. It was then prescribed to me not to drink wine; and having broken off the habit, I have never returned to it.'

In their nine days at Dunvegan Johnson dominated the company, and the company, particularly Boswell, wanted nothing more.

'I have often thought that if I were to keep a seraglio . . .'

Boswell laughed at the idea and requested the right of entry.

'Yes, if he were properly prepared; and he'll make a good eunuch,' Johnson told the company.

Boswell dwelled on the incident that evening in his journal.

It really hurt me. He made me quite contemptible for a moment. Luckily the company did not take it so clearly as I did.

On the Friday Johnson spoke of Pennant's book on Scotland.

'Pennant has greater variety than almost any man, and has told us more than perhaps one in ten thousand could have done, in the time that he took. He has not said what he has to tell; so you cannot find fault with him, for what he has not told. If a man comes to look for fishes, you cannot blame him if he does not attend fowls.'

Dunvegan Castle, set on a slab of rock commanding Loch Dunvegan.

One of the company intervened.

'But he mentions the unreasonable rise of rents in the Highlands, and says, "the gentlemen are for emptying the bag without filling it"; for that is the phrase he uses. Why does he not tell how to fill it?'

'If I tell you that many of the Highlanders go bare-footed, I am not obliged to tell how they may get shoes.'

The next day was Dr Johnson's birthday. He called Boswell in and forbade him to mention the fact. It was too late. Johnson was angry when he got downstairs, but Lady Macleod charmed him over breakfast. She said she was thinking of building a new house, about five miles from the castle. It would be so much more comfortable. Johnson would have none of it.

'Madam, if you once quit this rock, there is no knowing where you may settle. You move five miles first, then to St Andrews, as the late laird did; then Edinburgh; and so on till you end at Hampstead.'

He did not want to go, but Boswell was anxious to leave by Monday.

'I will not go before Wednesday. I want some more of this good.'

The weather was on Johnson's side. It poured and thundered, like the old man himself. Boswell had never seen weather like it. They were still island-bound on the Wednesday, when he watched the immigrant ship, *Margaret*, sail off towards America. 'It was a melancholy sight.' He climbed the castle's tower and saw the Outer Hebrides to the west and the peaks of the Cuillins to the south. They reminded him of Corsica.

The weather cleared a little on Thursday. It was time to leave the Highland Arcadia. They sailed towards Talisker to pick up their horses for the ride south. The rowing boat passed a small island, the isle of Isay. The laird, who was on the boat, offered it to the doctor on condition that he resided in it for three months a year. Johnson was delighted. He was collecting islands.

They came ashore and rode the mile to Talisker, where they stopped for the night. It was wilder and more desolate than Dunvegan.

'Talisker is the place beyond all that I have seen, from which the gay and the jovial seem utterly excluded; and where the hermit might expect to grow old in meditation,' Johnson wrote later.

What cheered them up was meeting the laird of Col[Coll], or simply Col, as they called him. He was likeable and invited them to his island to the south, off the Isle of Mull. Johnson wanted to go. Boswell did not. He had his sights set on Mull, Iona and the Catholic islands. Two days later they continued their journey to the south of the island. Boswell had won. They were going to Mull. Col went with them. They enjoyed his company.

On the way they saw an old woman by her croft, grinding oats with a quern, just as the Romans had done.

> The walls of the cottages in Skye, instead of being one compact mass of stones, are often formed by two exterior surfaces of stone, filled up with earth in the middle, which makes them very warm. The roof is generally bad. They are thatched, sometimes with straw, sometimes with heath, sometimes with fern. The thatch is secured with ropes of straw, or of heath; and, to fix the ropes, there is a stone tied at the end of each. These stones hang round the bottom of the roof, and make it look like a lady's hair in papers.

That night they stopped at the McKinnons' farm, Coirechatachan, again. Boswell got drunk. He slept until midday, and recovered from his hangover with another dram. The weather had turned again. There was no chance of a boat to Mull for several days. It was getting closer to winter. Boswell, after the initial enthusiasm of being somewhere with such delightful memories, was beginning to feel imprisoned. He could get no privacy, lovable as everyone was.

Johnson, on the other hand, was supremely happy. The McKinnon girls flirted with him. One of them sat on his knee and necked him.

'Do it again, and let us see who will tire first,' he said.

The weather cleared a little on the Tuesday and they set off for Ostig nearer the coast, only to see it turn again. It was rainy and windy. They were confined for five days and they could see the sea from their windows. Some of the time Johnson spent writing. He believed you could write anywhere, if you put your mind to it.

> Their winter overtakes their summer, and their harvest lies upon the ground drenched with rain. The autumn struggles hard to produce some of our early fruits. I gathered gooseberries in September; but they were small, and the husk was thick.

The soil was poor. So small were some of the patches cultivated that the sown land was divided between 'long land' and 'short land'. Long land was big enough to be turned by plough, short land by spade. Much was impossible to turn at all. One-third of the harvest had to be reserved for seed.

They were witnessing the end of the feudal system in Scotland. The defeat in '45 had ensured that. Yet in the Highlands, particularly in the islands, far away from central authority, traces of the old world survived. Eigg and Canna were still Catholic islands. St Kilda did not know money. There were tiny horses on Rhum, 'where perhaps no care is taken to prevent that diminution of size, which must always happen, where the greater and the less copulate promiscuously'.

A Scottish washerwoman: a drawing by Paul Sandby.

Now feudal obligations had gone, but nothing had replaced it. It was the problem of de-tribalization, and de-population.

'Where there was formerly an insurrection, there is now a wilderness.'

Then, one morning, the weather cleared. A flotilla of five herring buses transporting kelp were passing to Mull. A vessel from Skye was to set sail with them, and the master was anxious to leave. As they hastily packed their baggage the old man muttered something about man having the voyage of death before him, and being always ready for his Master's call. It was from Epictetus.

* * *

They set sail at 1 a.m. Dr Johnson felt seasick and went under cover, where he fell asleep. The wind came up. It began raining. Their destination was Mull, but the wind and the sea were blowing them south-west into the Hebrides Sea. Four of the herring buses that had managed to keep their course pulled ahead. Soon they had disappeared.

The sea got rougher. Col talked of trying to land at Eigg or Canna, or Col itself. The skipper told Col that if he could guide them into a safe anchorage there, he would sail for the island. Col was uncertain. It was getting rougher. The little ship was fighting against the storm. Finally Col undertook to take them into a harbour there.

'Then let us run for it, in God's name,' said the skipper.

They turned for Col. It was half-past eleven in the evening. They had been sailing for ten and a half hours.

Boswell was scared. 'The perpetual talking, or rather shouting, which is carried on in Erse, alarmed me still more. A man is always suspicious of what is saying in an unknown tongue.' Col gave him a rope to hold. It shut Boswell up. 'Thus did I stand firm at my post, while the wind and rain beat upon me.' It was still night when he saw the outline of Lochiern harbour.

'Thank God, we are safe!' Col shouted.

Boswell went below deck to wake Johnson. Except for a brief moment when he awoke, heard the word Col, and shouted, 'Col for my money', he had slept throughout the storm, with one of Col's greyhounds at his back to keep him warm.

They were taken into the home of Captain Lauchan Maclean. He was a kinsman of Col, and had served in India. Col, Joseph and some of the others caught a Shetland pony, put a straw hat on it, and sat Dr Johnson on its back. Joseph led the pony and its enormous burden up the hill to Captain Maclean's house. The rain poured down. Inside was a blazing peat fire, and tea for everyone.

The weather improved and the ship that had taken them to the island was set to sail on to Mull. The skipper offered Johnson and Boswell places. The two men declined. 'Having, contrarily to our own intentions, landed upon a new island,' said the doctor, 'we cannot leave it wholly unexamined.'

Next day they explored the island; Johnson, Boswell and Joseph on horseback, Col and Maclean walking. Their destination was Col's castle at Breacacha. They stopped on the way at the farm of one of Col's tennants, a Mr MacSweyn. He was nearly eighty, and looked younger than his son, who was a mere fifty. His wife was dressed in a tartan and could speak nothing but Erse. She served the visitors whiskey in little shells. It was an old custom. Dr Johnson, who would not drink whiskey, drank water out of his.

They sat and talked. After a while the two visitors were alone together.

'It would require great resignation to live in one of these islands,' said the older one.

'I don't know, sir; I have felt myself at times in a state of almost physical existence, satisfied to eat, drink, and sleep, and walk about, and enjoy my own thought; and I can figure a continuation of this.'

'Ay, sir; but if you were shut up here, your own thoughts would torment you: you would think of Edinburgh or London, and that you could not be there.'

They continued on to the family seat at Breacacha. Col himself had a new, and far more comfortable, house nearby.

It rained hard for several days. Boswell passed the hours reading Arthur Young's *Six Weeks Tour through the Southern Counties*. Both liked the place, in spite of the weather; and when the weather eased, Col showed them more of the island.

> Wherever we roved, we were pleased to see the reverence with which his subjects regarded him. He did not endeavour to dazzle them by any magnificence of dress: his only distinction was a feather in his bonnet; but as soon as he appeared, they forsook their work and clustered about him: he took them by the hand, and they seemed mutually delighted. He has the proper disposition of a chieftain. The bagpiper played regularly when dinner was served.

At one point they were riding over a strand, so flat they started galloping.

'Dr Johnson, mounted on a large bay mare without shoes, and followed by a foal, which had some difficulty in keeping up with him, was a singular spectacle,' Boswell recorded in his journal that evening.

Next day the weather was worse than he could ever remember, producing 'a kind of dismal quietness in the house'. They found themselves at MacSweyn's again. The doctor was fascinated.

'Life has not got at all forward by a generation in MacSweyn's family; for the son is exactly formed upon the father. What the father says, the son says; and what the father looks, the son looks.'

Then, on Wednesday, 13 October, Col called Boswell over to tell him that the weather was clearing for a passage to Mull. They sailed next morning in a ship carrying kelp. Col came with them.

Johnson was pensive. Boswell tried to cheer him up.

'We shall see Dr Maclean, who has written *The History of the Macleans*.'

'I have no great patience to stay to hear the history of the Macleans. I would rather hear the history of the Thrales.'

* * *

They left between six and seven in the morning, and at noon they arrived at the harbour of Tobermory, on the north-east corner of Mull. There were over a dozen vessels riding in the harbour. It was the next best thing to seeing a town, Boswell thought.

Col took them to a passable inn, where a dish of tea and some bread and butter improved the doctor's mood. Then he took them on to his aunt's. They found this a delight. The daughter, Miss Maclean, played the spinnet. Johnson listened contentedly. He himself had never learnt a musical instrument.

'If I had learnt music, I should have been afraid I would have done nothing else but play.'

He liked Miss Maclean.

'She is the most accomplished lady that I have found in the Highlands. She knows French, music and drawing, sews neatly, makes shell-work, and can milk cows; in short she can do everything,' he said when she was out of hearing. 'She talks sensibly, and is the first person whom I found that can translate Erse poetry literally.'

The country, however, he found dreary.

'All travel has its advantages. If the passenger visits better countries, he may learn to improve his own, if his fortune carries him to worse, he may learn to enjoy it.'

The weather cleared and they rode south-west across Mull. 'We were now long enough acquainted with hills and heath to have lost the emotion that they once raised, whether pleasing or painful, and had our mind employed only in our own fatigue,' Johnson wrote.

Their destination was Ulva, an island off the west coast of Mull. They arrived at the coast in the evening. There was no ferry. The master of an Irish vessel, seeing their predicament, sent over his long boat to take them to the island.

As usual Col was everywhere. 'Col does everything for us,' the doctor said. 'We will erect a statue to Col.'

They continued on to Inch Kenneth, a scrap of an island to the south of Ulva. It was as verdant as it was tiny. They stayed with the laird, Sir Allan Maclean, Col's feudal chief. He lived there alone, with his two daughters and his servants.

> Romance does not often exhibit a scene that strikes the imagination more than this little desert in these depths of western obscurity, occupied not by a gross herdsman, or amphibious fisherman, but by a gentleman and two ladies, of high birth, polished manners and elegant conversation, who, in a habitation raised not very far above the ground, but furnished with unexpected neatness and convenience, practised all the kindness of hospitality and refinement of courtesy.

Johnson wanted an island of his own like Inch Kenneth.

'I should build a fortification, if I came to live here; for, if you have it not, what should hinder a parcel of ruffians to land in the night, and carry off everything you have in the house, which, in a remote country, would be more valuable than cows and sheep? Add to all this the danger of having your throat cut.'

'I would have a large dog.'

'So you may, sir: but a large dog is of no use but to alarm.'

That evening Miss Maclean played the spinnet while Col, Boswell and her sister danced a reel. Johnson left early, to write a letter to Mrs Thrale.

The day after that they took leave of Col and left for Iona. Col meant much to them. The old man, in particular, had developed a lasting affection for him. They did not know that within a year he would be drowned in the Sound of Ulva.

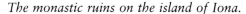

The day soon failed us, and the moon presented a very solemn and pleasing scene. The sky was clear, so that the eye commanded a wide circle: the sea was neither still nor turbulent: the wind neither silent nor loud. We were never far from one coast or another, on which, if the weather had become violent, we could have found shelter, and therefore contemplated at ease the region through which we glided in the tranquillity of the night, and saw now a rock and now an island grow gradually conspicuous and gradually obscure.

Johnson turned to Boswell. 'If this is not *roving among the Hebrides*, nothing is.'

Finally the travellers saw the lights of Iona, and the faint lines of the cathedral tower in the darkness. There was no jetty, so the two men were carried ashore. There they embraced. Boswell had talked so much of going to Iona that he was convinced that Johnson had talked as much about it himself. James Boswell was a Catholic of sorts. To him Iona was a 'sacred place'.

They spent the night in a large barn. There was nowhere else. They found some hay, borrowed some blankets from the village and used their portmanteaus as pillows. 'When I awaked in the morning, and looked round me, I could not help smiling at the idea of the Chief of the Macleans, the great English moralist, and myself, lying thus extended in such a situation.'

The monastic ruins on the island of Iona.

St Columba had landed on Iona 1,200 years before, bringing Christianity from Ireland, so naturally it was all very Irish. The man who showed them round was a descendant of St Columba's cousin.

Boswell was disappointed. Iona did not match his expectations. Johnson was not.

'That man is little to be envied, whose patriotism would not gain force upon the plain of Marathon, or whose piety would not grow warmer among the ruins of Iona.'

Boswell left Johnson and Sir Allan to breakfast in the barn and returned to the ruins of the abbey. The holyness of Holy Island had a profound effect on him, and backgrounds were important to him. Standing in the middle of the ruins he read the fifth chapter of St James and Ogden's tenth sermon out loud, then vowed to lead a better life.

'I suppose there has not been a sermon preached in this church since the Reformation. I had a serious joy in hearing my voice, while it was filled with Ogden's admirable eloquence, resounding in the ancient cathedral.'

They left Iona late that afternoon. Johnson looked back. 'The island, which was once the metropolis of learning and piety, has now no school of education, nor temple of worship, only two inhabitants that can speak English, and not one that can read or write,' he thought. 'Perhaps, in the revolutions of the world, Iona may be sometime again the instructress of the western regions.'

By midday they were back on Mull.

Johnson was at his worst next day, a braggart and an embarrassment, offending everyone with his English chauvinism. They were riding across the island to the laird of Lochbuie. He represented the last of pre-'45 Scotland, 'rough and haughty, and tenacious of his dignity'. He soon put Johnson in his place.

'Are you the Johnstons of Glencro or of Ardnamurchan?'

Johnson sulked. At breakfast Lady Lochbuie called him 'a dungeon of wit'.

*   *   *

That afternoon they made their last journey across the water, landing at Oban, where they found a tolerable inn.

They were now on the mainland. Next morning they set off on the last part of their journey, back to the world that they knew. It was pouring with rain. After some miles they reached a hut. Boswell changed into dry clothes. Johnson resolutely kept his own on, steaming by the turf fire and talking about Pope.

> The night came on while we had yet a great part of the way to go, though not so dark, but that we could discern the cataracts which poured down the hills, on one side, and fell into one general channel that ran with great violence on the other. The wind was loud, the rain was heavy, and the whistling of the blast, the fall of the shower, the rush of the cataracts, and the roar of the torrent, made a nobler chorus of the rough music of nature than it had ever been my chance to hear before.

They stopped at a good inn in Inveraray. Supper raised their spirits. They would soon be home. Dr Johnson even called for a gill of whiskey, which was unheard of. He drank all but a tiny bit at the bottom, which Boswell begged to be given to finish 'so I might say we drank whiskey together'. Boswell wanted to drink to Mrs Thrale, but the old man would not; so they drank to the Maclean girls instead.

> He said to me often that the time he spent on this tour was the pleasantest part of his life.

8
THE
FIRST
TOURIST

I bought here a map of England, folded for the pocket, with the roads and distances all marked upon it. I purchased also a book of the roads, in which not only the distances of every place in the kingdom from London, and from each other, is set down, but also the best inn in each place is pointed out, the name mentioned of every gentleman's seat near the road, and the objects which are most worthy a traveller's notice. Everything that can possibly facilate travelling seems to have been produced by the commercial spirit of this people.

Don Manual Espriella, *Letters from England*

IN 1807 A book was published recounting a very different kind of journey of discovery from that undertaken by James Boswell and Samuel Johnson. It was called *Letters from England*, and it comprised letters written by a Spaniard, Don Manual Alvarez Espriella, to his father confessor about a journey he made through England in 1802. Put together, the letters presented an extraordinary picture of Britain in the earliest days of the new century. The book had just been translated into English.

Don Manual Espriella arrived in England on Wednesday, 21 April 1802, twelve days out of Lisbon. It was a clear day. From his first sight of the Lizard he could see the coastline in all its detail. The ship anchored in Falmouth harbour about noon.

Though there was peace in Europe, Britain's war regulations still held. There were endless forms to fill in, and in the customs house Espriella was charged double duty on his baggage. He escaped from the port and found an inn. It seemed magnificent, he had never seen anything like it; but the food was appalling, the meat half-raw, the vegetables under-boiled, the bread salty, the wine dear and the beer better in Spain. The only decent things were the butter and cheese.

> The perpetual stir and bustle of this inn is as surprising as it is wearisome. Doors opening and shutting, bells ringing, voices calling to the waiter from every quarter, while he cries 'coming', to one room, and hurries away to another. Everybody is in a hurry here; either they are going off in the packets, and are hastening their preparations to embark; or they have just arrived, and are impatient to be on the road homeward. Every now-and-then a carriage rattles up to the door with a rapidity which

GLASGOW
Edinburgh

Newcastle
Carlisle
Durham

Keswick
Richmond

Windermere
Ripon

Lancaster
York
Halifax
Beverley
Preston
LEEDS
Kingston upon Hull

MANCHESTER
Doncaster
LIVERPOOL
Lincoln
Chester

Snowdon
Nottingham
Grantham
Derby
Lichfield
Stamford
Norwich
Shrewsbury
Peterborough
Leicester
Thetford
Ludlow
BIRMINGHAM
Ely
Coventry
Huntingdon
Bury St Edmunds
Warwick
Cambridge
Ipswich
Worcester
Stratford-on-Avon
Colchester

St David's
Gloucester
St Albans

Oxford
LONDON
Cardiff
Bristol
Bath
Canterbury
Wells
Tunbridge
Glastonbury
Wells
Dover
Salisbury
Taunton
Winchester
Southampton
Exeter
Dorchester
Launceston
Plymouth

Penzance
Falmouth
St Michael's
Mount

0   50   100 miles

———— Espriella's route
·—·—· return journey

Espriella's first impression of England: Falmouth Harbour (by J. M. W. Turner).

makes the very house shake. The man who cleans the boots is running in one direction, the barber with his powder-bag in another; here goes the barber's boy with his hot water and razors; there comes the clean linen from the washer-woman; and the hall is full of porters and sailors bringing in luggage, or bearing it away; – now you hear a horn blow because the post is coming in, and in the middle of the night you are awakened by another because it is going out. Nothing is done in England without a noise.

He rode in a chaise, four-wheeled, with room for three people facing forwards. Through the side windows he looked at the countryside, and through the front window at the posteriors of the two horses, as they cantered along at six miles an hour.

Breakfast at Truro was ruined by the bread, but the town astonished him. All the shops had glass windows. When he left Truro he realized why. The skies became dark and overcast. The Spaniard felt cold. 'Everything has a coarse and cold appearance: the heath looks nipt in its growth, and the hedge-plants are all mean and insignificant: nettles, and thistles, and thorns.'

The way was dreary and desolate. Mitchell was 'as miserable as any of our most decayed towns ... Mile after mile the road lay straight before us; up and down long hills, whose height only served to show how extensive was the waste.'

Espriella dined at Bodmin. The English coal fire fascinated him.

An Englishman's delight is to stir the fire; and I believe I shall soon acquire this part of their manners, as a means of self-defence against this raw and chilly atmosphere. The heath is furnished with a round bar to move the coals, a sort of forceps to arrange them, and a small shovel for the cinders; all of iron, and so shaped and polished as to be ornamental. Besides these, there is what they call the fender, which is a little moveable barrier, either of brass or polished steel, or sometimes of wire painted green and capped with brass, to prevent the live embers falling upon the floor. The grates which confine the fire are often very costly and beautiful, everything being designed to display the wealth of the people; even the bars, though they are necessarily blackened every day by the smoke, are regularly brightened in the morning by women.

They drove on and slept at Launceston. The view of the town and the ruins of the castle reminded him of the Moorish towns in southern Spain, 'and I would willingly for a while have exchanged the chaise for a mule, that I might have loitered to enjoy it at leisure'.

The chaise moved fast. Every so often they stopped at toll-gates. He had never seen toll-gates before. Soon they were overtaking convoys of gigantic eight-horse transport wagons, travelling slower than a funeral.

> The carrier walks beside them, with a long whip upon his shoulder, as tall again as himself, which he sometimes cracked in the air, seeming to have no occasion to exercise it in any other manner: his dress was different from any that I have seen, it was a sort of tunic of coarse linen, and is peculiar to this class of men.

They came into Okehampton. There was a ruined castle clad in ivy above a little river. Further on the land became more fertile, and was almost pretty by evening, when they arrived at Exeter.

> Exeter is an ancient city, and has been so slow in adopting modern improvements that it has the unsavoury odour of Lisbon. One great street runs through the city from east to west; the rest consists of dirty lanes. As you cross the bridge, you look down upon a part of the town below, intersected by little channels of water. The cathedral is a fine object from those situations where both towers are seen, and only half the body of the building, rising above the city. It cannot be compared with Seville, or Cordoba, or Burgos; yet certainly it is a noble pile.

Honiton, where they changed chaises, was uninteresting, but they were nearly killed when unbroken horses were put into the harness and bolted. The new horses were treated appallingly. Espriella was shocked by the Englishman's capacity for cruelty to animals.

Thomas Rowlandson's view of Honiton High Street, where Espriella changed chaises.

One of them had been rubbed raw by the harness. I was in pain the whole way, and could not but consider myself an accessory to an act of cruelty: at every stroke of the whip my conscience upbraided me, and the driver was not sparing of it.

Soon he was in Dorset, 'a dreary county'. The road was full of flints, and the horses' shoes 'struck fire at almost every step'. Only towards the end of the day – Espriella's third – did the road improve. He slept at Bridport.

The chaise was now driving across downland. This was sheep country. They passed through villages curled up in the folds of hills. He was surprised to notice that the English buried their dead around their churches – a morbid custom. The day's journey ended at Salisbury, a delightful city of trees, gardens and rivulets, 'the spire of the cathedral over-topping all'.

They drove on through Stockbridge and Basingstoke. Soon the chaise was crossing Bagshot Heath. 'Nothing but wild sheep, that run as fleet as hounds, are scattered over this dreary desert.' Next he crossed the Thames at Staines, by a crazy wooden bridge. It was over a hundred years old. There was another one made of iron. He thought it looked rusty, spidery and generally detestable. They were now riding over heathland, the haunt of highwaymen, or *bandetti*. Nothing happened.

They came on to the Great West Road at Hounslow. From Brentford it was one continuous street all the way into London.

The number of travellers perfectly astonished me, prepared as I had been for the gradual increase along the road; horsemen and footmen, carriages of every description and every shape, waggons and carts and covered carts, stage-coaches, long, square, and double, coaches, chariots, chaises, gigs, buggies, curricles, and phaetons; the sound of their wheels ploughing through the wet gravel was continuous and incessant as the roar of the waves on the sea beach.

Espriella came into London at Hyde Park Corner, and it was evening by the time he reached the house of J., an English merchant whom he had met in Spain. He was exhausted. He lay on his bed, but did not sleep.

Here was the watchman, whose business it is, not merely to guard the streets and take charge of the public security, but to inform the good people of London every half hour of the state of the weather. For the first three hours I was told it was a moonlight night, then it became cloudy, and at half-past three o'clock was a rainy morning.

There were a lot of rainy mornings, but the day he visited St Paul's it was relatively fine. From the dome he had a panorama of the whole city. All London lay mapped out below him: Westminster Abbey, the Monument, the Tower, the ships' masts on the Thames, and the hills of Hampstead and Highgate to the north and of Surrey to the south. The immensity of the place awed him. Between these landmarks, and far beyond them, as far as the eye could see, were houses, just houses, going on for ever, in every direction, filling every crevice.

I was looking down upon the inhabitants of a million of human beings; upon the single spot whereon was crowded together more wealth, more splendour, more ingenuity, more worldly wisdom, and alas! more worldly blindness, poverty, depravity, dishonesty and wretchedness, than upon any spot in the whole habitable earth.

He stayed in London some months, and the longer he stayed the more the English grew on him. They amused him, particularly their idea of a holiday. It was spent either on a freezing cold beach, at a spa trying to marry off a daughter, or climbing over mountains in Wales and the Lakes in search of the picturesque. The search for the picturesque was the most fashionable. Everyone was climbing mountains, or looking at them, or re-designing them.

On 1 July he set off on a journey through England, which would take him as far north as the Lake District. He had caught the bug for the picturesque himself.

*   *   *

He travelled by stage-coach, accompanied by an English friend, D. At 6 a.m., with a crack of the whip, the coach pulled out, rattled through the City, along Fleet Street and the Strand, to Piccadilly. There it picked up more passengers, some of them settling themselves on the roof. The whip cracked again, the coach rolled past Hyde Park Corner and took the Great West Road, bound for Oxford. Inside the coach no one spoke. It was perfectly understandable. This was England. But 'a fat vulgar woman who stored herself with cakes, oranges and cordials' soon told everyone her life story, and within hours the passengers were talking to each other. By the time they reached Oxford one of them, a fellow from Lincoln, had invited Don Manual and D. to visit his college. 'It must be admitted that though the English are in general inhospitable towards foreigners, no people can be more courteous to those who have been properly introduced.'

They breakfasted at Slough and could see Windsor Castle as the coach drove by, before crossing the Thames at Maidenhead. While the coachman was changing horses, Espriella's friend D. proposed that they join the more adventurous travellers on the roof. Espriella mounted with some trepidation. The two settled down, their feet resting on a narrow shelf and with nothing to hold on to but a low iron rail.

> At first it was fearful to look down over the driver, upon four horses going with such rapidity, or upon the rapid motion of the wheels immediately below us; but I soon lost all sense of danger, or, to speak more truly, found that no danger existed except in imagination.

At Maidenhead the Oxford road branched off the Great West Road and stopped in Henley, where they were within sight of the Thames again, 'still the same quiet and beautiful stream'.

> These stage coaches are admirably managed: relays of horses are ready at every post; as soon as the coach drives up they are brought out, and we are scarcely detained ten minutes. The coachman seems to know every body along the road; he drops a parcel at one door, nods to a woman at another, delivers a message at a third, and stops at a fourth to receive a glass of spirits or a cup of ale, which has been filled for him as soon as the sound of his wheels was heard.

Dinner was at Nettlebed. It was a good one, and at 5 p.m., sitting on the roof, Don Manual Espriella caught his first sight of Oxford, its towers, pinnacles, spires and domes rising above thick groves.

Espriella loved Oxford. He thought The High, its gentle curve resembling the Calle de Alcala in Madrid, 'the finest street in Europe'.

The first college he visited was Christ Church. It was beautiful and magnificent, far more so than the monasteries in his own country, though he *did* find the modern buildings out of harmony with the monastic character of the place. What was even

Broad Street, Oxford: the Sheldonian, Clarendon Building and Radcliffe Camera's dome.

more out of character was the piddly little fountain in the middle of the great square, Tom Quad: 'so pitiful that the famous *Manneke* of Brussels might well be placed in the midst of it, as the appropriate god of the puddle'.

Broad Walk in Christ Church Meadows was also beautiful. It was flanked by elm trees, their boughs forming perfect arches. He walked down to the River Isis. It was a typical Oxford day, languid. The students amused him. In a land where the clergy dressed like ordinary people, the students dressed like the clergy. Exams were over, and the students in their gowns and tassels were in rowing boats, punts and canoes. Espriella had never seen a canoe. On his right was the bridge where the medieval scholar Roger Bacon had lived in a bridge house. He had said that the house would not fall down until a wiser man than him had walked under it. The house had been demolished twenty-three years earlier.

At 9 p.m. Great Tom tolled the hour from Christ Church. 'It is of great size, and its tone full and sonorous.' He could see the students making their way into the college before the gates were shut. Next morning he woke to the chiming of so many bells that he did not know where he was.

Espriella and D. breakfasted with one of the coach travellers, the fellow from Lincoln, at his college. Its buildings included some of the oldest in Oxford. Front Quad had hardly changed since the fifteenth century, and Chapel Quad hardly since the seventeenth. It was all either medieval Gothic or Jacobean Gothic. Espriella found it 'small and gloomy', though the opulence of his fellow-traveller's rooms amazed him. Their next stop was Balliol College, mostly fifteenth-century except for the early sixteenth-century Tudor chapel, a corner range on The Broad and St Giles built in 1767, and some quite modern Regency 'Gothick' additions by James Wyatt in the hall. Espriella found it a college 'which, though not large, nor of the handsomest order, is very neat, and has of late received many improvements, in perfect good taste'. From Balliol they passed through into the gardens of Trinity College, where he was astonished by a wall of yew, though his friend, D., more in tune with gardening fashions, hated it. Then D. took him past the Sheldonian and the Bodleian to New College garden, where the college arms were cut in box and the alphabet grew in the

Great Tom, tolling the hour at Christ Church: a painting by J. M. W. Turner.

surrounding flowerbed. They went into the chapel. It was the largest in Oxford, and 'the most beautiful thing in the university'.

They stayed for a couple of days, then the two visitors sent their baggage on to Woodstock and set out from Oxford by boat for Blenheim. The Worcester coach left Oxford between 4 a.m. and 5 a.m. A night in Woodstock meant that they could catch the coach at a marginally more civilized hour – 6 a.m. They rowed up the Isis to Godstow, where they breakfasted at an alehouse by the waterside. The river was overhung by willow trees, and graced by meadows where cattle grazed. They disembarked near Woodstock and looked over the nunnery where Rosamund Clifford, Henry II's lover, was buried.

Their next stop was Blenheim. The deer in the park, standing in groups by clumps of trees, were splendid.

> Their branching antlers, their slender forms, their spotted skin, the way in which they spring from the ground and rebound as they alight, and the twinkling motion of their tails which are never at rest, made them beautiful accompaniments to the scenery.

They toured the house, then, exhausted by the pretentiousness of it, retired to the inn at Woodstock where their baggage awaited them.

They took the stage to Worcester at six the next morning. It was a fine day and they mounted the roof, stopping for breakfast at Moreton-in-Marsh. Further on Espriella was amazed by a great chalk horse carved into the hillside in the Vale of Evesham, 'one of the most fertile parts of England'. He liked Evesham, and he wanted to stay longer and examine the ruins of the abbey, but the stage-coach time-table would allow him no such Papist indulgence. The stage rolled on. The pear trees and hop cones, falling down in 'curly tresses' on either side of the road, were ripe and lovely. They reached Worcester at about three o'clock. Behind the city rose the Malvern Hills and the mountains of Wales.

The food in Worcester was splendid, particularly the salmon, fresh from the Severn. 'Were I an epicure, I should wish to dine every day at Worcester.' The perry reminded him of champagne.

The main industry was porcelain-making, and the workshops were so big you could fit a church into them.

> One dinner service you see painted with landscapes, every separate piece being a different picture; another represents flowers or fruit coloured to the life; another, the armorial bearings of the family for whom it has been fabricated, emblazoned with all the richness of heraldic colouring. These things are perfect in their kind: yet such are the effects of prejudice and habit, that the grotesque and tasteless patterns of the real china are frequently preferred; and the English copy the hair-lined eyebrows of the Chinese, their unnatural trees and distorted scenery, as faithfully as if they were equally ignorant of perspective themselves.

Late in the afternoon of the following day they took the Bristol–Birmingham coach. It carried sixteen people facing each other, with no windows, and was shaped like a coffin turned upside-down. It was hot. The twelve passengers said there were too many occupants already. No one was very talkative. The Spaniard rejoiced when they reached Birmingham and he could stretch his legs and gulp the cool air – even if it was not exactly fresh.

Whenever he thought of the wealth of England, Espriella wrote that evening, he would think of Birmingham. He did not know the exact human cost of that wealth – 'commerce sends in no returns of its dead and wounded'. Every man stank of grease and oil. 'Some I have seen with red eyes and green hair, the eyes affected by the fires to which they are exposed, and the hair turned green by the brass works.'

> The noise of Birmingham is beyond description; the hammers seem never to be at rest. The filth is sickening: it is active and moving, a living principle of mischief, which fills the whole atmosphere and penetrates everywhere, spotting and staining everything, and getting into the pores and nostrils. I felt as if my throat wanted sweeping like an English chimney.

He took the fast mail-coach to Manchester. Beside the driver sat the guard, armed with a blunderbuss and wearing the royal livery. It was a fine day. Espriella and D. mounted the roof. The coach cantered through the streets of Birmingham into the suburbs. It was a long time before Espriella began to breathe in fresh air. He looked back at the black columns of smoke rising above the city, 'not without satisfaction at thinking I should never see it again'.

The coach rumbled on. Industrialization was spreading from Birmingham to the towns and villages around. There were factory chimneys instead of church steeples, and children in rags, encrusted in soot and filth. A few miles on, Espriella was surprised to see smoke rising from the ground. He asked the driver the reason. It came from burning and abandoned coal mines.

'If you were to travel this road by night, sir, you would see the whole country afire, and might fancy you were going to hell.'

Public transport as Espriella knew it, in the earliest years of the nineteenth century.

Beyond Wolverhampton there were fields again. They rode through Stafford into Cheshire, passing a half-timbered Tudor moathouse on the way. 'No dress in an old picture was ever more curiously variegated with stripes and slashes.' It was Little Moreton Hall. When darkness came he was still sitting on the roof. Two hours later the mail clattered into Manchester. By the time they reached the Bridgwater Arms it was midnight. The inn was unlike anything he had experienced in the country.

> Here all is hurry and bustle; customers must come in the way of trade, and they care not whether you are pleased or not. We were led into a long room, hung round with greatcoats, spurs and horsewhips, and with so many portmanteaux and saddlebags lying out, that it looked like a warehouse.

Their first visit in the morning was to a cotton mill. D. had a letter of introduction to the mill owner, who proudly showed them around.

'You see these children, sir. In most parts of England children are a burden on their parents and to the parish; here the parish, which else would have to support them, is rid of all the expense; they get their bread almost as soon as they can run about, and by the time they are seven or eight years old bring in money. There is no idleness amongst us: they come at five in the morning; we allow them half an hour for breakfast, and an hour for dinner; they leave work at six, and another set relieves them for the night; the wheels never stand still.'

Espriella looked around at 'the unnatural dexterity' of the busy little workers. If Dante had peopled one of his hells with children, he could have found no better inspiration.

'They are as healthy as any children in the world could be. To be sure, many of them as they grow up go off in consumptions, but consumption is the disease of the English.'

Espriella asked if there was a shortage of this sort of labour.

'We are well-off for hands in Manchester, manufacturers are favourable to the population, the poor are not afraid of having a family here, the parishes therefore have always plenty of apprentices, and we take them as fast as they can supply us. In new manufacturing towns they find it difficult to get supply. Their only method is to send people round the country to get children from their parents. Women usually undertake the business; they promise the parents to provide for the children; one party is glad to be eased of the burden, and it answers well to the other to find the young ones in food, lodging and clothes, and receive their wages.'

Espriella and D. left the mill and walked through the grimy, sunless streets.

A place more destitute of interesting objects than Manchester is not easy to conceive. In size and population it is the second city of the kingdom, containing above fourscore thousand inhabitants. Imagine its multitude crowded together in narrow streets, the houses all built of brick and blackened with smoke; frequent buildings among them as large as convents, without their antiquity, without their beauty, without their holiness; where you hear from within, as you pass along, the everlasting din of machinery; and where when the bell rings it is to call wretches to their work instead of their prayers. Imagine this and you have the materials for a picture of Manchester.

They left on the Monday morning in a public long boat down the Manchester Ship Canal bound for Chester.

This is a new mode of travelling, and a delightful one it proved. The shape of the machine resembles the common representations of Noah's ark, except that the roof is flatter, so made for the convenience of passengers. Within this floating house are two apartments, seats of which are hired at different prices, the parlour and the kitchen. Two horses harnessed one before the other tow it along.

He wanted to travel further by canal. Looking at the map, the whole of England seemed criss-crossed with canals. It was a thoroughly modern form of transport. Yet already he had heard of something even more modern.

Excellent as these canals are, railroads are found to accomplish the same purpose at less expense. In these the wheels of the carriage move in grooves upon iron bars laid all along the road; where there is a descent no draught is required, and the laden waggons as they run down draw the empty ones up. These roads are always used in the neighbourhood of coalmines and founderies. It has been recommended by speculative men that they should be universally introduced, and a hope held out that at some future time this will be done, and all carriages drawn along by the actions of steam engines erected at proper distances.

They left the long boat at Warrington, and took a coach to Chester. On the way they passed two bodies swinging from gibbets, hanged, they were told, for murdering a postboy.

Espriella would remember Chester, with its streets cut out of red rock. Most memorable of all were the Rows, the pedestrian ways, which seemed to go through people's houses and contained the best shops in the city. The cathedral was mean, but from the city walls the view across the River Dee of the mountains of Wales was spectacular.

From Chester they took another canal to join the Mersey, then a ferry across to Liverpool. It was rough and wet. They went below but were driven up again by the stench of sea-sickness. It rained for the whole crossing.

The two drenched travellers arrived in Liverpool and found an inn. It was like the one in Manchester. 'They have a filthy custom in the inns of England, that when you

A country toll-bar. Private roads were the only reasonable roads in the 1800s.

pull off your boots, the man brings you a pair of old slippers, which serve for all travellers, and indeed are frequently worn-out shoes with the heels cut away.'

Next day he visited the city. It was enormous. Yet 'there is no cathedral, no castle, gate, town-hall or monument of antiquity, no marks of decay. Everything is the work of late years, almost of the present generation.'

Liverpool depressed Espriella. The two travellers took another coffin-shaped coach by stages to Kendal. The road out of Liverpool was drab, lined with cottages, kilns and brickworks all along the way. They crossed the River Ribble at Preston and reached Lancaster. At ten o'clock they arrived at Kendal, where Espriella bought Thomas West's best-selling *Guide to the Lakes* and a local map at the inn. That evening, like Celia Fiennes a century earlier, they supped on potted char, a Lakeland delicacy.

In Kendal it threatened to rain, so they bought umbrellas. The weather had been so bad, the shopkeeper smugly told them, that he had sold forty in a week. Equipped with knapsacks and umbrellas – not as picturesque as pilgrims' staffs, Espriella thought – they set off walking to Windermere. It took five hours. The sky was overcast. Twice it rained. 'Water and mountains have a grandeur, an awfulness, to which till now I have been a stranger,' he thought. They walked on to Bowness to get another view. Belle Island lay directly before them. From a ridiculous viewing platform above the inn they took in the beauty around, then, after dinner, took a boat across to the island, 'a liberty that is liberally allowed to strangers'.

They re-embarked on their boat, rowed to the far side of the lake and slept at the Ferry House, re-crossing the lake in the morning and taking the lakeside road north to Ambleside. 'The upper end of Windermere became more majestic as we advanced, mountains of greater height and finer form opened before us.' When they got to Ambleside they found that the inn was full, so they lodged in one of the village cottages. The streets were packed with tourists. 'New houses are building, old ones modernized, and marks of the influx of money to be seen everywhere.' They left Ambleside after a brief excursion to Rydal Water and Coniston Water, and hiked their way up to Kirkstone Pass, 'perhaps the longest and most laborious pass in England', where they encountered – of all people – a Jewish peddlar hawking barometers. On the far side of the pass they found themselves walking between two great walls of rock, which gradually opened up into a vale. The vale was scattered with cottages built of dry stone and roofed with uncut slates, so covered with moss and fern that they appeared part of the landscape.

They spent the night in Penrith and in the morning left for Keswick. Five hours later the vale of Keswick opened up before them, revealing Derwent Water, girdled by mountains. It began to rain. The inns were full. All those tourists in search of the picturesque. So they stayed – the two in one bed – at the local barber's. The simple hospitality of the barber and his family touched Espriella after so many nights in inns. Besides, he could hardly complain; the town was so crowded that some people had to sleep in their carriages.

After breakfast they took a boat on Derwent Water. Lodore Falls thundered down on the eastern shore. To the south the mountains parted at Borrowdale to let pass the River Derwent.

> Everything grows upon me. I become daily more and more sensible of the height of the mountains, observe their forms with a more discriminating eye, and watch with increased pleasure the wonderful changes they assume under the effects of clouds or of sunshine.

After another night at the barber's and an uncertain morning of changeable weather, they set out with a boy to guide them on the climb up Skiddaw. They had been told – wrongly – that it was the highest mountain in England. At first the climb seemed easy, but the way got harder the higher they got. Many times they stopped to rest. Finally they reached the top.

> We saw the sea through a hazy atmosphere, and the smoke of some towns upon the coast about six leagues off, when we were directed where to look for them: the Scotch mountains appeared beyond like clouds, and the Isle of Man, we were told, would have been visible had the weather been clearer.

They descended to Keswick and set off the following morning after an early breakfast, along the Borrowdale road, armed with West's *Guide to the Lakes* and hard-boiled eggs. The weather appeared kind – neither too hot, nor raining – but the insects tormented them. The road ran along the shoreline. They walked past Lodore Falls, 'glittering before us', towards Borrowdale, which 'became more beautiful the nearer we approached'. Soon they entered the vale of Borrowdale and a mile on came to a village called Grange.

> This village consists of not more than half a score cottages, which stand on a little rising by the riverside, built apparently without mortar, and that so long ago that the stones have the same weather-worn colour as those which lie upon the mountainside behind them. A few pines rise over them, the mountains appear to meet a little way on and form an amphitheatre, and where they meet their base is richly clothed with coppice wood and young trees. The river, like all the streams of this country, clear, shallow and melodious, washes the stone bank on which the greater number of the pines grow, and forms the foreground with an old bridge of two arches, as rude in construction as the cottages.

The River Derwent flowed directly beneath it, pale green-grey and translucent. They walked through Rosthwaite, Longthwaite and Seatoller, to Seathwaite, almost on the foothills of Scafell Pike, which *is* the biggest mountain in England. They made their way up to Stockley Bridge. It was raining.

When we had almost reached the extremity of this ascending vale, we came to a little bridge, as rude as work of human hands can be; the stream making a little cataract immediately under it. Here the ascent of the mountain began, a steep, wet and winding path, more like a goat's highway than the track of man. It rained heavily; but we consoled ourselves with remarking that the rain kept us cool, whereas we should otherwise have suffered much from heat.

Further on was a tarn, or mountain pool. It was called Sprinkling Tarn. Espriella felt lonely. Half a mile on they reached the top. There was little to see, the summits wrapped in clouds. They descended the west side, coming down to Wasdale, where the stones were all red, then continuing on through Ennerdale Forest to Ennerdale Water. 'The mountains seem to have planted their outworks in the lake; they rise directly up to a certain height on both sides, then leave an interval of apparently level ground, behind which they up again to a great height.'

They crossed Gale Fell, via Scale Force, to Crummock Water. It was raining again. They came to an inn.

Of all the scenes in the land of the Lakes, that from the middle of Crummock is assuredly the grandest. In colour the mountains almost rival the rainbow varieties of Wastwater, they rise immediately from the water, and appear therefore higher and more precipitous than any which we have seen. Honister Crag forms the termination, the steepest rock in the whole country, and of the finest form.

It was a good moment to leave the Lakes, but before returning to London they continued northwards, to Carlisle and the Scottish border. They took a chaise from Keswick. Skiddaw loomed above them on one side and Bassenthwaite spread below them on the other.

We now perceived the beauty of this water, which, because of its vicinity to Keswick, is contemptuously overlooked by travellers; and the sight of its wooded shores, its mountainous sides, with its creek and bays, and the grand termination formed by the Borrowdale mountains as we looked back, made us regret we had not devoted a day to exploring it.

The mountains and their outworks were soon behind him and he was in open country, broken by small hills and enclosures, that would appear, from the immaturity of the hedgerows, to have been just brought into cultivation.

The chaise-driver changed horses at Wigton, a prosperous town with good inns and well-dressed inhabitants, and rested them at Thursby, 'one of those townlets in which everything reminds us of the distance from a metropolis'. There were half a dozen houses forming an apology for a plaza, the grass grew between the paving stones and the children came clattering up to them in their wooden clogs and stared as if they had never seen a chaise before. Further on, the farms – with their dwellings and outhouses forming a circle around a courtyard, and with a dunghill in the middle for the cattle that were brought in each night – were as he imagined farms in Scotland to be.

The chaise rolled on. Before dusk came down they could see Carlisle over the plain. They hastened to what was left of the Norman cathedral (the Scots had sacked it during the civil war) while their dinner was being cooked. The outside was a disappointment. The tower was too small – it would have been too small on an ordinary parish church; it looked ridiculous on a cathedral. The inside fascinated Espriella, particularly the Early English and Decorated chancel, though he disliked the clear glass in the windows and the very un-Roman choir stalls. Behind the stalls were wall paintings of St Augustine, St Anthony and St Cuthbert. They had been plastered over in the Reformation and had been uncovered only twenty-four years before.

Outside the cathedral, walking through the streets Espriella found the city walls in decay, though the castle was still used by the military, ever-mindful of '45. Its old wooden portcullis was encast in iron. The town was full of Scottish and Irish immigrants who had poured in to the new factories opening up and had doubled the population. The inn's boot-cleaner was a Scotsman, polite to the point of being excruciating, asking if they would 'please to give him leave' to clean their boots.

They left early the next day, going south, looking down at Scottish drovers, returning home having taken their cattle to London. The drovers wore 'a sort of flat turban, and had a little mantle of grey chequered cloth round them, a costume far more graceful than the English'. One woman walked barefoot, carrying her shoes in her hand. ''Tis the way they do in Scotland,' the coachman said.

The landscape was wild and beautiful, the hills dotted with castles beyond their prime, 'the strongholds in former times of the *bandetti* of the Border'. The coach's route was along the Eden Valley, through Temple Sowerby, where the Knights Templars were once established; Kirkby Thore, where there was a Saxon church dedicated to the god Thor; and Appleby, where woods, castle and bridge presented an unforgettable scene. They continued up the valley into the foothills of the Pennines. The next stage lay across the Pennines, over the 'cold and desolate tract' of Stainmore into Yorkshire. Espriella had seen nothing so desolate. A single house at Greta Bridge was their next stage. It stood among woodland, with a clear stream running alongside it. From there the land was flat and dull, and the road a straight line, all the way to York. They drove under Bootham Bar and up High Petergate to an inn, where they ordered dinner. Then they set out to inspect the minster. 'Praise must be given to the English heretics, that they preserve these monuments of magnificent piety with a proper care, and do not suffer them to be disfigured by the barbarism of modern times.'

John Sell Cotman's watercolour study of Greta Bridge and its single house.

Ouse Bridge, built with houses on it like Old London Bridge, and York's only bridge.

They walked around the city and along the Ouse. 'There is a bridge over it of remarkable architecture, whose irregular arches with the old houses adjoining form a highly picturesque pile.'

They left at five next morning, departing as the minster's bell tolled the hour. It was cloudy. They passed through Tadcaster and came to Doncaster, 'one of the handsomest towns I have ever seen – though the country around is as insipid as the plains of Old Castille'. The landscape improved when they reached Nottinghamshire. The sun came out and they were driving past hop fields. They arrived in Lincoln that evening, after being cheated by a local coach that took them there the long way round. ('There was no remedy but the never-failing panacea of patience.') Finally, after the coach got bogged down and almost turned over, they saw Lincoln cathedral perched on a hill against a flat horizon. There were three towers. The two smaller ones were topped with spires. By the time they arrived it was too late to sightsee, so they ordered dinner – wild fowl fresh from the Fens. The cathedral would have to wait.

When they did see the cathedral, it compared easily with York. York had a plain exterior but exquisite interior, Lincoln an exquisite exterior and a plain interior. After climbing the highest tower and admiring the view, Espriella was taken to a second tower to inspect Great Tom, the largest bell in England. At first he was disappointed, but on closer view he admitted that he was impressed. It was big. A man could stand upright in it, and it was only rung on very solemn occasions, such as Whit Sunday, or the beginning of the Quarter Sessions.

From Lincoln they rode for two days in pouring rain, through Newark, Grantham and Stamford, to the Fenlands.

At length we came in sight of Cambridge. How inferior to the first view of Oxford, yet its lofty buildings and old trees gave it a characteristic appearance, and were more beautiful because in the midst of such a dreary land. The streets are narrow, and the greater number of colleges mean brick buildings; there is however one edifice, the chapel of King's College, which exceeds anything in Oxford, and probably in the world.

He walked up King's Parade, past Old Schools and Caius College to Trinity, where he pronounced the courtyard and the library magnificent. Further on Espriella found the round church of the Templars fascinating, but the Cam, flowing lazily through the Backs, and carrying all the rubbish and sewage of the colleges along with it, had little appeal.

They had an introduction to a fellow of one of the colleges and stayed in Cambridge for several days. It was vacation. The colleges – which the fellow had little love for – were deserted.

'The truth is,' he told them, 'that the institutions of men grow old like men themselves, and like women are always the last to perceive their own decay.'

They left Cambridge and went by chaise to London. The country was tame and Espriella was bored after the Lakes. They came into the city that evening. Soon he was back in the house of J. It was like coming home.

He remained in London into the new year, 1803, and through to the summer. It was not until 16 September that he began his journey back to Spain. He called his last day with his companion's family, knowing that they would never meet again, 'the most painful of my life'. He had been in England for sixteen months.

*   *   *

The coach taking Espriella back to Falmouth, where he had first set foot in England, was leaving at five; he rose at four. His host and wife were already up, preparing hot chocolate for him. He set off and boarded the coach, feeling apprehensive. 'For the first time I was now to travel alone in this country.'

They breakfasted at Maidenhead, then turned right on to the Bristol road. It was new to him. They passed through Hungerford and Marlborough, 'an old place, in which many of the houses are faced with tiles in the shape of fish scales'.

> There is something as peculiar as it is pleasing in the character of this country: the villages, with their churches, are all seated in the bottom, which is intersected by numberless little streams, in every respect unlike the mountain rivers of the north, but still beautiful; they flow slowly over weedy beds, sometimes through banks of osiers, sometimes through green fields.

They stopped at a small alehouse in West Kennett.

'If you have travelled this road before, sir, you will alight, of course; and if you have not, you must not pass by without tasting the best beer in England,' a fellow-passenger said to him.

He tasted it, saying, a little ambiguously, that if he had left England without tasting it, he would not have known what beer was. The landlady was so pleased that she took him to inspect her cellar, where she kept fifty full barrels.

They passed a white horse cut into the hills, close by Oldbury Castle. It was large, and on a clear day could be seen from sixteen miles away. He thought it was Saxon, which put him about 1,000 years out (it had been cut in the hillside in 1780). By the time he reached Chippenham it was dark. He was told that the country was beautiful but he could not verify it. The coach came into Bath about nine o'clock.

His fellow-travellers quickly left. He was landed at an inn – for the first time without a companion, 'and never more in need of one'. It was a depressing evening, his spirits falling with the barometer.

Bath was a modern city. 'It has no aqueduct, no palace, no gates, castle, or city walls, yet it is the finest and most striking town that I have ever seen.' He spent all morning there, visiting the cathedral, pump room and market.

> Since the Parades were built every addition to the town has been made upon the system, and with a view to its beauty; hence it presents the singular spectacle of a city of which parts are uniform yet the whole irregular – a few old streets still remaining to make the others more remarkable by contrast. The adjoining hills supply a soft freestone, which is easily worked, and becomes harder when exposed to the air; its colour is very beautiful when fresh, but it is soon blackened by the soot from the earth-coal fires, which is indeed exceedingly annoying to all the large towns. Still, blackened stones produce a far better effect than blackened bricks. There is a square in which the sides resemble so many palaces; ascend a handsome street from this, and you come into a Circus of like beauty, and near this is a Crescent built with equal, or even more magnificence, and overlooking the country.

Away from the centre the buildings became tattier, the suburbs dilapidating into building sites. 'It is plain that Bath has outgrown its beauty.'

Twelve miles on was Bristol, downstream on the River Avon. He had a fine view of the river, winding round a wooded hill, before coming into Keynsham, 'a little dirty town', named, so he was told, after Saint Keyna, a local hermit.

The Pump Room, Bath: detail from Humphrey Repton's watercolour and ink study.

Bristol was presently in sight, a huge city at the bottom, and extending up the adjoining hills, with many steeples, one of which inclines so much from the perpendicular, that I should be sorry to live within reach of its fall.

The streets were the filthiest and poorest he had seen in England, but the view of St Nicholas from the bridge compensated for the squalor. The inn stood opposite the Exchange, 'a fine edifice'. Behind the Exchange was the market, even finer than that at Bath, with separate buildings for meat, poultry and dairy products. He visited the cathedral. It was a disappointment. There had once been a gold lectern, but it had been sold. Outside he was told there had once been a cross in the square in front of the cathedral; it too had been sold. He found out what it looked like from a man who – though he could not remember the cross – remembered the gingerbreads shaped like the cross, which he ate as a child.

He visited Clifton, once the most beautiful village in England, and now a suburb of Bristol. 'Here too, as in Bath, is the dismal sight of streets and crescents that have never been finished, the most dolorous of all ruins. It stands upon a hill above the river, which runs between high rocks and a hanging wood.' Already the view was changing. The great rocks that so dominated the river were now being quarried. Bristol sold everything. It sold its lectern, its cross, and now 'they are selling the sublime and beautiful by the boat-load'.

Like Bath, Clifton had become a spa.

Several unhappy patients, who had been sent here to die at a distance from home, were crawling about upon the parade as if to take their last gasp of sunshine.

You would think it scarce possible that this scene of disease and death should be a place of amusement, where idlers of fashions resort to spend their summer, mingle in the pump room and in the walks with the dying, and have their card parties and dances within hearing of every passing bell.

At five the next morning he took his seat in the Plymouth coach. The journey out of the city was bone-wrecking. Bristol seemed to be the worst-paved city in the country. On the way he caught a glimpse of St Mary Redcliffe, 'the finest parochial church in the country'. Soon he could see the Bristol Channel, near Burnham.

They changed stages at Bridgwater and crossed the River Parrett on a hideous iron bridge built in 1795. Taunton was pretty, and the church of St Mary Magdalen's 'of uncommon beauty'. There Espriella had lunch, and continued by stages through Exeter to Plymouth, where the streets swarmed with sailors, but he was unable to visit the docks, because he was a foreigner.

He went on, by slow and uncomfortable stages, through Cornwall, changing horses at Liskeard, Lostwithiel ('a pretty place with slated roofs') and Truro. That evening he was in Falmouth, the port where he had first arrived in England. He was going home.

*   *   *

It may seem odd that the first tourist to survey Britain, and the last to hold up a looking-glass to it, should be a foreigner. But Don Manual Alvarez Espriella was no foreigner. He was the invention of an Englishman, Robert Southey, a future Poet Laureate, who shared a house with Mr and Mrs Coleridge in – would you guess? – the Lake District.

Such books as his, allowing the writer to wear the mask of naivity and observe his country as if for the first time, had a long pedigree. Daniel Defoe published a volume of *Letters Written by a Turkish Spy*, describing Europe through Moslem eyes, Goldsmith wrote *Citizen of the World*, supposedly the reactions of a Chinese visitor to Britain, and Horace Walpole wrote *Letter from Xo Ho to his friend Lien Chi*. Still, Mrs Coleridge did not like the book. She thought it 'rather a popular thing'.

Don Manual Espriella may have been the first modern tourist, but Robert Southey was the last British traveller to hold a mirror up to Britain and see it for what it was. Soon the roads would be trod by the likes of Cobbett, Barrow and the Victorian romantics, men who looked backwards to a pastoral and pre-industrial yesterday. From now on it would be the past, not the present, that travellers sought to discover. The looking-glass had become tinted and speckled, the image unclear.

As Johnson said to Boswell, 'We came too late.'

BIBLIOGRAPHY

General
Burton, Anthony, *Britain Revisited*, 1986.
Moir, Esther, *The Discovery of Britain*, 1964.
Pevsner, Nikolaus, *Buildings of England* series.

1   A Rumour of Britain
Worcestre, William, *Itineraries*, ed. J. H. Harvey, 1969.

2   Bare Ruin'd Choirs
Dobson, R. B., *Durham Priory*, 1973.
Knowles, David, *The Religious Orders of England*, vol. III, 1959.
Toulmin-Smith, Lucy (ed.), *The Itineraries of John Leland*, 1907.

3   The Clown, Three Hoorays and the Water Cabbie
Dyce, A. (ed.), *Kempe's Nine Day Wonder*, Camden Soc. 11.
Hammond, Lt, *A Relation of a short survey of 26 Counties*, ed. L. G. Wickham Legg, 1904.
—— *A Relation of the short survey of the Western Counties*, ed. L. G. Wickham Legg, 1936.
Taylor, John, *Works*, ed. C. Hindley, 1872.

4   The Weekend Guest
Morris, C. (ed.), *The Journeys of Celia Fiennes*, 1947.
Parkes, Joan, *Travel in England in the Seventeenth Century*, 1925.

5   A Wandering Disposition
Defoe, Daniel, *A Tour through the Whole Island of Great Britain*, ed. Pat Rogers, Penguin, 1971.
Moore, John, *Daniel Defoe, Citizen of the Modern World*, 1958.

6   Rural Revolutionary
Gazley, John, *Life of Arthur Young*, 1973.
Young, Arthur, *A Six Weeks Tour through the Southern Counties of England and Wales*, 1768.
—— *A Six Month Tour through the North of England*, 1770.
—— *A Farmer's Tour Through the East of England*, 1771.

7   The Discovery of Scotland
Boswell, James, *Journal of a Tour to the Hebrides*, ed. Peter Levi, Penguin, 1984.
Graham, H. G., *Social Life in Scotland in the Eighteenth Century*, 1950.
Johnson, Samuel, *Journey to the Western Islands of Scotland*, ed. Peter Levi, Penguin (published together with Boswell, *op. cit.*), 1984.
McLaren, Moray, *A Highland Jaunt*, 1954.

8   The First Tourist
Nicholson, Norman, *The Lakes*, 1955.
Southey, Robert, *Letters from England by Manual Espriella*, 1708.
West, Thomas, *Guide to the Lakes*, 1778.

INDEX